W9-DIM-544

Compressed Image
File Formats

WITHDRAWN

This book is published as part of the SIGGRAPH Books Series with ACM Press Books, a collaborative effort among ACM SIGGRAPH, ACM Press, and Addison-Wesley Publishing Company. The SIGGRAPH Books Series publishes books on theory, practice, applications, and imaging in computer graphics and interactive techniques, some developed from courses, papers, or panels presented at the annual ACM SIGGRAPH conference.

Editor: Stephen Spencer, The Ohio State University

Editorial Board:
Mike Bailey, San Diego Supercomputer Center
Wayne Carlson, The Ohio State University
George S. Carson, GSC Associates
Ed Catmull, Pixar
Tom DeFanti, University of Illinois, Chicago
Richard L. Phillips, Los Alamos National Laboratory
Andries van Dam, Brown University

MEMBERSHIP INFORMATION

Founded in 1947, ACM is the oldest and largest educational scientific society in the information technology field. Through its high-quality publications and its services, ACM is a major force in advancing the skill and knowledge of IT professionals throughout the world. From a dedicated group of 78, ACM is now 85,000 strong, with 34 special interest groups, including SIGGRAPH, and more than 60 chapters and student chapters.

For more than 25 years, SIGGRAPH and its conferences have provided the world's forum for the interchange of information on computer graphics and interactive techniques. SIGGRAPH members come from many disciplines and include researchers, hardware and software systems designers, algorithm and applications developers, visualization scientists, educators, technology developers for interactive visual communications, animators and special-effects artists, graphic designers, and fine artists.

For more information about ACM and ACM SIGGRAPH, contact:

ACM Member Services
1515 Broadway, 17th Floor
New York, NY 10036-5701
Phone: 1-212-626-0500
Fax: 1-212-944-1318
E-mail: acmhelp@acm.org

ACM European Service Center
108 Cowley Road
Oxford, OX4 1JF, United Kingdom
Phone: +44-1865-382388
Fax: +44-1865-381388
E-mail: acm_europe@acm.org

URL: http://www.acm.org

ROCKVILLE CAMPUS LIBRARY
ROCKVILLE, MARYLAND

Compressed Image File Formats

JPEG, PNG, GIF, XBM, BMP

John Miano

ACM Press • SIGGRAPH Series
New York, New York

ADDISON-WESLEY

An imprint of Addison Wesley Longman, Inc.

Reading, Massachusetts • Menlo Park, California • New York
Don Mills, Ontario • Harlow, England • Amsterdam • Bonn
Sydney • Singapore • Tokyo • Madrid • San Juan
Paris • Seoul • Milan • Mexico City • Taipei

249735

MAR 01 2001

Many of the designations used by manufacturers and sellers to distinguish their products are claimed as trademarks. Where those designations appear in this book, and Addison-Wesley was aware of a trademark claim, the designations have been printed in initial capital letters or all capital letters.

The author and publisher have taken care in the preparation of this book, but make no expressed or implied warranty of any kind and assume no responsibility for errors or omissions. No liability is assumed for incidental or consequential damages in connection with or arising out of the use of the information or programs contained herein.

The publisher offers discounts on this book when ordered in quantity for special sales. For more information, please contact:

Corporate, Government, and Special Sales Group

Addison Wesley Longman, Inc.
One Jacob Way
Reading, Massachusetts 01867

Library of Congress Cataloging-in-Publication Data
Miano, John, 1961–
    Compressed image file formats : JPEG, PNG, GIF, XBM, BMP / by John Miano
        p.   cm.
    Includes bibliographical references.
    ISBN 0-201-60443-4. — ISBN 0-201-61657-2 (CD-ROM)
    1. Image processing—Computer programs. 2. Data compression (Computer
    science) 3. Computer programming. 4. File organization (Computer science)
    I. Title
TA1637.M53   1999
005.74'6—dc21   99-15179
                                                                                    CIP

Copyright © 1999 by the ACM Press,
a division of the Association for Computing Machinery, Inc. (ACM).

All rights reserved. No part of this publication may be reproduced, stored in a retrieval system, or transmitted, in any form, or by any means, electronic, mechanical, photocopying, recording, or otherwise, without the prior consent of the publisher. Printed in the United States of America. Published simultaneously in Canada.

Text printed on recycled and acid-free paper.

ISBN 0201604434

2 3 4 5 6 7   MA   03 02 01 00

2nd Printing   January 2000

Contents

Preface

The purpose of this book is to instruct the reader on how to write software that can read and write files using various 2-D image formats. I wanted to write a book that explains the most frequently used file formats with enough depth for the reader to implement them, as opposed to one that covered many different formats at a high level or one that avoided the more difficult image formats. As a result, I chose to cover the image file formats that are associated with Web browsers. Those covered in this book (BMP, XBM, JPEG, GIF, and PNG) represent the vast majority of image files that can be found on the Internet. They employ a wide range of encoding techniques and range in implementation difficulty from simple to very complex.

The inspiration for this book was my own frustration resulting from the lack of information on how to implement encoders and decoders for the more complex file formats. Most of the information available was at too high a level, left major gaps, or was very difficult to decipher. I have tried to create a bridge between the programmer and the standards documents.

One issue I faced at the start of this project was which programming language to use for the examples. The intention was to create a book on graphics file formats rather than one on how to write programs to read and write graphics files in a particular language. Therefore, I debated using a language that is easy to read (e.g., Pascal or Ada) or the one most people are likely to use (C++). In the end I felt that its widespread use made C++ the best choice. To make the examples more understandable for non-C++ programmers, I have carefully avoided certain C++ language constructs (e.g., expressions with side effects and integer/boolean interchangeability) that would make the code difficult for them to understand.

In order to make the encoding and decoding processes as clear as possible, I have used a Pascal-like pseudo-code. C++ is used for complete function implementations and pseudo-code for illustrative fragments. These fragments generally contain no error checking.

Because of their generally large size, it was not possible to include working source code for the formats in the book itself. Instead, the accompanying CD-ROM contains the complete source code for encoders and decoders for almost all of the image formats covered.[1] The reader should use the pseudo-code in the text to learn how processes work and the C++ examples on the CD to see how to implement them.

Generally, the decoders implement more features than to the encoders. In the decoders I have implemented all of the features needed to decode files that a reader will have any likelihood of encountering on the Internet. For the sake of clarity, the encoders generally implement a smaller feature subset.

In writing the programming examples I have given clarity precedence over execution efficiency and instant portability. The source examples will compile, without modifications, on Microsoft Windows using both Borland C++Builder V3.0 and Microsoft Visual C++ V5.0. Other compilers generally require some modifications to the code.

The descriptions of the encoders and decoders for the various file formats frequently employ the term "user" to describe the source of certain input parameters to the encoding or decoding process. By this I mean the user of the encoder or decoder, not necessarily the person typing at the keyboard. Since image encoders and decoders are incorporated into other applications, such as image viewers and editors, the user in this case would most likely be another piece of software. However, in many situations the "user" application may get some of these parameters directly from a human.

Just as this is not intended to be a book on C++ programming, it is also not intended to be a book on programming in a specific environment. For that information readers will need a book for their particular system.

---

[1]The unfortunate exception is GIF because of legal issues.

Acknowledgments

A project as large as producing a book requires the involvement of many people. Mike Bailey, Eric Haines, Tom Lane, Shawn Neely, and Glenn Randers-Pehrson reviewed the manuscript and provided many invaluable suggestions. Glenn also arranged for me to get the latest proposed PNG standards for the CD. My fellow aviator, Charlie Baumann, was kind enough to provide several of the photographs. Ralph Miano and Margaret Miano assisted with preparing the manuscript. Jean-Loup Gailley answered all my questions on ZLIB. Albert "The Chipster" Copper compiled examples on systems I did not have access to. Most important, Helen Goldstein at AWL guided the process from start to finish.

John M. Miano
Summit, New Jersey
miano@colosseumbuilders.com

Chapter 1

Introduction

In this chapter we cover the fundamental aspects of image file formats. Here you will be introduced to bitmap images, the methods used to display images, the representation of color, and compression methods.

The Representation of Images

In most computer displays, the screen image is composed of discrete units called *pixels*. Each pixel occupies a small rectangular region on the screen and displays one color at a time. The pixels are arranged so that they form a 2-dimensional array.

Objects are drawn on the screen by adjusting the color of individual pixels. Figure 1.1 shows an ideal triangle and one broken down into pixels. The pixel representation has jagged edges and is not very pleasing to the eye. The more densely pixels are packed on a display device, the less noticeable the jagged edges become.

Over the years the number of pixels displayed on PC monitors has increased dramatically. Not too long ago 640 × 480 (307,200 pixels) displays were standard. Now monitor resolutions of 1024 × 768 (786,432), 1280 × 1024 (1,310,720), and even higher are common. The amount of video memory and the capabilities of

Figure 1.1
Ideal Image and
Pixel Image

 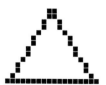

1

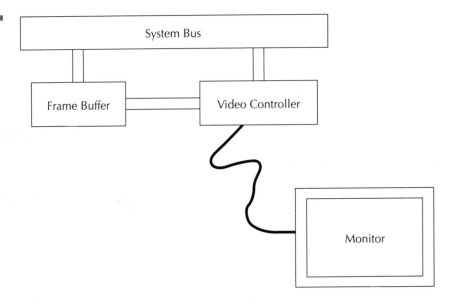

Figure 1.2
Simple Video
System

the monitor and video adapter limit the number of pixels a computer system can display.

Figure 1.2 illustrates the components of a typical video system. The frame buffer is a block of video memory that controls the color of each pixel on the monitor. Each pixel has a corresponding memory location, usually ranging in size from 1 to 32 bits. On many systems, video memory can be read from and written to just like any other memory location. An application can change the color displayed on the monitor just by changing a memory value. The video controller converts the values in the frame buffer to a signal that can be displayed by the monitor.

Computer printers are also used to display images. These days most printers employ a similar mechanism to video systems. They divide the image into a number of pixels, but with a much higher density than a computer monitor does, typically 300 or 600 pixels per inch for an office printer. Printers designed for typesetting applications use even higher densities. The printer contains memory analogous to the frame buffer, except that data is transmitted over a serial or parallel cable rather than directly through the system bus. The image gets built in the printer's memory and then gets written to the printed page.

Not all printers work by mapping memory to pixels. Plotters used for drafting and other engineering work have pens controlled by commands, such as draw a line from one point to another, draw an ellipse within a specified rectangle, or draw text using a specified font at some location.[1]

---

[1]Back in the old days, computer monitors for graphics worked this way as well.

Vector and Bitmap Graphics

Just as display devices have two general methods of operation, graphics file formats can be divided into two general classes. vector and bitmap.[2] Vector graphics formats use a series of drawing commands to represent an image. A Windows metafile is a commonly used vector graphics format. Figure 1.3 contains a simple vector image created using commands to draw two arcs and a rectangle.

Figure 1.3
Simple Vector Image

Vector graphics formats are not limited to output devices, such as plotters, that create images through drawing commands. Computer monitors and laser printers usually have software that converts vector commands into pixels.

There are two main drawbacks with vector graphics. First, they are not suitable for reproducing photographs or paintings. A painting such as *Whistler's Mother* would require tens of thousands of drawing commands —simply determining which commands to use to represent the painting would be a monumental task. Second, complex images take a long time to display. On most display systems, each vector object has to be converted to a pixel image.

All of the image formats covered in this book are bitmap image formats. Such formats represent images as 2-dimensional arrays where each array element represents a color to be displayed at a specific location. When displayed on a computer screen, each element is generally mapped to a single screen pixel. If pixels are close enough on the display device, it becomes difficult for the human eye to detect the array structure that composes the image.

The greatest advantage of bitmap images is their quality. As the amount of disk space and memory has increased along with the speed of processors, the use of bitmap images has expanded as well. One of the most visible examples of this is in the computer game industry. Currently even games that require high performance, such as flight simulators and shoot-em-ups, use bitmap graphics. Contrast the graphics in games like Quake and Doom to the vector graphics of Tank or even the Death Star graphics in the original *Star Wars* movie.

A major drawback with bitmap images is the amount of data required to hold them. The size of an image in bytes (not counting overhead) is

$$\frac{width \times height \times bits\ per\ pixel + 7}{8}$$

Thus, an 800×600 image with 24 bits per pixel requires 1,440,000 bytes of memory to display or disk space to store. As the amount of memory on computers has grown, so has the number and size of images that can be displayed at the

---

[2]*Raster graphics format* is a common synonym for *bitmap graphics format.*

same time. Compression is usually used to reduce the space an image file occupies on a disk, allowing a larger number of images to be stored.

Another drawback with bitmap images is that they are size dependent and not suitable for extensive editing. With vector formats, it is easy for drawing programs to add, delete, and modify individual elements. It is also simple to perform transformations such as perspective, enlarging, and scaling on a vector image.

With bitmap images, even changing the size causes problems. Reducing them requires throwing away information; enlarging them produces blocking effects. Figure 1.4 illustrates the problem with increasing the size of a bitmap image by duplicating pixels. Smoothing techniques exist to improve the appearance of resized images.

Table 1.1 summarizes the advantages of vector and bitmap graphics. The important thing to notice is that neither method is better than the other—they simply have different uses. In fact, some applications use a combination of the two techniques.

Figure 1.4
Bitmap Image and
an Enlargement

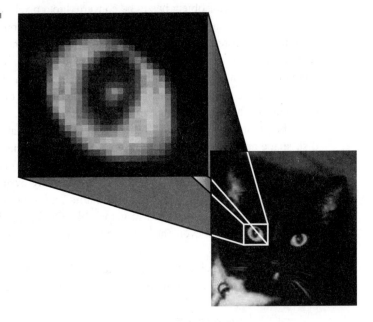

Table 1.1
Bitmap Graphics
versus Vector
Graphics

	Bitmap Graphics	Vector Graphics
Display speed	X	
Image quality	X	
Memory usage		X
Ease of editing		X
Display independence		X

Color Models

In the previous section we saw that in a bitmap image each pixel has a value that specifies its color. So, how does a numerical value get translated to a color?

There are many ways to represent colors numerically. A system for representing colors is called a *color model*. Color models are usually designed to take advantage of a particular type of display device.

On most color monitors there are three phosphors (red, green, and blue), or light emitters, for each pixel. Adjusting the intensity of the individual phosphors controls the color of the pixel. When all three phosphors are at their minimum intensity the pixel appears black. At their maximum intensity the pixel appears white. If the red phosphor is the only one active, the pixel appears red. When the red and green phosphors are on they combine to produce shades of yellow, and when all three phosphors are at full intensity the pixel appears white.

The most common color model used in computer applications is known as *RGB* (Red-Green-Blue). The RGB model mimics the operation of computer displays. In RGB, colors are composed of three component values that represent the relative intensities of red, green, and blue. Figure 1.5 shows the relationship of colors in the RGB color model. The range of colors that can be represented by a color model is known as a *colorspace*. In Figure 1.5, the RGB colorspace is the cube in the diagram.

In mathematical discussions of color, component values are often represented as real numbers normalized to the range 0.0 to 1.0. In programming and image formats, unsigned integer component values are almost always used. The range of values for a color component is determined by the *sample precision,* which is the number of bits used to represent a component. For photographic

Figure 1.5
RGB Color Model

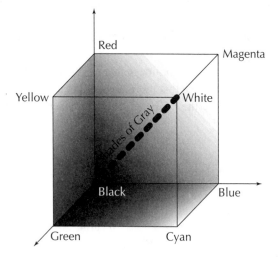

images, 8 is the most commonly used sample precision. However, 1, 2, 4, 12, and 16 are also common.

Integer component values can range from 0 to $2^{Sample\ Precision} - 1$. To convert from the normalized real number representation of a color to the integer representation you simply multiply by $2^{Sample\ Precision} - 1$.

On Windows the sample precision is almost always 8 bits, so the operating system (but not necessarily the underlying hardware) recognizes 256 different shades of each primary color. Other systems may use a larger or smaller sample precision.

Grayscale

Some display devices, such as laser printers, cannot display colors at all but rather shades of gray. These are known as *grayscale devices.* Shades of gray can be represented by a single component in the range 0 (black) to $2^{Sample\ Precision} - 1$ (white). In Figure 1.5 you can see that shades of gray occur in the RGB model along the line where R=G=B.

YCbCr Color Model

RGB is not the only color model in use. At one time the HSB (Hue-Saturation-Brightness) color model was commonly used in computer systems and still is used by some image processing applications. JPEG images are almost always stored using a three-component color space known as YCbCr. The Y, or *luminance,* component represents the intensity of the image. Cb and Cr are the *chrominance* components. Cb specifies the blueness of the image and Cr gives the redness.

The YCbCr color model is similar to the one used in television sets that allows color images to be compatible with black and white sets. In the YCbCr color model, the Y component on its own is a grayscale representation of the color image.

The relation between the YCbCr and RGB models as used in JPEG is represented in Equation 1.1.

Figure 1.6 shows a color image that has been separated into its Y, Cb, and Cr components. You can see that the Y component contributes the most information to the image. Unlike the RGB color model, where all components are roughly

Equation 1.1
YCbCr/RGB
Colorspace
Conversion

$$Y = 0.299R + 0.587G + 0.114B$$
$$Cb = -0.1687R - 0.3313G + 0.5B + 2^{Sample\ Precision/2}$$
$$Cr = 0.5R - 0.4187G - 0.0813B + 2^{Sample\ Precision/2}$$

$$R = Y + 1.402Cr$$
$$G = Y - 0.34414\left(Cb - 2^{Sample\ Precision/2}\right) - 0.71414\left(Cr - 2^{Sample\ Precision/2}\right)$$
$$B = Y + 1.722\left(Cb - 2^{Sample\ Precision/2}\right)$$

Figure 1.6
Color Image
Separated into Its
Y, Cb, and Cr
Components

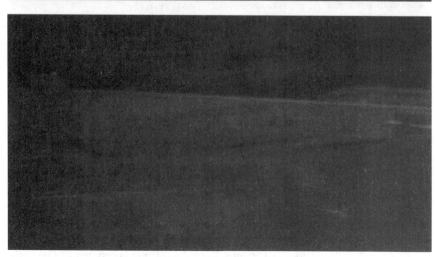

equal, YCbCr concentrates the most important information in one component. This makes it possible to get greater compression by including more data from the Y component than from the Cb and Cr components.

CMYK Color Model

One other color model worth mentioning at this point is a four-component model known as CMYK (cyan, magenta, yellow, black), which is frequently used in color printing. Most printing is done on white paper with ink added to create darker colors. This is the opposite of what happens on a computer monitor. The CMYK colorspace follows the printing model. The components represent the four inks commonly used in color printing.

The color models we have looked at so far are known as *additive,* which means the components add light to the image. The higher the component values are, the closer the color is to white. However, in CMYK, larger component values represent colors close to black. This is known as *subtractive.* Cyan, magenta, and yellow are the complements for red, blue, and green. A pure cyan surface absorbs all the red light directed at it. If yellow and magenta inks are combined, they absorb the green and blue light, which results in red. Cyan, magenta, and yellow combine to absorb all light, resulting in black—in theory, anyway.

In practice, cyan, magenta, and yellow inks do not combine on a white piece of paper to produce a pure black. Even if you could get a good shade of black by combining colors, it would require three times as much ink as simply using black alone. Since most printing is done in black anyway, it makes sense to use black ink to produce black and shades of gray.

On a computer monitor, the relationship between RGB and CMYK can be approximated as shown in Equation 1.2.

Equation 1.2
CMYK/RGB
Colorspace
Conversion

$$K = \left(2^{Sample\ Precision/2} - 1\right) - MAX(R,G,B)$$
$$C = \left(2^{Sample\ Precision/2} - 1\right) - R - K$$
$$Y = \left(2^{Sample\ Precision/2} - 1\right) - G - K$$
$$M = \left(2^{Sample\ Precision/2} - 1\right) - B - K$$

$$R = \left(2^{Sample\ Precision/2} - 1\right) - K - C$$
$$G = \left(2^{Sample\ Precision/2} - 1\right) - K - Y$$
$$B = \left(2^{Sample\ Precision/2} - 1\right) - K - M$$

When the C, M, and Y component values are equal, the color is a shade of gray. Notice how the conversion from RGB to CMYK replaces cyan, magenta, and yellow ink with shades of gray produced by black ink. The result of this substitution is that at least one of the CMY components will always be zero if this conversion process is followed exactly as shown here. The CMYK color model does not require the value of one component to be zero—this is simply a result of converting from RGB. Applications that use the CMYK color model will allow any combination of component values to give complete control over the printed colors and allow for variations among various types of ink.

Another thing to notice about the CMYK color model is that there is not a one-to-one mapping between it and RGB. Instead, multiple CMYK values map to the same RGB value.

True Color versus Palette

The examples in this book assume that the output device uses the RGB color model to display images and that each component is represented using 8 bits and is in the range 0–255.[3] This is the color representation used by most personal computer systems. Such a system can produce 16,777,216 (256^3) distinct colors. There are computer systems that use more bits to represent color, for example the 12-bit grayscale frequently used for medical images. Some image formats support data with more than 8 bits per component (12 for JPEG, 16 for PNG). For the remainder of this discussion we are going to assume that you are working on a system that uses 8 bits per component.

Two methods are commonly used to assign one of the possible colors to a pixel. The simplest is to store the color value for each pixel in the compressed data. For images with 24 bits per pixel, each pixel has a 3-byte color value associated with it. Images that use 24 bits or more are called *true color* because over the range of colors a monitor can display, 24 bits per pixel is the limit of color differences that a human can distinguish.

The problem with 24-bit graphics is that while a system may be capable of displaying 16,777,216 different colors, it may not be able to do so simultaneously. Older computers may not even have a video card capable of using a 24-bit display mode. Newer computers may not have enough video memory to operate in 24-bit mode at higher screen resolutions. A display on a personal computer set at a resolution of 1024×768 pixels would require 2,359,296 ($1024 \times 768 \times 3 = 2.25$ MB) of video memory to display 24-bit images. If the computer had only 2 MB of video memory it could not display 24-bit images at this resolution but could do so at a lower resolution of 800×600 ($800 \times 600 \times 3 = 1.4$ MB).

The solution devised to represent colors before the days of displays capable of 24 bits per pixel was to define a color palette that selects a subset of the possible colors. Conceptually the palette is a 1-dimensional array of 3-byte elements that specify the color. Rather than directly specifying the color, each pixel value is an index into the color palette. The most common size for a palette is 256 entries where each pixel value consists of 8 bits. Most computers today can

---

[3]To avoid dealing too deeply with specific system implementations, this section contains some simplifications as to the behavior of display devices.

display 8-bit graphics in all their display resolutions, but very old computers were limited to even smaller palette sizes.

 Images with 24 or greater bits per pixel images never use a palette because it would take more bits to specify the index into the palette than to specify the color directly.

Bitmap image file formats represent colors in essentially the same way computer displays do. Some specify the color value for each pixel, some use a color palette, and others support both methods. Table 1.2 shows the methods used to represent colors for various image formats.

A file format that uses a palette may use pixel values with fewer than 8 bits in order to reduce the size of the file. A 4-bit-per-pixel image requires half as much storage as an 8-bit-per-pixel image of the same size. For images that use a limited number of colors, such as cartoons, a simple method to reduce the file size is to reduce the sample precision.

Table 1.2
Color
Representation
Methods

	Palette	Color Value
BMP	X	X
JPEG		X
GIF	X	
PNG	X	X

Compression

Since color bitmap images typically require over a megabyte of storage, most image file formats incorporate compression techniques. Compression techniques take advantage of patterns within the image data to find an equivalent representation that occupies less space. Completely random data cannot be compressed.

The following are brief descriptions of the compression techniques used by the image formats in this book. Table 1.3 shows the techniques used by each format.

Table 1.3
Compression
Methods Used by
Various File Formats

	BMP	GIF	PNG	JPEG
RLE	X			X
LZ		X	X	
Huffman			X	X
DCT				X

Run Length Encoding (RLE). Consecutive pixels with the same value are encoded using a run length and value pair. For example, an image with the pixel value 8 repeated 9 times could be represented as the 2-byte sequence

$$09_{16} \; 08_{16}$$

rather than

$$08_{16} \; 08_{16} \; 08_{16} \; 08_{16} \; 08_{16} \; 08_{16} \; 08_{16} \; 08_{16}$$

LZ Encoding. The compressor maintains a dictionary containing pixel value sequences that have already been encountered. The compressed stream contains codes that represent entries in the dictionary.

Huffman Coding. Rather than using a fixed number of bits to represent component values, variable length codes are used. More frequently used values are assigned shorter codes.

Discrete Cosine Transform (DCT). Blocks of pixels are represented using cosine functions of different frequencies. The high frequencies, which generally contribute less information to the image, are discarded.

The effectiveness of a compression technique depends upon the type of data. Figure 1.7 is a photograph and Figure 1.8 is a drawing. The photograph contains many areas with small changes in color, while the drawing has large areas with the same color.

Figure 1.7
IRENE.BMP

Figure 1.8
STARS.BMP

Figure 1.9 shows the relative file sizes when the photograph in Figure 1.7 is compressed using various formats: Uncompressed BMP, BMP with RLE encoding, GIF, PNG, and JPEG. Notice that BMP-RLE and GIF produce very little compression while PNG and, especially, JPEG produce significant reductions in file size.

Figure 1.10 contains a similar graph, this time using the drawing in Figure 1.8. You can see that the other file formats nearly catch up to JPEG with this image.

Lossless versus Lossy Compression

Most image file formats use what is known as *lossless compression*. By this we mean that if we take an image, compress it using a lossless technique, and expand it again, the resulting image is bit-by-bit identical to the original.

Some compression methods (notably JPEG) are *lossy*. Using the compression sequence described above, lossy compression produces an image that is

Figure 1.9
Percent of Original
Size Compressing
IRENE.BMP

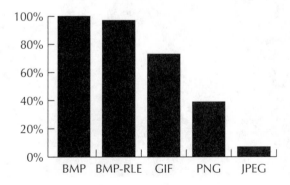

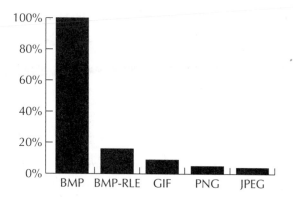

Figure 1.10
Percent of Original
Size Compressing
STARS.BMP

close to the original but not an exact match. That is, a pixel with an RGB color value of (128,243,118) in an image that is compressed may produce (127,243,119) when it is expanded. In image compression, lossy techniques take advantage of the fact that the eye has a hard time distinguishing between nearly identical colors.

The reason for using lossy compression is that it generally gives significantly greater compression than lossless methods do. In many situations, small losses of data are acceptable in exchange for increased compression.

Byte and Bit Ordering

All bitmap image files contain integers stored in binary format. For single-byte integers there is no compatibility problem among different processor types. This is not the case with multi-byte integers. When reading multi-byte integers there is the issue of how to order the bytes from the input stream in the integer. Suppose that an image file contains these two bytes in succession.

$$0\ 1\ 1\ 0\ 0\ 0\ 1\ 1\quad (63_{16})$$
$$0\ 0\ 0\ 1\ 1\ 1\ 0\ 1\quad (1D_{16})$$
$$\downarrow \qquad\qquad \downarrow$$

Most Significant Bit   Least Significant Bit

If these bytes represent a 2-byte integer should they be interpreted as

$$0\ 0\ 0\ 1\ 1\ 1\ 0\ 1\ \ 0\ 1\ 1\ 0\ 0\ 0\ 1\ 1\quad (1D63_{16})\ 75{,}231_{10}$$

or

$$0\ 1\ 1\ 0\ 0\ 0\ 1\ 1\ \ 0\ 0\ 0\ 1\ 1\ 1\ 0\ 1\quad (631D_{16})\ 25{,}373_{10}$$

In other words, in a multi-byte integer does the most significant byte occur first or last in the file?

The answer to this question depends upon the type of file. Some formats require that the most significant byte be stored first; others require that the least significant be first.

Why not order bytes in an image file so that a simple read operation like this reads integers correctly?

```
unsigned int value ;
inputstream.read ((char *) &value, sizeof (value)) ;
```

The problem is that different types of processors order integers differently, and blindly reading raw bytes into an integer variable will not work for all of them. Most processors in common use, including the Motorola 680x0 and Sun SPARC families, store integers with the most significant byte first. This byte ordering is known as *big-endian*. It is also known as *network order* because it is used by Internet protocol. Processors that store integers with the least significant byte first are known as *little-endian*. The Intel 80x86 family of processors used in personal computers is the most common little-endian processor.

This code example produces different output depending upon whether it is run on a big-endian or a little-endian system.

```
#include <iostream>
using namespace std ;
main ()
{
    unsigned short value = 1 ;
    unsigned char *ptr = (unsigned char *) &value ;
    if (*ptr == 1)
        cout << "I'm Little-Endian" << endl ;
    else
        cout << "I'm Big-Endian" << endl ;
    return 0 ;
}
```

Converting between little-endian and big-endian formats is simply a matter of swapping bytes, and the conversion is the same in either direction. For 2-byte integers the conversion is

```
unsigned short SwapBytes (unsigned short source)
{
    unsigned short destination ;
    destination = ((source & 0xFF) << 8) | ((source & 0xFF00) >> 8) ;
    return source ;
}
```

and 4-byte integers are converted as

```
unsigned long SwapBytes (unsigned long source)
{
    unsigned long destination ;
    destination = ((source & 0x000000FFL) << 24)
                | ((source & 0x0000FF00L) << 8)
                | ((source & 0x00FF0000L) >> 8)
                | ((source & 0xFF000000L) >> 24) ;
    return destination ;
}
```

 In these programming examples we assume that long is 32 bits and short is 16 bits. This is correct for most environments, but not for all.

Whatever the processor type, when processing an entire byte the ordering of bits within a byte is the same. However, the ordering of bit strings within individual bytes is a more subtle issue. Computer processors deal only with complete bytes. When processing compressed data one frequently has to process bit strings that are not aligned on byte boundaries. Bit strings can be extracted from bytes, but their ordering is determined entirely by the image format.

Suppose that you need to read three 3-bit strings from the 2-byte sequence

```
1st Byte  0 0 0 1 1 1 0 1
2nd Byte  0 1 1 0 0 0 1 1
```

Depending upon whether the bit strings are read from the most significant bit to least significant bit and whether the bits in the second byte are made the most significant or least significant, the resulting bit strings could be one of these four possibilities:

1. 000 111 010
2. 000 111 001
3. 101 011 001
4. 101 011 100

The ordering of bit strings within bytes is specified by the image format.

Except for XBM, in all image file formats in this book that support images with fewer than 8 bits per pixel, the most significant bits within a byte contain the values of the leftmost pixel. One should view the bit ordering in these formats as

```
                Data Byte
          | 7 6 5 4 | 3 2 1 0 |    4 bits per pixel
          | 7 6 | 5 4 | 3 2 | 1 0 |    2 bits per pixel
          |7|6|5|4|3|2|1|0|    1 bit per pixel
    Leftmost Pixel            Rightmost Pixel
```

Color Quantization

The JPEG and PNG formats covered in this book can contain image data that uses 24 bits or more per pixel. How can you display a 24-bit JPEG image on an output device that supports only 8 bits per pixel? Likewise, how can you convert a JPEG file to the GIF format, which supports a maximum of 8 bits per pixel? The answer is a process known as color quantization, a fancy name for the process of reducing the number of colors used in an image. The topic of color quantization falls outside the scope of this book; therefore, we are only going to cover enough to allow you to display images if you are using a display that does not support 24-bit images and to convert to such formats.

The method we are going to use is called *median cut quantization.* In it we create a three-dimensional count of the number of times each pixel color value is used. Such a counting would look something like that shown in Algorithm 1.1

Now we have a cubic region containing all the color frequencies. The next step, shown in Algorithm 1.2, is to divide the cube into two rectangular regions in such a manner that each part has half the frequency values. This fragment divides the frequencies in half along the blue axis.

Figure 1.11 shows the result of the first application of the process in Algorithm 1.2. We apply the process recursively, dividing the rectangular regions in half using a different color axis until we have 256 boxes with roughly the same total frequency. Figures 1.12 and 1.13 show sample divisions of the RGB color-space along the other axes.

Keep in mind that this is a rough outline. If 4-byte integers were used to store frequency values, the FREQUENCIES array defined in Algorithm 1.1 would

Algorithm 1.1
Gathering
Frequencies in the
Median Cut
Algorithm

```
Global FREQUENCIES [0..255][0..255][0..255]
Global IMAGE [1..IMAGEHEIGHT][1..IMAGEWIDTH]

Procedure GatherFrequencies
    Begin
    For II = 1 To IMAGEHEIGHT Do
        Begin
        For JJ = 1 To IMAGEWIDTH Do
            Begin
            RED = IMAGE [II][JJ].RED
            GREEN = IMAGE [II][JJ].GREEN
            BLUE = IMAGE [II][JJ].BLUE
            FREQUENCIES [RED][GREEN][BLUE] =
                FREQUENCIES [RED][GREEN][BLUE] + 1
            End
        End
    End
```

Algorithm 1.2
Dividing the
Colorspace in Half

```
GLOBAL FREQUENCIES [0..255][0..255][0..255]
Function DivideBlueInHalf
     Begin
     COUNT = 0
     For BLUECUT = 0 To 255 Do
          Begin
          For II = 0 To 255 Do
               Begin
               For JJ = 0 To 255 Do
                    Begin
                    COUNT = COUNT + FREQUENCIES [II][JJ][BLUECUT]
                    End
               End
          If COUNT > IMAGEHEIGHT * IMAGEWIDTH / 2 Then
               Return BLUECUT
          End
     Return 255
     End
```

be 64 megabytes. Even in this era of cheap memory, this is too large for a practical implementation. In fact, the size of the FREQUENCIES array is larger than the pixel data for most images, so in practice we have to reduce the precision of each color value, use dynamic data structures, or use a combination of both. A simple method to reduce the array size is to drop some of the least significant bits from each component value. Using 6 instead of 8 bits reduces the size of the FREQUENCIES array to just 1 megabyte ($4 \times 2^6 \times 2^6 \times 2^6$).

Figure 1.11
Example of the RGB
Colorspace Being
Divided Using the
Process in
Algorithm 1.2

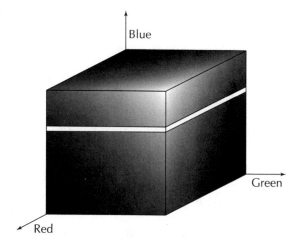

Figure 1.12 RGB Colorspace in Figure 1.11, Now Divided along the Green Axis As Well

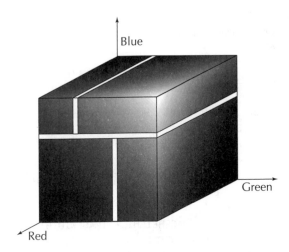

Figure 1.13 RGB Colorspace in Figure 1.12, Now Divided along the Red Axis As Well

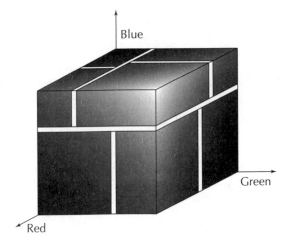

A Common Image Format

A typical application for viewing image files will be able to read and store images using several file formats, and convert files from one format to another. Rather than having a function for viewing each type of file and a separate function for each possible format conversion, it is useful to have a common uncompressed image format that can be used for all types of files supported by the application.

With a common uncompressed format you need only write one display function for the common format. If each image file format has a function for reading into the common format and a function for writing from the common format, you have everything you need to display, save, and convert among all file formats.

In addition to supporting all of the anticipated image formats, a common image format ideally is easy to display and portable across various hardware platforms. Unfortunately, ease of display and portability are somewhat exclusive. You do not want a common image format and a separate display format. The format in our examples is a compromise, designed to be as easy as possible to use in the Windows environment while at the same time concealing Windows-specific behavior. It is capable of storing images using 1, 4, 8, and 24 bits per pixel. PNG and JPEG are the only formats that store data using other formats. The PNG decoder will convert the data to one of the formats above; the JPEG decoder will only read files with 8-bit sample data.

Datatype Definitions

The source code examples in this book use typedefs for integers that are expected to be a specific size. Table 1.4 lists the integer types used. They are defined in the file datatype.h, which also defines a function for performing endian conversions of integers. The existing definitions are suitable for most 32-bit little-endian systems, so if you are porting the code to another type of system, this is the first file you need to modify.

Common Image Class

BitmapImage is the name of the common image format class. It is defined in the file bitimage.h. The general process followed by all of the encoders and decoders in this book for reading and writing images is

```
BitmapImage image ;
XYZDecoder decoder ;
XYZEncoder encoder ;
ifstream input ("INPUT.XYZ", ios::binary) ;
decoder.ReadImage (input, image) ;
ofstream output ("OUTPUT.XYZ", ios::binary) ;
encoder.WriteImage (output, image) ;
```

where XYZDecoder and XYZEncoder are the decoder and encoder classes for the image type.

Table 1.4
Types Defined in
datatype.h

Type	Use
BYTE1	Signed 8-bit integer
UBYTE1	Unsigned 8-bit integer
BYTE2	Signed 16-bit integer
UBYTE2	Unsigned 16-bit integer
BYTE4	Signed 32-bit integer
UBYTE4	Unsigned 32-bit integer

The implementation of this class is tailored for Microsoft Windows. However, the interface is designed to conceal system-specific behavior. The BitmapImage class has two main storage areas: the color map and the pixel data. An application can store an image in a BitmapImage object by using one of the image decoders in this book (or one you write yourself) or by using the SetSize, ColorMap, and [] operators to write store raw image data.

SetSize
The SetSize function allocates the dynamic memory used to store image data within a BitmapImage object. An application must call this function before attempting to store image data into the object.

ColorMap
The ColorMap functions are used to access the image's color palette. For images with a bit depth of 8 or fewer the application must fill in the color map. If the image has a bit depth of 24 this function should not be used.

[] (Subscript) Operator
The subscript operator is used to access individual bytes in the image pixel data. The format of this data depends upon the bit depth of the image. For images that use 8 bits per pixel each data byte is an index into the color map (accessed through the ColorMap functions). If the bit depth is fewer than 8, multiple color indices are packed into the data bytes. The higher-order bits contain the leftmost pixel values. For 24-bit images each pixel is represented by 3 bytes. The usual ordering for color bytes in a 24-bit image is RGB, but Windows expects the values in BGR order. The BitmapImage class defines the values RedOffset, GreenOffset, and BlueOffset used by the programming examples to specify the ordering of these bytes. If your system does not use BGR ordering, you can change the values of these offsets.

Another Windows'ism that the subscript operator conceals is Windows images will be stored starting with the bottommost row. In order to make displaying an image as easy as possible on Windows, this implementation of the BitmapImage class stores the rows in bottom-to-top order, as Windows expects them to be. However, the subscript operator reverses the row order so that [0] returns the topmost row of the image. Windows also expects the length of each image row to be a multiple of 4 bytes. The subscript operator automatically takes this padding into account so that [N][0] always returns the first pixel byte for the Nth row. By making the implementation of BitmapImage independent of the interface it is possible to change the implementation to support different systems without affecting the image encoders and decoders.

There are two implementations of the subscript operator. If the CHECK_RANGE preprocessor symbol is defined, the subscript operator performs range checking on all values. If CHECK_RANGE is not defined, no range checking is done. The latter implementation is significantly faster, but the former is better for use while debugging.

GetRGB

The GetRGB function returns the RGB color value for a given pixel in the image. An image encoder can use this function to get pixel values without having to deal with different sample precision values.

EightBitQuantization

The EightBitQuantization function converts a 24-bits-per-pixel image to an 8-bits per pixel image using the mean cut processes. About half of the source code for the BitmapImage function is devoted to color quantization. This implementation makes two passes through the image. On the first pass the FindColorUsage function creates a ColorUsage structure for each color used in the image. These structures are inserted into three linked lists sorted by the Red, Green, and Blue component values. Next the recursive SplitAreaInHalf function repeatedly divides the RGB colorspace into two areas that contain half of the weighted color values of the original.

At this point we have defined the 256 color areas for the image. The CreateColor function defines a single color that is the average for a box. This gives the "best" colors to use for the image. Finally, QuantizeSourceImage makes a second pass over the image data to replace the colors in the source image with a color from among the 256 colors that were defined in the preceding passes.

Conclusion

In this chapter we covered the basics of bitmap image formats. We explained the difference between bitmap and vector image formats and the way images are displayed on output devices. We also covered the representation of color and described some of the color models used by graphics file formats. The chapter presented a brief introduction to color quantization and the compression techniques used by the file formats covered in this book.

Foley et al. (1996) describes the operation of computer displays in greater detail than we have here. It also contains excellent descriptions of colorspaces. Brown and Shepherd (1995) and Murray and van Ryper (1994) contain introductory descriptions of a large number of graphics file formats.

In this book we will cover only the specific compression techniques used by file formats under discussion. Nelson (1992) is the best introduction to compression techniques available and an excellent source for their history and relationships.

The medium cut algorithm is described in Heckbert (1982). Lindley (1995) and (Rimmer (1993) describe this algorithm and take a different approach to implementing it.

Chapter 2

Windows BMP

Format: Windows BMP
Origin: Microsoft
Definition: Windows SDK

The first image format we are going to cover is one of the simplest. Windows BMP is the native image format in the Microsoft Windows operating systems. It supports images with 1, 4, 8, 16, 24, and 32 bits per pixel, although BMP files using 16 and 32 bits per pixel are rare. BMP also supports simple run-length compression for 4 and 8 bits per pixel. However, BMP compression is of use only with large blocks with identical colors, making it of very limited value. It is rare for Windows BMP to be in a compressed format.

Over the years there have been several different and incompatible versions of the BMP format. Since the older forms have completely disappeared, version incompatibilities are not a problem. The discussion here deals with the BMP format in use since Windows version 3 (common) and the format introduced with OS/2 (rare but supported).

Data Ordering

Multi-byte integers in the Windows BMP format are stored with the least significant bytes first. Data stored in the BMP format consists entirely of complete bytes so bit string ordering is not an issue.

File Structure

File Header
Image Header
Color Table
Pixel Data

Figure 2.1
Bitmap File
Structure

The BMP file structure is very simple and is shown in Figure 2.1. If you are developing on Windows, the BMP structures are included from the windows.h header file. If you are not working on Windows, you can create your own structures from the tables below. For some reason Microsoft insists on adding confusing prefixes to the names of structure fields. To be consistent with Microsoft's documentation we have included these prefixes in the field names.

File Header

Every Windows BMP begins with a BITMAPFILEHEADER structure whose layout is shown in Table 2.1. The main function of this structure is to serve as the signature that identifies that file format.

Three checks can be made to ensure that the file you are reading is in fact a BMP file:

- The first two bytes of the file must contain the ASCII characters "B" followed by "M."

- If you are using a file system where you can determine the exact file size in bytes, you can compare the file size with the value in the bfSize field

- The bfReserved1 and bfReserved2 fields must be zero.

The file header also specifies the location of the pixel data in the file. When decoding a BMP file you must use the bfOffbits field to determine the offset from the beginning of the file to where the pixel data starts. Most applications place the pixel data immediately following the BITMAPINFOHEADER structure or palette, if it is present. However, some applications place filler bytes between these structures and the pixel data so you must use the bfOffbits to determine the number of bytes from the BITMAPFILEHEADER structure to the pixel data.

Table 2.1
BITMAPFILEHEADER
Structure

Field Name	Size in Bytes	Description
bfType	2	Contains the characters "BM" that identify the file type
bfSize	4	File size
bfReserved1	2	Unused
bfReserved2	2	Unused
bfOffBits	4	Offset to start of pixel data

Image Header

The image header immediately follows the BITMAPFILEHEADER structure. It comes in two distinct formats, defined by the BITMAPINFOHEADER and

BITMAPCOREHEADER structures. BITMAPCOREHEADER represents the OS/2 BMP format and BITMAPINFOHEADER is the much more common Windows format. Unfortunately, there is no version field in the BMP definitions. The only way to determine the type of image structure used in a particular file is to examine the structure's size field, which is the first 4 bytes of both structure types. The size of the BITMAPCOREHEADER structure is 12 bytes; the size of BITMAPINFOHEADER, at least 40 bytes.

The layout of BITMAPINFOHEADER is shown in Table 2.2. This structure gives the dimensions and bit depth of the image and tells if the image is compressed. Windows 95 supports a BMP format that uses an enlarged version of this header. Few applications create BMP files using this format; however, a decoder should be implemented so that it knows that header sizes can be larger than 40 bytes.

The image height is an unsigned value. A negative value for the biHeight field specifies that the pixel data is ordered from the top down rather than the normal bottom up. Images with a negative biHeight value may not be compressed.

Table 2.2 BITMAPINFOHEADER Structure	Field Name	Size	Description
	biSize	4	Header size—Must be at least 40
	biWidth	4	Image width
	biHeight	4	Image height
	biPlanes	2	Must be 1
	biBitCount	2	Bits per pixel—1, 4, 8, 16, 24, or 32
	biCompression	4	Compression type—BI_RGB=0, BI_RLE8=1, BI_RLE4=2, or BI_BITFIELDS=3
	biSizeImage	4	Image Size—May be zero if not compressed
	biXPelsPerMeter	4	Preferred resolution in pixels per meter
	biYPelsPerMeter	4	Preferred resolution in pixels per meter
	biClrUsed	4	Number of entries in the color map that are actually used
	biClrImportant	4	Number of significant colors

BITMAPCOREHEADER Structure

The BITMAPCOREHEADER structure is the other image header format. Its layout is shown in Table 2.3. Notice that it has fewer fields and that all have analogous

Table 2.3 BITMAPCOREHEADER Structure	Field Name	Size	Description
	bcSize	4	Header size—Must be 12
	bcWidth	2	Image width
	bcHeight	2	Image height
	bcPlanes	2	Must be 1
	bcBitCount	2	Bit count—1, 4, 8, or 24

fields in the BITMAPINFOHEADER structure. If the file uses BITMAPCOREHEADER rather than BITMAPINFOHEADER, the pixel data cannot be compressed.

Color Palette

The color palette immediately follows the file header and can be in one of three formats. The first two are used to map pixel data to RGB color values when the bit count is 1, 4, or 8 (biBitCount or bcBitCount fields). For BMP files in the Windows format, the palette consists of an array of $2^{bitcount}$ RGBQUAD structures (Table 2.4). BMP files in OS/2 format use an array of RGBTRIPLE structures (Table 2.5).

Table 2.4
RGBQUAD *Structure*

Field	Size	Description
rgbBlue	1	Blue color value
rgbGreen	1	Red color value
rgbRed	1	Green color value
rgbReserved	1	Must be zero

Table 2.5
RGBTRIPLE *Structure*

Field	Size	Description
rgbtBlue	1	Blue color value
rgbtGreen	1	Red color value
rgbtRed	1	Green color value

The final format for the color palette is not really a color mapping at all. If the bit count is 16 or 32 and the value in the biCompression field of the BITMAPINFOHEADER structure is BI_BITFIELDS (3), in place of an array of RGBQUAD structures, there is an array of three 4-byte integers. These three values are bit masks that specify the bits used for the red, green, and blue components respectively. In each mask the nonzero bits must be contiguous. In addition, no bit set in one bit mask may be set in any other bit mask. Images using 24 bits as well as 16- and 32-bit images without the biCompression field set to BI_BIT-FIELDS do not have a color palette.

In a 32-bit image, the three 32-bit values

$$0\,0\,0\,0\,0\,0\,0\,0\,0\,0\,0\,0\,0\,0\,0\,0\,0\,0\,0\,0\,0\,0\,1\,1\,1\,1\,1\,1\,1\,1\,1\,1_2 \quad \text{Red}$$
$$0\,0\,0\,0\,0\,0\,0\,0\,0\,0\,0\,0\,1\,1\,1\,1\,1\,1\,1\,1\,1\,1\,0\,0\,0\,0\,0\,0\,0\,0\,0\,0_2 \quad \text{Green}$$
$$0\,0\,1\,1\,1\,1\,1\,1\,1\,1\,1\,1\,0\,0\,0\,0\,0\,0\,0\,0\,0\,0\,0\,0\,0\,0\,0\,0\,0\,0\,0\,0_2 \quad \text{Blue}$$

specify that that each component is represented by 10 bits. The logical AND of the three values must be zero, and the bit range for each component must be contiguous.

Pixel Data

The pixel data follows the palette or bit masks if they are present. Otherwise, it follows the BITMAPINFOHEADER or the BITMAPCOREHEADER structure. Normally the data follows immediately, but there may be intervening fill bytes. You must use the bfOffBits field in the BITMAPFILE header to determine the offset from the BITMAPFILEHEADER structure to the pixel data.

Pixel rows are ordered in the file from bottom to top. The number of data rows is given by the biHeight or bcHeight field in the image header. Row size is determined from the biBitCount and biWidth or bcBitCount and bcWidth fields. The number of bytes per row is rounded up to a multiple of four and can be determined as follows (Using integer division):

$$bytes\ per\ row = \frac{\left(\dfrac{width\ \times\ bit\ count\ +\ 7}{8}\right) + 3}{4}$$

The format of the pixel data depends upon the number of bits per pixel.

1 and 4 Bits per Pixel. Each data byte is subdivided into either eight or two fields whose values represent an index into the color palette. The most significant bit field represents the leftmost pixel.

8 Bits per Pixel. Each pixel in the row is represented by 1 byte that is an index into the color palette.

16 Bits per Pixel. Each pixel is represented by a 2-byte integer value. If the value of the biCompression field in the BITMAPINFOHEADER structure is BI_RGB (0), the intensity of each color is represented by 5 bits, with the most significant bit not used. The default bit usage is shown in Figure 2.2.

Figure 2.2
Format for 16 Bits per Pixel

15	14	13	12	11	10	9	8	7	6	5	4	3	2	1	0
	Red					Blue					Green				

If the biCompression field is set to BI_BITMAP, the three 4-byte bit masks that follow the BITMAPINFOHEADER structure specify the bits used for each color component. The bit masks are ordered red, blue, green.

24 Bits per Pixel. Each pixel is represented by three consecutive bytes that specify the blue, green, and red component values, respectively. Note that this ordering is the reverse of that used in most image file formats.

32 Bits per Pixel Each pixel is represented by a 4-byte integer. If the value of the biCompression field in the BITMAPINFOHEADER is set to BI_RGB, the three low-order bytes represent the 8-bit values for the blue, green, and red components in that order. The high-order byte is not used. This format is just like 24 bits per pixel with a wasted byte at the end.

If the biCompression field contains the value BI_BITFIELD, the three 4-byte bit masks that follow the BITMAPINFOHEADER specify the bits to be used for each component. The bit masks are ordered red, blue, green.

Compression

The BMP format supports simple run-length encoding of 4- and 8-bit-per-pixel images. A 4-bit-per-pixel image is compressed if the value of the biCompression field of the BITMAPINFOHEADER structure is BI_RLE4 (=2), and an 8-bit-per-pixel image is compressed if the value is BI_RLE8 (=1). No other bit depths may be compressed.

Run-length encoding is one of the simplest compression techniques. In it data is stored so that repeated values are replaced by a count. This type of compression is suitable only for images that have many repeated values, such as a cartoon drawing. For many types of images, run-length encoding will produce a larger file (negative compression). The compressed data format depends upon the number of bits per pixel.

RLE8

In RLE8, compressed data is broken down into 2-byte pairs. The first byte gives the count of pixel values, and the second gives the pixel value to be repeated. In 8-bit-per-pixel images the byte sequence

$$08_{16} \ 00_{16}$$

expands to the pixel values

$$00_{16} \ 00_{16} \ 00_{16} \ 00_{16} \ 00_{16} \ 00_{16} \ 00_{16} \ 00_{16} \ 00_{16}$$

A repeat count of zero is used as an escape code. A zero value followed by another zero means advance to the next line in the image. A zero value followed by a 1 marks the end of the image. Zero followed by a byte containing the value 2 changes the current position in the image. The next two bytes are unsigned values that give the number of columns and rows, respectively, to advance. This code allows a large number of pixels with the value zero to be skipped. This encoded sequence:

$$04_{16} \ 15_{16} \ 00_{16} \ 00_{16} \ 02_{16} \ 11_{16} \ 02_{16} \ 03_{16} \ 00_{16} \ 01_{16}$$

expands into these two rows:

$$15_{16} \ 15_{16} \ 15_{16} \ 15_{16}$$
$$11_{16} \ 11_{16} \ 03_{16} \ 03_{16}$$
End of Image

A zero escape code followed by a value greater than two gives a count of literal bytes to copy to the image. The literal bytes immediately follow the count. If the count is odd, one fill byte is stored after the data bytes. This code is used to store uncompressed data.

It is worth noting from the preceding description that if the image contains no consecutive bytes with the same value, the resulting image data will be larger than the equivalent uncompressed data.

RLE4

The RLE4 format is almost identical to the RLE8 format. The major difference is that when encoding color runs, the data byte that follows the count contains two pixel values. The value in the four high-order bits is used to encode the first and all subsequent odd pixels in the run, while the four low-order bits are used to encode the second and remaining even pixels. Thus, the RLE4 format can encode runs of the same pixel value or two alternating values. This encoded pair

05_{16} 56_{16}

expands to this sequences of 4-bit values:

5 6 5 6 5

All of the escape commands for RLE4 are the same as for RLE8 with the exception of coding absolute values. A zero escape value followed by a byte value greater than two gives the number of absolute pixel values that follow. These values are packed into 4 bits each with the high-order bits coming first. If the run is not a multiple of four, padding follows so that the number of absolute data bytes (not pixels) is a multiple of two.

Conclusion

If you are developing software to read and write graphics files in the Windows environment, Windows BMP is your best choice to use for testing. It is simple to implement, easy to debug, and can be viewed without special tools.

Unlike all of the other formats in this book, the definition of Windows BMP is under the complete control of one company. Microsoft can be expected to make upwardly compatible enhancements to the format in the future. Microsoft's definition of the BMP format can be found in Microsoft (1993). Murray and van Ryper (1994) contains a description that includes older BMP versions. Swan (1993) also has a good explanation of BMP.

The accompanying CD contains source code for a Windows BMP encoder (BmpEncoder) and decoder (BmpDecoder). The following illustrates how these classes are used to read and write BMP files:

```
#include "bitimage.h"
#include "bmpdecod.h"
#include "bmpencod.h"

BitmapImage image ;

ifstream input ("INPUT.BMP", ios::binary) ;
BmpDecoder decoder ;
decoder.ReadImage (input, image) ;
ofstream output ("OUTPUT.BMP", ios::binary) ;
BmpEncoder encoder ;
encoder.WriteImage (output, image) ;
```

When you read and write binary image files you must open them in binary mode. Otherwise, your library may translate the contents of the files in unexpected ways.

The CD also contains the source code for a Windows application (viewer.cpp) that displays a BMP file. This application can be easily modified to use the decoder for any of the other formats covered in this book.

Chapter 3

XBM

Format: XBM
Origin: X Consortium
Definition: Informal

XBM is the simplest format covered in this book as well as the most unusual. Native to the X Windows system and rarely used outside that environment, it is much more limited than Windows BMP. It only supports two color images. An XBM file is actually more analogous to an icon file on Windows than to a BMP.[1]

File Format

The XBM image file format is completely unlike the other formats described in this book. Rather than containing binary data, an XBM file contains C source code. When writing user interface code for the X-Window system, you can include predefined icons in the XBM format simply by including a source file in the application and then compiling and linking the image into the application. This serves roughly the same function as a resource file in Windows. Applications containing an XBM decoder, such as web browsers and image editors, can read XBM files and display the image contained in them without compiling and linking to it.

The format of an XBM file is shown in Figure 3.1. The string `imagename` represents the unique name assigned to the image in an application that includes

---

[1]There is a similar, more capable X-Windows format called XPM.

Figure 3.1
XBM File format

```
#define imagename_width 16
#define imagename_height 2
#define imagename_hot_x 1
#define imagename_hot_y 1
static unsigned char imagename_bits [] = { 0x10, 0x10,
0x10, 0x01 } ;
```

many different XBM files. When an XBM file is read to display the image, this name has no significance.

The image dimensions are defined with a pair of `#define` preprocessor directives. The preprocessor symbols with the suffixes `_width` and `_height` specify the image width and height in pixels. These definitions are required.

XBM files can define a hot spot that is used when the image is used as an icon. The position of the hot spot is specified by two `#define` directives that create preprocessor symbols with the suffixes `_hot_x` and `_hot_y`. The definition of the hot spot is optional within an XBM file, but one symbol may not be present without the other symbol.

The last statement in the image definition is an array of bytes that defines the pixel values for the image. Each byte represents the value for eight pixels in the image. The image data is stored from top to bottom, left to right; pixel values are not split across rows. If the image width is not a multiple of eight, the extra bits in the last byte of each row are not used. The total number of bytes in the image must be

$$bytes = height \times \frac{width + 7}{8}$$

using integer division. XBM files contains no color information. Bits set to zero are drawn in the current background color, and bits set to one are drawn in the current foreground color.

Byte Ordering

Byte ordering is not an issue with XBM files since all the data consists of single bytes. Within a byte the least significant bit represents the leftmost pixel. This is the opposite of the Windows BMP format (and all the other formats in the book).

Sample Image

The following code is a sample XBM file that produces the image shown in Figure 3.2.

```
#define myimage_height 12
#define myimage_width 12
static unsigned char myimage_bits[] = {
    0xF0, 0x00,
```

```
                        0xF0, 0x00,
                        0xF0, 0x00,
                        0xF0, 0x00,
                        0xFF, 0x0F,
                        0xFF, 0x0F,
                        0xFF, 0x0F,
                        0xFF, 0x0F,
                        0xF0, 0x00,
                        0xF0, 0x00,
                        0xF0, 0x00,
                        0xF0, 0x00 } ;
```

Figure 3.2
Sample XBM Image

File Syntax

An XBM image file is a C source file. However, no one is going to implement a complete C preprocessor and parser to read an image file. C is a free-format language, making it relatively difficult for a simple parser to handle. Consequently, a legal XBM file and an XBM file that can be displayed by a given image-viewing application are two different things.

Unfortunately, the difference between the two is not specified, so we can only give some guidelines when creating XBM files:

- Use no blank lines.

- Use no comments.

- Follow the exact statement ordering shown in Figure 3.1.

- Use decimal values for integers in the #define directives.

- Use no spaces between the # and define.

- Use hexadecimal values for integers in the pixel data.

Violating any of these rules, even though it results in perfectly valid C, can make your XBM image unreadable. Interestingly, there are XBM decoders that will correctly display images stored in files that contain certain errors in C syntax.

Reading and Writing XBM Files

Creating XBM files is a trivial process. All an encoder has to do is output a simple text file using the format described above.

On the other hand, reading XBM files is rather difficult, especially considering the limited capabilities of the format. One approach is to apply compiler writing techniques. The decoder is logically broken down into two passes: One breaks the file into a sequence of tokens while the other parses the tokens to create the image. Tools like LEX and YACC can be used to generate the two passes, but the format is simple enough to create them by hand.

Conclusion

While the XBM format is very limited outside the X Windows environment, it is supported by all of the major Web browsers. It also illustrates an unusual approach to storing images within a file. Scheiffler and James (1990) is the closest thing to an official description of the XBM format. Nye (1988) gives an alternate description.

Chapter 4

Introduction to JPEG

> Format: JPEG
> Origin: Joint Photographic Experts Group
> Definition: ISO 10918-1
>   JFIF V1.02

JPEG has become the most commonly used format for storing photographic images, yet in spite of its widespread use, the inner workings of JPEG compression remain something of a black art. Since JPEG is a very complex image format we have divided the JPEG material into eight chapters. In this chapter we will cover the fundamentals. Subsequent chapters will examine specific aspects.

JPEG is an acronym for "Joint Photographic Experts Group." This organization created a standard for compressing images under the authority of international standards bodies. The JPEG standard is fairly complex because, rather than defining an image file format, it defines a number of related image compression techniques.

The power of the JPEG format is that, for photographic images, it gives the greatest compression of any bitmap format in common use. A photograph that takes 1 MB to store in a Windows BMP file can usually be compressed down to 50 KB with JPEG. Although JPEG is computationally intensive, its outstanding compression generally outweighs the processing required.

As good as JPEG is, it is not suitable for some applications. All of the JPEG compression methods in general use are lossy, which makes them unsuitable for an intermediate storage format when you are repeatedly editing an image file. JPEG is also not as good at compressing text and drawings as it is at compressing photographs.

JPEG Compression Modes

The original JPEG standard defined four compression modes: hierarchical, progressive, sequential, and lossless. In addition, the standard defined multiple encoding processes for the modes. Figure 4.1 shows the relationship of the major JPEG compression modes and encoding processes. While there is some commonality among them, for the most part they must be implemented as completely different techniques.

Sequential

Sequential is the plain vanilla JPEG mode. As the name implies, *sequential-mode* images are encoded from top to bottom. Sequential mode supports sample data with 8 and 12 bits of precision.

In sequential JPEG, each color component is completely encoded in a single *scan*—a block of compressed data that contains a single pass through the image for one or more components. In most formats, the entire compressed pixel data is stored in one contiguous region in the file. In JPEG, each pass through the image is stored in a distinct data block called a scan.

Within sequential mode, two alternative entropy encoding processes are defined by the JPEG standard: one uses Huffman encoding; the other uses arithmetic coding. We will speak more of these two processes shortly.

 Almost every JPEG file you are likely to come across will use sequential JPEG with Huffman encoding and 8-bit sample data.

The JPEG standard also defines another sequential encoding process that uses Huffman encoding. This is the *baseline* process, a subset of the sequential mode with Huffman coding. A decoder that can handle the extended process should be able to handle baseline transparently. Baseline images can have only 8-bit samples and are restricted to fewer Huffman and quantization[1] tables than extended sequential images.

Progressive

In *progressive* JPEG images, components are encoded in multiple scans. The compressed data for each component is placed in a minimum of 2 and as many as 896 scans, although the actual number is almost always at the low end of that range. The initial scans create a rough version of the image while subsequent scans refine it. Progressive images are intended for viewing as they are decoded.

---

[1]Huffman tables and quantization tables are described starting in the next chapter.

JPEG										
Sequential				Progressive				Lossless		Hierarchical
Huffman		Arithmetic		Huffman		Arithmetic		Original Lossless	JPEG-LS	
8-Bit	12-Bit	8-Bit	12-Bit	8-Bit	12-Bit	8-Bit	12-Bit			

Figure 4.1
JPEG Modes

They are useful when an image is being downloaded over a network or used in a Web browser because they allow the user to get an idea of what the image contains after as little data as possible has been transmitted.

Figure 4.2 shows an image that has been encoded with four scans using progressive JPEG. You can see that with each scan the image becomes clearer. Notice that from only the first scan you can tell that the image is an airplane. Say you wanted to download the image of a car over a slow network connection. With progressive JPEG you would be able to determine that you had the wrong picture after a relatively small amount of data had been transmitted.

The main drawbacks of progressive mode are that it is more difficult to implement than sequential and that, if the image is viewed as it is downloaded, it requires much more processing. Progressive JPEG is most suitable when the relative processing power exceeds the relative transmission speed of the image. In general, progressive-mode image files tend to be about the same size as their sequential counterparts.

Progressive mode is rarely used, but Huffman-encoded images with 8-bit samples are becoming more common.

Hierarchical

Hierarchical JPEG is a super-progressive mode in which the image is broken down into a number of subimages called *frames*.[2] A frame is a collection of one or more scans. In hierarchical mode, the first frame creates a low-resolution version of the image. The remaining frames refine the image by increasing the resolution.

Advocates claim that hierarchical is better than progressive when low transmission rates are used. If only a low resolution of an image is desired, not all of the frames are required to get the desired result.

---

[2]The other modes have one frame per image.

Figure 4.2
Sample Progressive
Image

The obvious drawback of hierarchical mode is its complexity. Its implementation has all of the complexity of the other modes and then some. Hierarchical JPEG clearly requires much more processing than the other modes, and using multiple frames increases the amount of data that must be transmitted.

 Not surprisingly, hierarchical JPEG is not in general use.

Lossless

The original JPEG standard defined a *lossless* compression mode that always preserves the exact, original image. A lossless mode could never hope to compress as well as a lossy one. Moreover, for most applications it did not compress as well as formats that were already available, so there was no compelling reason to use it. A new lossless compression method known as JPEG-LS has been created that, for all practical purposes, has made the original lossless format obsolete.

What Part of JPEG Will Be Covered in This Book?

The JPEG standard is so vast that we could not hope to cover it all in one book. Fortunately, only a small subset of the JPEG standard is in general use. That subset is what we will be covering in the following chapters: sequential and progressive JPEG with Huffman coding and 8-bit samples.

Twelve-bit data is used in some specialized applications, such as medical imaging (although it is not used to exchange pictures over the Internet). Our descriptions of JPEG structures include information on items specific to 12-bit data, but it is not implemented in the examples because it would require either duplicate 12-bit versions of many functions or conditional compilation. If you need to use 12-bit data, the sample programs are structured so that it should not be difficult to make the modification.

It is worth pointing out some of the reasons that so little of the JPEG standard is in common use, especially considering how widespread is the use of some of its pieces. The primary reason is that the JPEG standard simply defines too many ways to do the same thing—a decoder that can handle every possible JPEG stream would be a monster.

Another major reason is that the arithmetic coding modes are covered by patents, and to use them you need to pay licensing fees to the patent holders. Huffman coding and arithmetic coding are used by different processes to perform identical functions. If two methods do the exact same thing and one requires license fees and the other does not, which should you choose? Besides the issue of licensing fees, patents make it impossible to create freely available implementations of certain JPEG features.

This leads to the most critical reason that most of the JPEG encoding modes are rarely used in the real world. In order for a graphics file format to gain general acceptance someone has to implement software to handle that format and make it available to others.[3] An image format that cannot be used to exchange data among many different applications is of little use. The implementation problem is exacerbated by the fact that the JPEG standard is not freely available. The standards for every other major graphics file format circulate freely; not so with JPEG.[4] You have to purchase a copy from your national representative to ISO and it is not cheap. If a format is too complex, of limited value, or requires licensing fees, it is unlikely people will take the trouble to create code for it and make the code available.

What Are JPEG Files?

One of the most striking things about the JPEG standard, especially considering how sprawling it is, is what it did not define: a file format. The JPEG standard does not specify what an application needs to do in order to create images that can be exchanged among different applications. For example, it says nothing about how colors are represented, but deals only with how component values are stored. Nor is there any definition of how the components values are mapped within a colorspace. An implementer of JPEG software is not told if component one is red, two is green, three is blue, or even if the RGB color model is used at all. While a standard that is independent of colorspace is flexible, it is also impossible to implement.

Nature abhors a vacuum, and into this one came JFIF (JPEG File Interchange Format), created by Eric Hamilton. This specification fills in the gaps left by JPEG in creating files that can be exchanged among applications. "JFIF" has become synonymous with "JPEG File." While other file formats, such as TIFF, use JPEG compression, a file with a JPG or JPEG extension invariably is in the JFIF format. JFIF is what we are going to cover in this book.

SPIFF File Format

The JPEG organization recently released a file format standard called SPIFF (Still Picture Interchange File Format) that is intended to supplant JFIF. Unfortunately, SPIFF is probably a case of too much too late. JFIF has been in use for so long that it is probably here to stay.

---

[3] In the case of JPEG the main force for this was the Independent JPEG Group.

[4] That is the way it is supposed to be. However, the JPEG standards documents can be found easily on the Internet.

SPIFF presents some issues for implementers of JPEG software, because it is simply too inclusive. Most formats in use support only one color model. SPIFF supports thirteen, including three variations on YCbCr. Are JPEG decoders going to implement this many colorspaces? Clearly not, so what subset of SPIFF should be implemented for exchanging images among the most applications? Since JPEG is already in widespread use it is unlikely that a useful SPIFF subset is going to evolve on its own. From a practical point of view, JFIF remains the best choice of a file format for implementers of JPEG software.

Byte Ordering

Integers in JPEG files are stored with the most significant byte first, that is, in big-endian format. Bit-strings are encoded within bytes starting at the most significant bits. When a bit string crosses a byte boundary the bits in the first byte are more significant than the bits in the second.

Sampling Frequency

In JPEG, a *sampling frequency* is the relative frequency a component is sampled at. This is probably easiest to understand in the context of converting a photograph to a bitmap. Unlike an image on a computer display, a photograph can have continuous variations in color. To convert a photograph to a digital image, you scan the image and measure the component values at regular intervals. Figure 4.3 on page 42 shows a continuous function and samplings of the function at various frequencies. You can see that the more frequently samples are taken, the better the approximation of the original image.

So why bother with sampling frequencies, as it appears that they only affect the resolution of the image? Since most applications deal with data that has already been scanned there seems to be no need for them.

In most graphics file formats, all the color components are sampled at the same frequency. JPEG allows individual components to be sampled at different frequencies. Sampling frequencies allow images to be compressed while varying the amount of information contributed by each component. You saw in Chapter 1 that in the YCbCr color model the Y component is the most important. Reducing the amount of information included from the Cb and Cr components is a simple way to reduce the size of the compressed image.

Suppose you were creating a JPEG file from a color image. By adjusting the sampling frequencies you could include each pixel's Y component value in the compressed data and 1 value for every 4 pixels from the other components. Instead of storing 12 values for every 4 pixels, you would be storing 6—a 50% reduction.

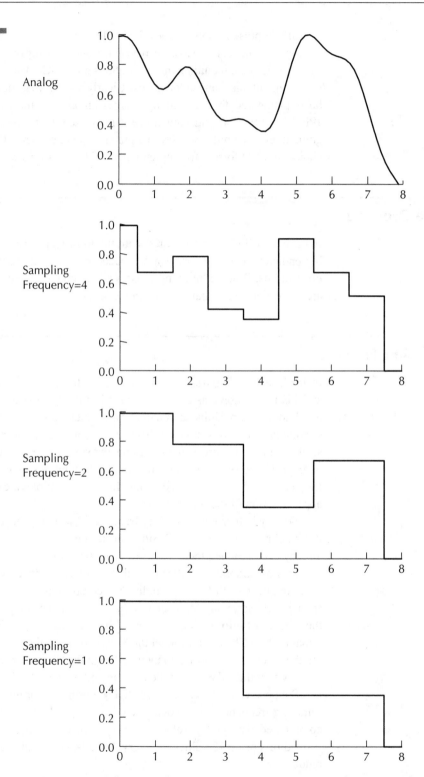

Figure 4.3
An Analog Signal
Sampled at Various
Frequencies

Analog

Sampling
Frequency=4

Sampling
Frequency=2

Sampling
Frequency=1

There is no requirement that the Y component be sampled at higher frequencies than the Cb and Cr components. It is possible to create a JPEG file with the Cb or Cr component having a higher sampling frequency than the Y component.

What makes sampling frequencies confusing when programming with graphics files is that generally the data you are dealing with has already been digitized. Instead of converting analog data to digital, in JPEG programming sampling is generally used to reduce the amount of data from one or more components. In most applications, what you are really doing with sampling frequencies is shrinking and stretching component values across multiple pixels.

When an image is compressed using JPEG, each component is assigned a horizontal and vertical sampling frequency that can range from 1 to 4. The higher the sampling frequency, the more data used for the component. The number of samples for a component is relative to the maximum sampling frequency in each dimension for the image.

Say, for example, that Y has a horizontal sampling frequency of 4, Cb 2, and Cr 1. This means that in the horizontal direction there are 2 Y component values for every Cb value and 4 for every Cr value. If, for each component, the vertical sampling frequency were the same as the horizontal sampling frequency, each Y component value would be mapped to a single pixel, each Cb component to 4 pixels, and each Cr component to 16 pixels. Figure 4.4 illustrates such a sampling.

The process of reducing the number of data points a component contributes is called *down-sampling*. An encoder can implement down sampling by encoding only every second, third, or fourth pixel or by taking an average value. The reverse process of stretching down-sampled pixels is called *up-sampling*. The simplest method for implementing down sampling is to repeat a data value across multiple pixels. Sometimes filtering processes are used to reduce blocking effects.

*Figure 4.4
Component
Sampling
Frequencies*

Y: H=4, V=4
Cb: H=2, V=2
Cr: H=1, V=1

Y: H=4, V=4
Cb: H=4, V=2
Cr: H=2, V=2

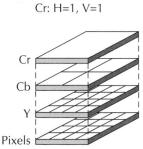

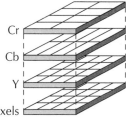

Note that it is entirely possible to create an image where the Y component is down-sampled when an image is compressed. This is not normally done except for experimentation since it tends to produce images that contain flaws when decompressed. Another sampling trap is that the JPEG standard does not forbid combinations of sampling frequencies that result in the need to sample fractions of pixels. Suppose the Y component has a vertical sampling frequency of 3, the Cb component a sampling frequency of 2. This means that each data value for the Cb component in the vertical direction represents $1\frac{1}{2}$ pixels. Most JPEG applications do not permit this kind of fractional sampling.

JPEG Operation

Figure 4.5 shows the steps of JPEG encoding. The following are brief descriptions of the steps.

Sampling.   The first stage in JPEG encoding is sampling. In this phase pixel data is converted from the RGB to the YCbCr colorspace and down sampling is performed.

Discrete Cosine Transform.   JPEG images are compressed in 8   8 pixel blocks called *data units.* The discrete cosine transform (DCT) converts the data unit values into a sum of cosine functions.

Quantization.   The quantization phase of JPEG compression gets rid of discrete cosine transform coefficients that are not essential for recreating a close approximation of the original. Quanitization is the main process that makes JPEG a lossy compression scheme.

Huffman Coding.   The Huffman code phase encodes the quantized DCT coefficients while eliminating runs of zero values. In the JPEG standard this phase is referred to as entropy coding because the JPEG standard allows arithmetic coding to be used in place of Huffman coding.

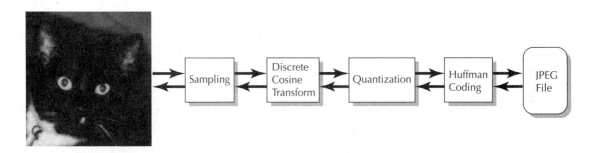

Figure 4.5
JPEG Encoding
Overview

Interleaved and Noninterleaved Scans

Earlier in this chapter we said that a scan could contain data for one or more components. A scan with one component is referred to as *noninterleaved.* In a noninterleaved scan, the data units are encoded one row at a time, top to bottom, left to right.

If a scan has data from more than one component, it is known as *interleaved.* Interleaved scans are encoded as groups of data units known as *minimum coded units,* or *MCUs.* A component's vertical sampling frequency specifies the number of data unit rows it contributes to an MCU, and its horizontal frequency gives the number of columns. (In a noninterleaved scan an MCU is always 1 data unit.) Within an MCU the data units for each component are encoded from top to bottom, left to right. Components are not interleaved within an MCU.

Figure 4.6 shows how the data units would be encoded in an MCU in an image with three components and with horizontal and vertical sampling frequencies of 4×2, 2×4, and 1×1. Each tiny square represents a single pixel. The thick rectangles show how sampling groups the pixels into data units. The numbers show the order in which each data unit is encoded within the MCU.

The maximum horizontal and vertical sampling frequency values are both 4, so each MCU will represent a 32×32 (8×4 by 8×4) block of pixels. The sampling frequencies for each component specify the relationship of the component to the MCU. The first component has a horizontal sampling frequency of 4, so it contributes 4 columns of data units. The vertical sampling frequency is 2, so the component contributes 2 rows of data units.

Scans are always encoded with complete MCUs. If the image height or width is not a multiple of the MCU size, extra pixel values are inserted into the image data so that the compressed data always contains complete MCUs. The JPEG

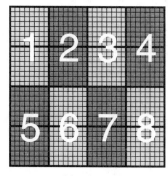
H=4,V=2

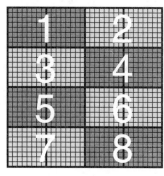
H=2,V=4

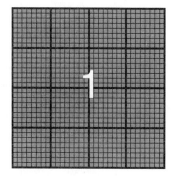
H=1,V=1

Figure 4.6
MCU Ordering

standard recommends duplicating the last column or row of pixels to fill out incomplete data units. Keep in mind that the numbers of MCU rows and columns are determined from the maximum sampling frequencies for the components in an image, not from the maximum in a scan.

Suppose we have an image that is 129×129 pixels in size. If we were to encode it with one component having vertical and horizontal sampling frequencies of 4 and the other components having vertical and horizontal sampling frequencies of 1, each MCU would represent a 32×32 block of pixels. Four complete rows and columns of MCUs as well as one fractional MCU row and column would be required to encode the image. Since fractional MCUs are not allowed, the image would be encoded using five rows and columns of MCUs.

To encode the first components in a noninterleaved scan, each MCU would consist of 1 data unit. For the first component, each data unit represents an 8×8 block of pixels, so 17 rows and columns would be used to encode the scan. Each data unit for the other components represents a 32×32 block of pixels so 5 rows and columns of data units would be required.

Conclusion

In this chapter we covered the basics of JPEG: sampling frequencies, scans, data units, MCUs, and interleaving. JPEG is not a single method but rather a collection of related compression techniques. Only a small subset of the JPEG standard is in general use.

Because of copyright restrictions, the official JPEG standard (JPEG 1994) is not included on the CD. The standard comes in two parts: the actual standard and information about compliance testing. Only the first part is essential for implementing JPEG. (There are moreover ten patents related to arithmetic coding listed in Annex L of this document.) These documents can be ordered from your local ISO representative (ANSI, in the United States). Besides containing information on JPEG modes not covered in this book, Pennebaker and Mitchell (1993) includes copies of draft specifications for both parts of the JPEG standard.

At this moment the JPEG-LS standard is in a draft stage and is not included in any of the sources mentioned above. Because of copyright restrictions we could not include a copy of this draft standard on the CD, either. However, the draft JPEG-LS standard is available on the Internet at *www.jpeg.org*.

Chapter 5

JPEG File Format

This chapter continues the discussion of the JPEG format. In it we cover the structure of JPEG files, which includes every part of a file except for the compressed data. The descriptions here take into account only the subset of JPEG covered by this book, so you will find some discrepancies with the JPEG standard.

Markers

Markers are used to break a JPEG stream into its component structures. They are 2 bytes in length, with the first byte always having the value FF_{16}. The second byte contains a code that specifies the marker type. Any number of bytes with the value FF_{16} may be used as a fill character before the start of any marker. A byte in a JPEG stream with a value of FF_{16} that is followed by another FF_{16} byte is always ignored.

JPEG markers can be grouped into two general types. Stand-alone markers consist of no data other than their 2 bytes; markers that do not stand alone are immediately followed by a 2-byte-long value that gives the number of bytes of data the marker contains. The length count includes the 2 length bytes but not the marker length itself. JPEG stand-alone markers are listed in Table 5.1 and markers with data are listed in Table 5.2. You can see from the tables that most of the markers are not used in the modes we are working with.

The JPEG standard is fairly flexible when it comes to the ordering of markers within a file. Its strictest rule is that a file must begin with an SOI marker and end with an EOI marker. In most other cases markers can appear in any order.

The main requirement is that if the information from one marker is needed to process a second marker, the first marker must appear before the second. The specific rules regarding marker ordering are described in the next section.

Table 5.1 Stand-Alone JPEG Markers	Value	Symbol Used in JPEG Standard	Description
	FF01*	TEM	Temporary for arithmetic coding
	FFD0–FFD7	RST_0–RST_7	Restart marker
	FFD8	SOI	Start of image
	FFD9	EOI	End of image

*Not used by any of the techniques covered in this book.

Table 5.2 JPEG Markers with Data	Value	Symbol Used in JPEG Standard	Description
	FFC0	SOF_0	Start of frame, baseline
	FFC1	SOF_1	Start of frame, extended sequential
	FFC2	SOF_2	Start of frame, progressive
	FFC3*	SOF_3	Start of frame, lossless
	FFC4	DHT	Define Huffman table
	FFC5*	SOF_5	Start of frame, differential sequential
	FFC6*	SOF_6	Start of frame, differential progressive
	FFC7*	SOF_7	Start of frame, differential lossless
	FFC8*	JPG	Reserved
	FFC9*	SOF_9	Start of frame, extended sequential, arithmetic coding
	FFCA*	SOF_{10}	Start of frame, progressive, arithmetic coding
	FFCB*	SOF_{11}	Start of frame, lossless, arithmetic coding
	FFCC*	DAC	Define arithmetic coding conditions
	FFCD*	SOF_{13}	Start of frame, differential sequential, arithmetic coding
	FFCE*	SOF_{14}	Start of frame, differential progressive, arithmetic coding
	FFCF*	SOF_{15}	Start of frame, differential lossless, arithmetic coding
	FFDA	SOS	Start of scan
	FFDB	DQT	Define quantization tables
	FFDC*	DNL	Define number of lines
	FFDD	DRI	Define restart interval
	FFDE*	DHP	Define hierarchical progression
	FFDF*	EXP	Expand reference components
	FFE0–FFEF	APP_0–APP_{15}	Application-specific data
	FFFE	COM	Comment
	FFF0–FFFD*	JPG_0–JPG_{13}	Reserved
	FF02–FFBF*	RES	Reserved

*Not used by any of the techniques covered in this book.

We use the subscript *n* when referring to certain markers collectively. For example, RST_n means any of the restart markers RST_0 to RST_7; SOF_n means any start of frame marker.

Compressed Data

The compressed component data is the only part of a JPEG file that does not occur within a marker. Compressed data always immediately follows an SOS marker. Since it has no length information, in order to find the end of the compressed data without expanding it, you have to scan for the next marker (other than RST_n). RST_n markers are the only ones that can occur within the compressed data, and they cannot be placed anywhere else.[1]

The JPEG compression method is designed so that it will rarely produce the compressed value FF_{16}. When this value is required in the compressed data, it is encoded as the 2-byte sequence FF_{16} followed by 00_{16}. This makes it easy for applications to scan a JPEG file for specific markers.

Marker Types

This section describes all of the markers used by the JPEG modes we are working with. The tables that illustrate marker structure omit the 2-byte marker and the 2-byte length field.

The individual marker descriptions specify where in the file the marker can occur. They do not repeat the following restrictions:

- Only RST and DNL markers may appear in compressed data.
- An image must start with an SOI marker followed by an APP_0 marker.[2]
- The last marker in the file must be an EOI, and it must immediately follow the compressed data of the last scan in the image.

APP$_n$

The APP_0–APP_{15} markers hold application-specific data. They are used by image-processing applications to hold additional information beyond what is

---

[1] The JPEG standard allows DNL markers to appear with compressed data. A DNL marker is used to define or redefine the image size within the compressed data rather than within the SOF_n marker. In practice DNL markers are not used and most applications cannot handle them. Therefore, we will not consider them further.

[2] That an APP_0 marker immediately follow the SOI marker is a JFIF requirement. Some applications, such as Adobe Illustrator, can create JPEG files that are not JFIF.

specified in the JPEG standard. The format of these markers is application specific. The length field after the marker can be used to skip over the marker data. Except for the APP0 markers used by the JFIF format, an application can ignore the APP markers it does not recognize. If an application needs to store information beyond the capabilities of JPEG and JFIF, it can create APP_n markers to hold this information. An APP_n marker may appear anywhere within a JPEG file.

By convention, applications that create APP_n markers store their name (zero-terminated) at the start of the marker to prevent conflicts with other applications. An application that processes APP_n markers should check not only the marker identifier but also the application name.

COM

The COM (Comment) marker is used to hold comment strings such as copyright information. Its interpretation is application specific, but a JPEG encoder should assume that the decoder is going to ignore this information. A COM marker, rather than an APP_n marker, should be used for plain comment text. It may appear anywhere within a JPEG file.

DHT

The DHT (Define Huffman Table) marker defines (or redefines) Huffman tables, which are identified by a class (AC or DC[3]) and a number. A single DHT marker can define multiple tables; however, baseline mode is limited to two of each type, and progressive and sequential modes are limited to four. The only restriction on the placement of DHT markers is that if a scan requires a specific table identifier and class, it must have been defined by a DHT marker earlier in a file.

The structure of the DHT marker is shown in Table 5.3. Each Huffman table is 17 bytes of fixed data followed by a variable field of up to 256 additional bytes. The first fixed byte contains the identifier for the table. The next 16 form an array of unsigned 1-byte integers whose elements give the number of Huffman codes for each possible code length (1–16). The sum of the 16 code lengths is the number of values in the Huffman table. The values are 1 byte each and follow, in order of Huffman code, the length counts. The structure of Huffman tables is described in more detail in Chapter 6.

The number of Huffman tables defined by the DHT marker is determined from the length field. An application needs to maintain a counter that is initialized with the value of the length field minus 2. Each time you read a table you subtract its length from the counter. When the counter reaches zero all the tables have been read. No padding is allowed in a DHT marker, so if the counter becomes negative the file is invalid.

---

[3]The significance of AC and DC is explained in Chapter 7.

Table 5.3
DHT Format

Field Size	Description
1 byte	The 4 high-order bits specify the table class. A value of 0 means a DC table, a value of 1 means an AC table. The 4 low-order bits specify the table identifier. This value is 0 or 1 for baseline frames and 0, 1, 2, or 3 for progressive and extended frames.
16 bytes	The count of Huffman codes of length 1 to 16. Each count is stored in 1 byte.
Variable	The 1-byte symbols sorted by Huffman code. The number of symbols is the sum of the 16 code counts.

DRI

The DRI (Define Restart Interval) marker specifies the number of MCUs between restart markers within the compressed data. The value of the 2-byte length field following the marker is always 4. There is only one data field in the marker—a 2-byte value that defines the restart interval. An interval of zero means that restart markers are not used. A DRI marker with a nonzero restart interval can be used re-enable restart markers later in the image.

A DRI marker may appear anywhere in the file to define or redefine the restart interval, which remains in effect until the end of the image or until another DRI marker changes it. A DRI marker must appear somewhere in the file for a compressed data segment to include restart markers.

Restart markers assist in error recovery. If the decoder finds corrupt scan data, it can use the restart marker ID and the restart interval to determine where in the image to resume decoding.

The following formula can be used to determine the number of MCUs to skip:

$$MCUs\ to\ Skip = Restart\ Interval \times ((8 + Current\ Marker\ ID - Last\ Marker\ ID)MOD8)$$

Example   Assume that the restart interval is 10. After 80 MCUs have been decoded, the RST_7 marker is read from the input stream. If the decoder encounters corrupt data before reading the next restart marker (RST_0), it stops decoding and scans the input stream for the next restart marker.

If the next marker is RST_3, the decoder skips 40 MCUs ($= 10 \times ((8 + 3 - 7)MOD8)$) from the last known point (80). The decoder resumes decoding at the 121st MCU in the image.

DQT

The DQT (Define Quantization Table) marker defines (or redefines) the quantization tables used in an image. A DQT marker can define multiple quantization tables (up to 4). The quantization table definition follows the marker's length field. The value of the length field is the sum of the sizes of the tables plus 2 (for the length field).

The format of a quantization table definition is shown in Table 5.4. Each table starts with 1 byte that contains information about the table. If the 4 high-order bits of the information byte are zero, the quantization table values are 1 byte each and the entire table definition is 65 bytes long. If the value is 1, the size of each quantization value is 2 bytes and the table definition is 129 bytes long. Two-byte quantization values may be used only with 12-bit sample data.

The 4 low-order bits assign a numeric identifier to the table, which can be 0, 1, 2, or 3. The information byte is followed by 64 quantization values that are stored in JPEG zigzag order (defined in Chapter 7).

DQT markers can appear anywhere in an image file. The one restriction is that if a scan requires a quantization table it must have been defined in a previous DQT marker.

Table 5.4
Quantization Table
Definition in a DQT
Marker

Field Size	Description
1 byte	The 4 low-order bits are the table identifier (0, 1, 2, or 3). The 4 high-order bits specify the quanization value size (0 = 1 byte, 1 = 2 bytes).
64 or 128 bytes	64 1- or 2-byte unsigned quantization values

EOI

The EOI (End of Image) marker marks the end of a JPEG image. An EOI marker must be at the end of a JPEG file and there can only be one EOI marker per file and no other markers may follow the EOI marker. The EOI marker stands alone.

RST$_n$

The restart markers RST_0–RST_7 are used to mark blocks of independently encoded compressed scan data. They have no length field or data and may only occur within compressed scan data.

Restart markers can be used to implement error recovery. The interval between them is defined by the DRI (Define Restart Interval) marker. Thus, if the restart interval is zero, then restart markers are not used. Restart markers must occur in the sequence RST_0, RST_1, ... RST_7, RST_0, ... in the scan data.

SOI

The SOI (Start of Image) marker marks the start of a JPEG image. It must be at the very beginning of the file and there can only be one per file. The SOI marker stands alone.

SOF$_n$

The SOF$_n$ (Start of Frame) marker defines a frame. Although there are many frame types, all have the same format. The SOF marker consists of a fixed header after the marker length followed by a list of structures that define each component used by the frame. The structure of the fixed header is shown in Table 5.5, and the structure of a component definition is shown in Table 5.6.

Components are identified by an integer in the range 0 to 255. The JFIF standard is more restrictive and specifies that the components be defined in the order {Y, Cb, Cr} with the identifiers {1, 2, 3} respectively. Unfortunately, some encoders do not follow the standard and assign other identifiers to the components. The most inclusive way for a decoder to match the colorspace component with the identifier is to go by the order in which the components are defined and to accept whatever identifier the encoder assigns.

There can be only one SOF$_n$ marker per JPEG file and it must precede any SOS markers.

Field Size	Description
1 byte	Sample precision in bits (can be 8 or 12)
2 bytes	Image height in pixels
2 bytes	Image width in pixels
1 byte	Number of components in the image

Table 5.5
*Fixed Portion of an
SOF Marker*

Field Size	Description
1 byte	Component identifier. JPEG allows this to be 0 to 255. JFIF restricts it to 1 (Y), 2 (Cb), or 3 (Cr).
1 byte	The 4 high-order bits specify the horizontal sampling for the component. The 4 low-order bits specify the vertical sampling. Either value can be 1, 2, 3, or 4 according to the standard. We do not support values of 3 in our code.
1 byte	The quantization table identifier for the component. Corresponds to the identifier in a DQT marker. Can be 0, 1, 2, or 3.

Table 5.6
*Component-
Specific Area of an
SOF Marker*

SOS

The SOS (Start of Scan) marker marks the beginning of compressed data for a scan in a JPEG stream. Its structure is illustrated in Table 5.7. After the component count comes a component descriptor for each component (shown in Table 5.8). This is followed by 3 bytes of data used only in progressive mode. The compressed scan data immediately follows the marker.

Table 5.7 SOS Marker Structure	Field Size	Description
	1 byte	Component count
	2 component count bytes	Scan component descriptors (see Table 5.8)
	1 byte	Spectral selection start (0–63)
	1 byte	Spectral selection end (0–63)
	1 byte	Successive approximation (two 4-bit fields, each with a value in the range 0–13)

Table 5.8 SOS Marker Scan Descriptor	Field Size	Description
	1 byte	Component identifier
	1 byte	The 4 high-order bits specify the DC Huffman table and the 4 low-order bits specify the AC Huffman table.

The component descriptors are ordered in the same sequence in which the components are ordered within MCUs in the scan data. While not all of the components from the SOF_n marker must be present, their order in the SOS marker and in the SOF_n marker must match. The component identifier in the scan descriptor must match a component identifier value defined in the SOF_n marker. The AC and DC Huffman table identifiers must match those of Huffman tables defined in a previous DHT marker.

The JPEG standard allows 1 to 4 components in a scan, but there are some other restrictions on the number. JFIF limits an image to 3 components. In progressive scans there can be only 1 component if the spectral selection start is not zero. The JPEG standard also places a rather low arbitrary limit of 10 on the number of data units that can be in an MCU, which can limit the number of components in a scan.

In a sequential scan, the spectral selection start must be zero, the spectral selection end 63, and the successive approximation zero. In a progressive scan, if the spectral selection start is zero the spectral selection end must also be zero. Otherwise, the spectral selection end must be greater than or equal to the spectral selection start. These values will be explained in more detail in Chapter 10.

An SOS marker must occur after the SOF_n marker in the file. It must be preceded by DHT markers that define all of the Huffman tables used by the scan and DQT markers that define all the quantization tables used by the scan components.

JFIF Format

For all practical purposes a "JPEG file" means "a JPEG file in the JFIF format." The JFIF standard defines the following:

Start of Image (SOI)

APP0 JFIF Marker

Optional APP0 JFIF
Extension Header

Tables

Start of Frame

Tables

Start of Scan 1

Scan 1 Data

Tables

Start of Scan 2

Scan 2 Data

⋮

Tables

Start of Scan *n*

Scan *n* Data

End of Image (EOI)

Figure 5.1
Structure of a JFIF
File

- A signature for identifying JPEG files
- Colorspace
- Pixel density for device independent display of an image
- Thumbnails
- The relationship of pixels to sampling frequency

The general layout of a JFIF file is shown in Figure 5.1. Because all of the JFIF-specific information is stored within APP0 markers, JFIF files are completely compatible with the JPEG standard. JFIF requires that the SOI that starts the file be immediately followed by an APP0 marker in the format shown in Table 5.9.

JFIF specifies that the YCbCr colorspace be used. The conversion between RGB and YCbCr specified by JFIF was shown in Chapter 1. Color images should have all three components, and their component identifiers should be Y=1, Cb=2, and Cr=3. Grayscale images should have only the Y component.

A JFIF file can be identified by reading the first 11 bytes and ensuring that the first 4 bytes are FF_{16} $D8_{16}$ FF_{16} $E0_{16}$ (SOI marker followed by APP_0 marker). After skipping 2 bytes the next 5 bytes should be J, F, I, F followed by 00_{16}. A file that starts with this pattern is unlikely to be anything other than a JFIF file.

The JFIF APP_0 header may be followed by another APP_0 used to embed a thumbnail in a format other than the RGB triple format defined by the header. The format of the data following the length field for the optional APP_0 header is shown in Table 5.10.

If the JFIF extension header has an `extension_code` of 10_{16} the `extension_data` field contains a JPEG encoded image. Colors are encoded according to the JFIF standard, but the compressed data does not contain a JFIF APP_0 header. The format for the `extension_data` when the `extension_code` is 11_{16} is shown in Table 5.11; the format for 12_{16} is shown in Table 5.12.

Your applications should avoid creating APP_0 markers other than those required by the JFIF standard. There are fifteen other APP_n markers available, and this should be sufficient for any conceivable situation. When applications create APP_n markers, it should place the application name at the start of the data area. This allows the marker's creator to be identified.

Table 5.9 JFIF APP0 Header Format	Field Name	Size	Description
	Identifier	5 bytes	The zero-terminated string `JFIF`
	Version major ID	1 byte	The major ID of the file version. For the current JFIF version (1.2) this value is 1.
	Version minor ID	1 byte	The minor ID of the file version. For the current JFIF version (1.2) this value is 2.
	Units	1 byte	Units for the X and Y pixel densities. Zero means that no densities are used. The next two fields specify the aspect ratio. One means that the next two fields specify pixels per inch. Two means that they specify pixels per cm.
	`Xdensity`	2 bytes	Horizontal pixel density
	`Ydensity`	2 bytes	Vertical pixel density
	`Xthumbnail`	1 byte	Width of the optional thumbnail image. This value may be 0.
	`Ythumbnail`	1 byte	Height of the optional thumbnail image. This value may be 0.
	Thumbnail	Variable	An optional thumbnail image. The size of this field is 3 × `Xthumbnail` × `Ythumbnail`. The image is stored with 3 bytes per pixel with the colors in RGB order.

Table 5.10 JFIF Extension Header Format	Field Name	Size	Description
	Identifier	5 bytes	The zero terminated string `JFXX`
	`extension_code`	1 byte	Specifies the format of the `extension_data` field below. 10_{16} means that the thumbnail is encoded using JPEG. 11_{16} means that the thumbnail is encoded with 1 byte per pixel. 12_{16} means that the thumbnail is encoded with 3 bytes per pixel.
	`extension_data`	Variable	

Table 5.11 `extension_data` Format for JFIF Extension Type 11_{16}	Field Name	Size	Description
	`Xthumbnail`	1 byte	Thumbnail width
	`Ythumbnail`	1 byte	Thumbnail height
	Palette	768 bytes	Array of 3-byte RGB color values
	Pixels	Variable (`Xthumbnail` × `Ythumbnail`)	Indices into the palette for each pixel in the thumbnail

	Field Name	Size	Description
Table 5.12 extension_data Format for JFIF Extension Type 12_{16}	Xthumbnail	1 byte	Thumbnail width
	Ythumbnail	1 byte	Thumbnail height
	RGB	Variable (3 × Xthumbnail × Ythumbnail)	RGB color values for each pixel in the image

 While most of the structures in the JFIF standard are devoted to defining formats for thumbnail images, these are rarely used.

Conclusion

After reading this chapter you should understand the internal structure of a JPEG file. As you go through the subsequent JPEG chapters, you will probably need to refer to this one frequently. The original JPEG standard did not define a file format, but the unofficial JFIF format has become universally accepted as such. The text of the JFIF standard and the text of the official SPIFF standard are included on the accompanying CD. JPEG (1994) defines the rest of the JPEG format. The remaining JPEG chapters in this book deal with the compressed data within SOS markers.

The accompanying CD contains the source code for an application called JPEGDUMP that analyzes the structure of a JPEG file. It outputs a text version of the contents of a JPEG file's markers. It supports all JPEG markers to some degree, even those not covered in this chapter, but it would be surprising if you ever came across any of these markers in an actual JPEG file.

To run this application enter `jpegdump somefile.jpg` at the command prompt.

Figure 5.2 shows sample output from the JPEGDUMP program for a color image. This is fairly typical of most JPEG images you will encounter. Notice that the quantization and Huffman tables are defined in pairs and that the Y component uses one of the tables in each pair and the Cb and Cr components share the other. This assignment of tables is not specified by the standard but it is usual practice.

Figure 5.2
Sample JPEGDUMP
Output

```
{ Start Of Image }
{ APP0 Marker
  Length: 16
  Version: 1.1
  Density Unit: (pixels per inch)
  X Density: 72
  Y Density: 72
  Thumbnail Width: 0
  Thumbnail Height: 0
}
{ Define Quantization Table
  Length: 132
  Table Index: 0
  Table Precision: 0
  Table Values:
        6 4 4 4 5 4 6 5
        5 6 9 6 5 6 9 11
        8 6 6 8 11 12 10 10
        11 10 10 12 16 12 12 12
        12 12 12 16 12 12 12 12
        12 12 12 12 12 12 12 12
        12 12 12 12 12 12 12 12
        12 12 12 12 12 12 12 12
  Table Index: 1
  Table Precision: 0
  Table Values:
        7 7 7 13 12 13 24 16
        16 24 20 14 14 14 20 20
        14 14 14 14 20 17 12 12
        12 12 12 17 17 12 12 12
        12 12 12 17 12 12 12 12
        12 12 12 12 12 12 12 12
        12 12 12 12 12 12 12 12
        12 12 12 12 12 12 12 12
}
{ Start Of Frame
Type: Baseline (Huffman)
  Length: 17
  Precision: 8
  Height: 383
  Width: 262
  Component Count: 3
   Component 1
    Horizontal Frequency: 2
    Vertical Frequency: 2
    Quantization Table: 0
   Component 2
    Horizontal Frequency: 1
    Vertical Frequency: 1
    Quantization Table: 1
   Component 3
    Horizontal Frequency: 1
    Vertical Frequency: 1
    Quantization Table: 1
}
{ Define Huffman Table
```

```
             Length: 418
              Table Index 0
               Table Class: DC
               Code Counts: 0 0 7 1 1 1 1 1 1 0 0 0 0 0 0 0
               Code Values:  4  5  3  2  6  1  0  7  8  9  a  b
              Table Index 1
               Table Class: DC
               Code Counts: 0 2 2 3 1 1 1 1 1 0 0 0 0 0 0 0
               Code Values:  1  0  2  3  4  5  6  7  8  9  a  b
              Table Index 0
               Table Class: AC
               Code Counts: 0 2 1 3 3 2 4 2 6 7 3 4 2 6 2 73
               Code Values:  1  2  3 11  4  0  5 21 12 31 41 51  6 13 61 22
                            71 81 14 32 91 a1  7 15 b1 42 23 c1 52 d1 e1 33
                            16 62 f0 24 72 82 f1 25 43 34 53 92 a2 b2 63 73
                            c2 35 44 27 93 a3 b3 36 17 54 64 74 c3 d2 e2  8
                            26 83  9  a 18 19 84 94 45 46 a4 b4 56 d3 55 28
                            1a f2 e3 f3 c4 d4 e4 f4 65 75 85 95 a5 b5 c5 d5
                            e5 f5 66 76 86 96 a6 b6 c6 d6 e6 f6 37 47 57 67
                            77 87 97 a7 b7 c7 d7 e7 f7 38 48 58 68 78 88 98
                            a8 b8 c8 d8 e8 f8 29 39 49 59 69 79 89 99 a9 b9
                            c9 d9 e9 f9 2a 3a 4a 5a 6a 7a 8a 9a aa ba ca da
                            ea fa
              Table Index 1
               Table Class: AC
               Code Counts: 0 2 2 1 2 3 5 5 4 5 6 4 8 3 3 6d
               Code Values:  1  0  2 11  3  4 21 12 31 41  5 51 13 61 22  6
                            71 81 91 32 a1 b1 f0 14 c1 d1 e1 23 42 15 52 62
                            72 f1 33 24 34 43 82 16 92 53 25 a2 63 b2 c2  7
                            73 d2 35 e2 44 83 17 54 93  8  9  a 18 19 26 36
                            45 1a 27 64 74 55 37 f2 a3 b3 c3 28 29 d3 e3 f3
                            84 94 a4 b4 c4 d4 e4 f4 65 75 85 95 a5 b5 c5 d5
                            e5 f5 46 56 66 76 86 96 a6 b6 c6 d6 e6 f6 47 57
                            67 77 87 97 a7 b7 c7 d7 e7 f7 38 48 58 68 78 88
                            98 a8 b8 c8 d8 e8 f8 39 49 59 69 79 89 99 a9 b9
                            c9 d9 e9 f9 2a 3a 4a 5a 6a 7a 8a 9a aa ba ca da
                            ea fa
       }
       { Start Of Scan
         Length: 12
         Scan Count: 3
          Component ID: 1
           AC Entropy Table: 0
           DC Entropy Table: 0
          Component ID: 2
           AC Entropy Table: 1
           DC Entropy Table: 1
          Component ID: 3
           AC Entropy Table: 1
           DC Entropy Table: 1
         Spectral Selection Start: 0
         Spectral Selection End: 63
         Sucessive Approximation High: 0
         Sucessive Approximation Low: 0
       }
       { End Of Image }
```

Chapter 6

JPEG Huffman Coding

In this chapter we continue our discussion of JPEG with an explanation of Huffman coding, one of the compression techniques used within JPEG. While the chapter deals specifically with its application to JPEG, Huffman coding is also used in the PNG image format.

Usage Frequencies

In English, certain letters are used much more frequently than others. *E* and *T* are used with great frequency, while *X* and *Q* are quite rare. Table 6.1 shows the normalized frequency for each letter as it is used in the King James version of the Bible. You can see that *E*, the most frequently used letter, occurs about 5 times more often than *U* and *M* in the middle of the pack, and about 400 times more often than *Q*, which brings up the rear.

Table 6.1
Letter Frequencies in the King James Bible

Frequency	Letter	Frequency	Letter	Frequency	Letter
0.1272	E	0.0489	D	0.0151	B
0.0981	T	0.0401	L	0.0133	P
0.0875	H	0.0258	F	0.0094	V
0.0852	A	0.0257	U	0.0069	K
0.0750	O	0.0247	M	0.0027	J
0.0695	N	0.0202	W	0.0009	Z
0.0598	I	0.0181	Y	0.0004	X
0.0587	S	0.0170	G	0.0003	Q
0.0525	R	0.0169	C		

Morse Code	Letter	Morse Code	Letter	Morse Code	Letter
.	E	− . .	D	− . . .	B
−	T	. − . .	L	. − − .	P
. . . .	H	. . − .	F	. . . −	V
. −	A	. . −	U	− . −	K
− − −	O	− −	M	. − − −	J
− .	N	. − −	W	− − . .	Z
. .	I	− . − −	Y	− . . −	X
. . .	S	− − .	G	− − . −	Q
. − .	R	− . − .	C		

Table 6.2
Morse Code

The frequency of letter usage was taken into account in the design of Morse Code (Table 6.2), in which the more frequently used letters tend to have shorter codes. Thus, E and T, have 1-character codes while the least frequently used letters have 4-character codes.

In the computer world, character sets for Western alphabets are almost always represented using fixed-length encoding methods, such as ASCII or EBCDIC, that do not take usage into account. Each character takes up a fixed number of bits no matter how frequently it is used. For the fastest execution speed, this is very efficient. However, in applications such as image compression, where data size is the most important consideration, variable-length codes make a lot of sense.

The best known scheme for generating variable-length codes for symbols based upon usage is called *Huffman coding,* invented by D. A. Huffman in 1952. The procedure for creating Huffman codes for a set of values based on their frequency of usage is quite simple. It involves creating a binary tree containing the symbols from the bottom up, with the least frequently used symbols being farthest from the root. First, we create a pool that contains either values or tree nodes. Initially this pool contains all the values and no nodes. The following procedure is repeated until the pool contains one tree node and no more symbols.

1. Locate the two values or tree nodes with the lowest frequencies and remove them from the pool. If more than one item has the lowest frequency, the tie can be broken using an arbitrary choice.[1]

2. Create a new tree node and make the items in the previous step its two branches.

3. Make the frequency of the new tree node the sum of the frequencies of the children.

4. Add the new node to the pool.

---

[1]Choices made to break ties affect only the codes generated for the values. They do not affect compression.

After all of the values have been joined into a single tree, we assign the value 0 to one branch of each tree node and the value 1 to the other. The Huffman code for each value is found by following the path from the root of the tree to the value appending the code of each branch in the path. Keep in mind that with Huffman codes we are working with bit strings. A Huffman code consists of a variable number of bits—in other words, it is a variable-length string that can consist of 0s or 1s. The set of values and their associated codes are known as a Huffman table.

Huffman Coding Example

We will use the following palindrome as an example of how Huffman coding works. It consists of eight different characters with the frequencies shown in Table 6.3.

A MAN A PLAN A CANAL PANAMA.

In Table 6.3 the symbols C and the period are the least frequently used. To begin the Huffman coding process we use these two symbols to create a tree node. Assign a frequency value for the node using the sum of all the leaves below it.

```
A   L M N  P  <space>  ┌─┬─┐
10  2 2 4 (1)    6     │ 2 │
                       C   .
                       1   1
```

Among the remaining items in the pool, four are tied at the lowest frequency of 2. We take P and the tree node and join them together to create a new tree node with a combined frequency of 4.

```
A   L M N <space>  ┌─┬─┐
10  2 2 4    6     │ 4 │
                   P   ┌─┬─┐
                   2   │ 2 │
                       C   .
                       1   1
```

Table 6.3	Value	Frequency	Value	Frequency
Frequencies for Symbols in the Palindrome	A	10	N	4
	C	1	P	2
	L	2	SPACE	6
	M	2	. (period)	1

L and M now have the lowest frequency. Since all of the existing branches in the tree have greater frequencies, we have to start a new tree node using these letters.

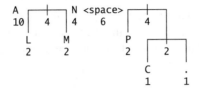

Now we have the two tree nodes and N tied with the lowest frequency. We choose to join N to the tree.

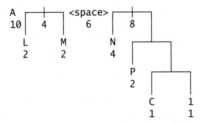

The space character and the L–M tree have the lowest frequency, so we join them.

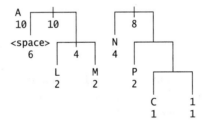

There are now two tree nodes and the letter A remaining. We arbitrarily choose to join the two trees.

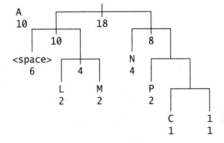

Finally we add the letter A to complete the tree and then mark each left branch with 0 and each right branch with 1.

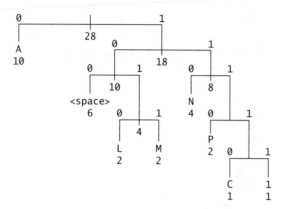

We create the Huffman code for each symbol by appending the 0 or 1 code on the path from the root to the value. Table 6.4 shows the Huffman codes generated for each value. Using the Huffman coding shown in Table 6.2 the palindrome can be encoded using 74 bits, whereas if we were to use fixed-length codes, it would require 3 bits to represent each character and 84 (3 × 28) to represent the entire string. While the compression in this example is a modest 12%, keep in mind that we have a fairly short text and there is not a large variation in frequencies among the symbols. You cannot have frequency variations on the order of 300:1 in a 28-character text string.

Notice in Table 6.4 that no code is a prefix to any other code. For example, the code for N is 110, and no other code in the table starts with the bit-string 110. The same is true for all the other codes. This is an important property because without it, it would be impossible to decode a Huffman-encoded string.

Table 6.4
Huffman Codes for Symbols in the Palindrome

Value	Huffman Code	Length	Frequency	Bit Usage
A	0	1	10	10
C	11110	5	1	5
L	1010	4	2	8
M	1011	4	2	8
N	110	3	4	12
P	1110	4	2	8
Space	100	3	6	18
. (period)	11111	5	1	5
			Total	74

Huffman Coding Using Code Lengths

While a tree structure makes it easy to understand how Huffman coding works, this is not the simplest way to generate Huffman codes. Another method is to generate the code length for each symbol and from these generate the Huffman

codes. In this method we have symbols with an associated code length and lists
of values with an associated frequency. Initially we assign each value a code
length of 0 and place each value in a separate list whose frequency is assigned
the frequency of its value. For the palindrome this gives us a structure like

To generate the code lengths, join the two lists with the lowest frequencies.
When we join two lists, the frequency of the new list is the sum of the frequencies of the two old ones. Each time we join a list we increment the frequency of
each symbol in the list by one. We repeat the process until we have one list of
codes. In case of ties for the lowest frequency we always select the list that is
nearest the end.

The lists with the period and the C have the lowest frequencies, so we join
them and increment the code length for the two symbols.

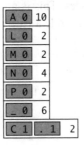

This leaves four lists tied with 4 as the lowest frequency. We select the two
lists closest to the bottom and join them, giving:

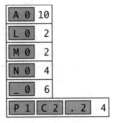

Repeating the process results in the following steps.

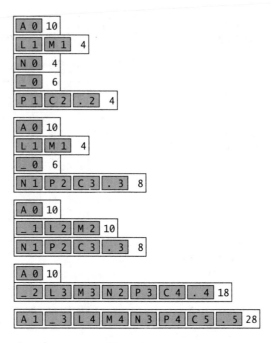

If we sort the symbols by code length, we get the code lengths shown in Table 6.5. We can generate Huffman codes from the sorted list by using Algorithm 6.1 (page 70). The input to this function is an array of Huffman code lengths, such as the one in Table 6.5 and the number of elements in the array. The output is an array of Huffman codes generated for the code lengths. Figure 6.1 shows the process of generating the Huffman codes from the sorted list of Huffman code lengths shown in Table 6.5.

You can see that the Huffman codes in Figure 6.1 are not identical to the codes in Table 6.4, but this does not matter. It takes the same number of bits to encode the palindrome using either Huffman table. The differences in the code values are a result of arbitrary choices made during the encoding processes.

The number of Huffman values will be larger than the length of the longest code. The code lengths can be represented in a more compact manner if, instead

	Symbol	Code Length
Table 6.5 *Palindrome Symbols Sorted by Code Length*	A	1
	Space	3
	N	3
	L	4
	M	4
	P	4
	C	5
	. (period)	5

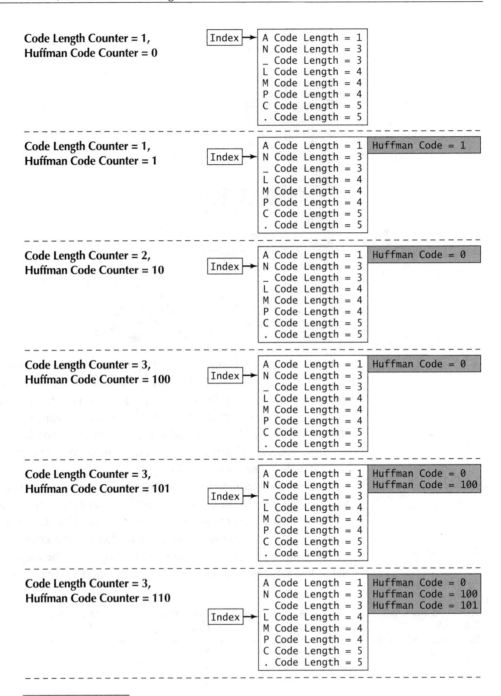

Figure 6.1
Generation of
Huffman Codes
from Code Lengths

Code Length Counter = 4,
Huffman Code Counter = 1100

Index →

```
A Code Length = 1    Huffman Code = 0
N Code Length = 3    Huffman Code = 100
_ Code Length = 3    Huffman Code = 101
L Code Length = 4
M Code Length = 4
P Code Length = 4
C Code Length = 5
. Code Length = 5
```

- -

Code Length Counter = 4,
Huffman Code Counter = 1101

Index →

```
A Code Length = 1    Huffman Code = 0
N Code Length = 3    Huffman Code = 100
_ Code Length = 3    Huffman Code = 101
L Code Length = 4    Huffman Code = 1100
M Code Length = 4
P Code Length = 4
C Code Length = 5
. Code Length = 5
```

- -

Code Length Counter = 4,
Huffman Code Counter = 1110

Index →

```
A Code Length = 1    Huffman Code = 0
N Code Length = 3    Huffman Code = 100
_ Code Length = 3    Huffman Code = 101
L Code Length = 4    Huffman Code = 1100
M Code Length = 4    Huffman Code = 1101
P Code Length = 4
C Code Length = 5
. Code Length = 5
```

- -

Code Length Counter = 4,
Huffman Code Counter = 1111

Index →

```
A Code Length = 1    Huffman Code = 0
N Code Length = 3    Huffman Code = 100
_ Code Length = 3    Huffman Code = 101
L Code Length = 4    Huffman Code = 1100
M Code Length = 4    Huffman Code = 1101
P Code Length = 4    Huffman Code = 1110
C Code Length = 5
. Code Length = 5
```

- -

Code Length Counter = 5,
Huffman Code Counter = 11110

Index →

```
A Code Length = 1    Huffman Code = 0
N Code Length = 3    Huffman Code = 100
_ Code Length = 3    Huffman Code = 101
L Code Length = 4    Huffman Code = 1100
M Code Length = 4    Huffman Code = 1101
P Code Length = 4    Huffman Code = 1110
C Code Length = 5
. Code Length = 5
```

- -

Code Length Counter = 5,
Huffman Code Counter = 11111

Index →

```
A Code Length = 1    Huffman Code = 0
N Code Length = 3    Huffman Code = 100
_ Code Length = 3    Huffman Code = 101
L Code Length = 4    Huffman Code = 1100
M Code Length = 4    Huffman Code = 1101
P Code Length = 4    Huffman Code = 1110
C Code Length = 5    Huffman Code = 11110
. Code Length = 5
```

- -

Code Length Counter = 5,
Huffman Code Counter = 100000

```
A Code Length = 1    Huffman Code = 0
N Code Length = 3    Huffman Code = 100
_ Code Length = 3    Huffman Code = 101
L Code Length = 4    Huffman Code = 1100
M Code Length = 4    Huffman Code = 1101
P Code Length = 4    Huffman Code = 1110
C Code Length = 5    Huffman Code = 11110
. Code Length = 5    Huffman Code = 11111
```

of maintaining a code length for each value, we maintain the count of codes for each code length. It is easy to convert a list of Huffman code lengths to a list containing the count of codes of a given length, as shown in Algorithm 6.2.

The codes generated in Figure 6.1 create the code length counts shown in Table 6.6.

Algorithm 6.1
Generation of
Huffman Codes
from Code Lengths

```
Procedure GenerateHuffmanCodes (NUMBEROFCODES,
                                CODELENGTHS[0..NUMBEROFCODES-1],
                                CODES [0..255])
    Begin
    HUFFMANCODECOUNTER = 0
    CODELENGTHCOUNTER = 1
    For INDEX = 0 TO NUMBEROFCODES - 1 Do
        Begin
        If CODELENGTHS [INDEX] = CODELENGTHCOUNTER Then
            Begin
            CODES [INDEX] = HUFFMANCODECOUNTER
            HUFFMANCODECOUNTER = HUFFMANCODECOUNTER + 1
            End
        Else
            Begin
            HUFFMANCODECOUNTER = HUFFMANCODECOUNTER LeftShift 1
            CODELENGTHCOUNTER = CODELENGTHCOUNTER + 1
            End
        End
    End
```

Algorithm 6.2
Converting Code
Lengths to Length
Counts

```
Procedure LengthsToCounts (CODELENGTHS [1..CODECOUNT],
                           CODECOUNT,
                           LENGTHCOUNTS [1..16])
    Begin
    For INDEX = 1 TO CODECOUNT Do
        Begin
        LENGTHCOUNTS [CODELENGTHS [INDEX]]
            = LENGTHCOUNTS [CODELENGTHS [INDEX]] + 1
        End
    End
```

Table 6.6
Count of Code
Lengths for
Palindrome Symbols

Code Length	Count
1	1
2	0
3	2
4	3
5	2

Converting backwards, from the code length counts to a list of code lengths, is just as easy, as shown in Algorithm 6.3.

In Chapter 5 we looked at how Huffman tables are stored in a JPEG file. Each table in a DHT marker is stored with a 16-byte list of code counts followed by a variable-length list of Huffman values sorted by increasing Huffman codes. We can convert the information in the DHT marker to a Huffman code and code length using Algorithms 6.1 and 6.3.

Algorithm 6.3
Converting Length
Counts to Code
Lengths

```
Procedure CountsToLengths (LENGTHCOUNTS [1..MAXIMUMLENGTH],
                           MAXIMUMLENGTH,
                           CODELENGTHS [0..255])
    Begin
    INDEX = 1
    For II = 1 To MAXIMUMLENGTH Do
        Begin
        For JJ = 1 To LENGTHCOUNTS [II] Do
            Begin
            CODELENGTHS [INDEX] = II
            INDEX = INDEX + 1
            End
        End
    End
```

Huffman Coding in JPEG

In the JPEG modes we will be using in this book, the possible Huffman values are the integers 0 to 255. We have seen that, depending upon how the Huffman coding algorithm is applied, different codes can be generated from the same symbol values and frequency data. The JPEG standard does not specify exactly how Huffman codes are generated. The Huffman codes for values in JPEG files do not have to be optimal. In fact, as we shall see in a moment, there are times when they cannot be. It is possible to define the Huffman tables so that the least frequently used values have the shortest code. The result would be terrible compression, but it is not illegal.

The JPEG standard puts two restrictions on Huffman codes. A Huffman-encoded bit-string consisting of all 1-bits must be a prefix to a longer code. This means that no Huffman code can consist of all 1-bits. In Table 6.4 and Figure 6.1 you can see that the only code consisting of all 1-bits is the one generated for the period. If we got rid of the period, the problem with all 1-bit codes would go away.

Using Algorithm 6.1, the only code that will consist of all 1-bits is the one for the last value when the values are sorted by code length. If we insert a dummy value with a usage frequency of 1 at the start of Huffman coding and sort the values so that the dummy value winds up at the end of the list, the dummy value will be the only one assigned a code consisting of all 1-bits. At the end of the coding process we simply discard the dummy code. In the palindrome example, our dummy code is the period.

Limiting Code Lengths

Limiting code lengths to 16 bits is a little more difficult, even though in practice the Huffman code generation process does not often result in codes longer than that. On those rare occasions when the Huffman algorithm generates longer codes you must use a less than optimal coding.

The longest Huffman code length we generated for the palindrome was 5, but suppose we wanted to limit the maximum code length to 4. We could easily accomplish this by shifting nodes in the tree. Figure 6.2 is a representation of the tree generated for the results in Figure 6.1, showing how nodes could be moved to reduce the maximum code length to 4.

It is much simpler to do the transform shown in Figure 6.2 on an array of length counts than on an actual tree structure. The basic method is to find a symbol with a code length of at least 2 less than the code you want to reduce. You

Figure 6.2
Shifting Tree Nodes
to Reduce Code
Length

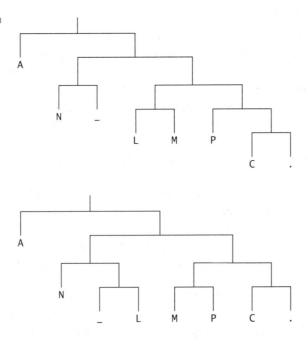

Algorithm 6.4
Limiting Code
Lengths to 16 Bits

```
Procedure LimitTo16Bits (LENGTHCOUNTS [1..32])
    Begin
    For II = 32 DownTo 17
        Begin
        While LENGTHCOUNTS [II] <> 0 Do
            Begin
            JJ = II - 2
            While LENGTHCOUNTS [JJ] = 0 Do
                JJ = JJ - 1
            // Replace a tree node with a value.
            LENGTHCOUNTS [II] = LENGTHCOUNTS [II] - 2
            LENGTHCOUNTS [II - 1] = LENGTHCOUNTS [II-1] + 1
            // Replace a value with a tree node.
            LENGTHCOUNTS [JJ + 1] = LENGTHCOUNTS [JJ + 1] + 2
            LENGTHCOUNTS [JJ] = LENGTHCOUNTS [JJ] - 1
            End
        End
    End
```

replace the symbol with a branch and then shift all the longer codes across. The complete process is shown in Algorithm 6.4.

Decoding Huffman Codes

When we read a JPEG image file we get a set of counts for each Huffman code and a list of symbol values sorted by Huffman code. From this information we need to set up tables for converting the Huffman codes in the input stream to the correct symbol. Since Huffman codes vary in length, we have to read them one bit at a time. Our first problem is how to tell when we have read a complete Huffman code.

The obvious method for decoding Huffman values is to create a binary tree containing the values arranged according to their codes. Start at the root of the tree and, using the value of bits read from the input stream to determine the path, search for the values in the tree.

A simpler method to implement is to use the list of values sorted by Huffman code in conjunction with an array of data structures with one element per Huffman code length. Each structure contains the minimum and maximum Huffman code for a given length and the index of the first value with a Huffman code of that length in the sorted value array. Figure 6.3 shows how these structures would look for the Huffman table in Figure 6.1.

Algorithm 6.5 shows how to decode Huffman-encoded values using this data structure. This algorithm relies on the Huffman codes for a given length being consecutive.

Figure 6.3
Huffman Decoding
Data

Sorted Values

1. A
2. N
3. <space>
4. L
5. M
6. P
7. C
8. .

Length	Minimum Code	Maximum Code	First Value
1	0	0	1
2			
3	100	101	2
4	1100	1110	4
5	11110	11111	7

Algorithm 6.5
Decoding Huffman
Values

```
GLOBAL VALUES [256]
GLOBAL MINCODE [1..16]
GLOBAL MAXCODE [1..16]
GLOBAL FIRSTDATA [1.16]
FUNCTION HuffmanDecode
   Begin
   CODE = 0
   CODELENGTH = 1
   While CODELENGTH <= 16 Do
      Begin
      CODE = CODE LeftShift 1
      CODE = CODE Or NextBitFromInput ()
      CODELENGTH = CODELENGTH + 1
      If CODE <= MAXCODE [CODELENGTH] Then
         Begin
         INDEX = FIRSTCODE [CODELENGTH] + CODE - MINCODE [CODELENGTH]
         Return VALUES [INDEX]
         End
      End
   // Error If We Get Here
   End
```

Using the Huffman codes in Figure 6.3, suppose the next bits in the input stream are 110100. During the next passes through the loop, the code value and maximum code lengths will be:

Length	Code	Maximum
1	1	0
2	11	
3	110	101
4	1101	1110

After we have read 4 bits the code value is less than or equal to the maximum value for length 4. This means we have read in the entire Huffman code. Since the minimum code value of length 4 is 1100_2, 1101_2 is the second Huffman code of length 4 ($1101_2 - 1100_2 = 1$). The first value with a Huffman code of length 4 is the fourth value in the value array, so the value we are looking for is the fifth, which is M. If you look back at Figure 6.1 you can see that this is correct.

Conclusion

In this chapter we introduced Huffman coding and covered it's implementation in JPEG compression. Huffman coding is also used in PNG compression, and the basic method is the same in both formats. In Chapter 14 we will cover the specific requirements for implementing Huffman coding in PNG. Nelson (1992) has a more general description of Huffman coding. Huffman (1952) contains its original description. The JPEG standard JPEG (1994) is the source for the JPEG-specific requirements of Huffman coding.

The source code for this chapter on the accompanying CD-ROM contains classes for JPEG Huffman encoding (JpegHuffmanEncoder and JpegHuffmanDecoder). There is also an application called HUFFCOMP for compressing a file using Huffman coding, in which the command

```
HUFFCOMP SOURCE-FILE COMPRESSED-FILE
```

creates a compressed output file. This application reduces the size of the King James Bible by about 44 percent.

The CD contains a corresponding application for expanding files, in which the command

```
HUFFDECO COMPRESSED-FILE DESTINATION-FILE
```

expands a file compressed with HUFFCOMP to its original state.

Chapter 7

The Discrete Cosine Transform

The Discrete Cosine Transform (DCT) is the heart of JPEG compression. This chapter describes the forward and inverse DCTs as they are used in JPEG and how to perform them using matrix operations.

A transform is an operation that maps members of one set to members of another set.[1] A simple example is the mapping of letters to integers using ASCII codes; a more complicated one is the rotation of geometric figures around the z-axis.

The input to the DCT is a set of numeric values and the output is a set of the same size. The DCT is an invertible transform, which means that its output coefficients can be used to recreate the original input values. The reverse of the DCT is called the Inverse Discrete Cosine Transform (IDCT). The DCT is often referred to as the Forward DCT (FDCT).

The DCT transforms the set of input values into a set of coefficients to cosine functions with increasing frequencies. Each of the original values is transformed into the sum of cosines. In this the DCT is closely related to the Fourier transform.

The DCT is commonly used to process data organized in either one or two dimensions. The number of input values is usually a power of two. In JPEG the DCT and IDCT are always in two dimensions on data arranged in 8×8 blocks. To show how the DCT and IDCT work we will first look at the 1-dimensional case.

---

[1] In mathematics a transform or mapping is indistinguishable from a function. In the computer world we generally think of a function as an operation that returns a single numeric value.

DCT in One Dimension

The 1-dimensional DCT of an array V of N numbers into an array T of N numbers is defined as

Equation 7.1
The 1-D Discrete
Cosine Transform

$$T[i] = c(i) \sum_{n=0}^{N-1} V[n] \cos \frac{(2n+1)i\pi}{2N}$$

where

$$c(0) = \sqrt{\frac{1}{N}}, c(k) = \sqrt{\frac{2}{N}}, k \neq 0$$

The 1-dimensional IDCT is used to reverse the process. It is defined as

Equation 7.2
The 1-D Inverse
Discrete Cosine
Transform

$$V[i] = \sum_{n=0}^{N-1} c(n) T[n] \cos \frac{(2i+1)n\pi}{2N}$$

The following code examples show the definitions of the DCT and IDCT converted into a form more familiar to programmers.

```
void DCT (unsigned int NN, double input [], double output [])
{
 double cc = 1.0 / sqrt (NN) ;
 for (unsigned int ii = 0 ; ii < NN ; ++ ii)
 {
   output [ii] = 0 ;
   for (unsigned int jj = 0 ; jj < NN ; ++ jj)
   {
   output[ii] += cc * (input [jj])
                  * cos ((2*jj+1)*ii * M_PI/2.0/NN) ;
   }
   cc = sqrt (2.0/NN) ;
 }
 return ;
}

void IDCT (unsigned int NN, double input [], double output [])
{
  for (unsigned int ii = 0 ; ii < NN ; ++ ii)
  {
     double cc = 1 / sqrt (NN) ;
     output [ii] = 0.0 ;
     for (unsigned int jj = 0 ; jj < NN ; ++ jj)
     {
     output [ii] += cc * input [jj]
                   * cos((2*ii+1)*jj*M_PI/2.0/NN) ;
     cc = sqrt (2.0/NN) ;
     }
  }
  return ;
}
```

The value of the function

$$y = \cos(x\pi)$$

is shown in Figure 7.1. The cosine function is cyclic so that as x increases the function values start over each time x reaches a multiple of 2π. We can change the frequency with which the cosine function repeats itself by including a constant value n in the function.

$$y = \cos(xn\pi)$$

The larger the value of n, the more often the cosine function repeats. Thus, it repeats twice as often when n is 2 than when n is 1.

By multiplying the cosine function by another value, the amplitude of the cosine wave can be adjusted. Since the value of the function ranges from -1 to 1, in the function

$$y = A \cos(xn\pi)$$

the constant value A is the amplitude of the cosine wave.

If you substitute

$$2x = \frac{2i+1}{2N}$$

and

$$A = c(n)T[n]$$

into the IDCT function in Equation 7.2, you can clearly see that the IDCT is summing cosine functions of increasing frequency where the DCT coefficient is the amplitude of each cosine function in the summation. Figure 7.2 shows a contrived group of eight input values and the resulting DCT coefficients. This is followed by the IDCT calculation for $n = 1$.

In the JPEG modes we will be using in this book, sample values are represented using 8-bits so they can range from 0 to 255. JPEG requires that 128 be subtracted from each input value to bring it into the range -128 to 127 before per-

Figure 7.1
The Cosine
Function

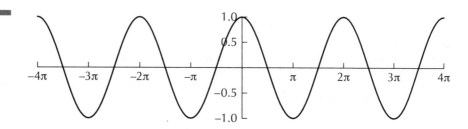

n	0	1	2	3
Input	128	88	40	0
DCT	181.0	0.0	136.6	0.0

$$181.0\sqrt{\tfrac{1}{8}}\cos(0) + 0.0\sqrt{\tfrac{2}{8}}\cos\left(\tfrac{3\pi}{16}\right) + 136.6\sqrt{\tfrac{2}{8}}\cos\left(\tfrac{6\pi}{16}\right) + 0.0\sqrt{\tfrac{2}{8}}\cos\left(\tfrac{9\pi}{16}\right)$$

n	4	5	6	7
Input	0	40	88	128
DCT	0.0	0.0	4.6	0.0

$$+ 0.0\sqrt{\tfrac{2}{8}}\cos\left(\tfrac{12\pi}{16}\right) + 0.0\sqrt{\tfrac{2}{8}}\cos\left(\tfrac{15\pi}{16}\right) + 4.6\sqrt{\tfrac{2}{8}}\cos\left(\tfrac{18\pi}{16}\right) + 0.0\sqrt{\tfrac{2}{8}}\cos\left(\tfrac{21\pi}{16}\right)$$

$$= 64.0 + 0.0 + 26.1 + 0.0 + 0.0 - 2.1 + 0.0$$

$$= 88.0$$

forming the DCT calculation. This has the effect of reducing the magnitude of the first DCT coefficient, but it does not affect the value of any of the others. After performing the IDCT we have to add 128 to bring the results back into the correct range.

If the DCT and IDCT are performed in sequence using infinite precision, the result will always be exactly the same as the input. Unfortunately, computers do not work with infinite precision. In addition, during JPEG compression all DCT values are rounded to integers, which means that the DCT process used in JPEG introduces a rounding error when we compress and then decompress an image. The error is small, but exists nonetheless.

Table 7.1 contains a set of eight sample values extracted from a row at the middle of the image IRENE.JPG (Figure 7.3) and the DCT coefficients calculated from them. We can use the DCT coefficients to recreate the original sample values (with rounding errors), but they take up no less space than those values. Why then use the DCT in image compression at all?

The clue to the value of the DCT can be seen in the decreasing magnitude of the coefficient values in Table 7.1. The magnitudes of the coefficients for the lower values of n are much smaller than those for the higher values.

Graphing the IDCT should make the purpose of the DCT in JPEG much clearer. Figure 7.4 on pages 82 and 83 shows eight graphs of the data from Table 7.1 plotted with the IDCT value calculated using 1 to 8 DCT coefficients.

Input	190	184	186	182	167	123	63	38
n	0	1	2	3	4	5	6	7
DCT coefficients	38.5	143.81	−67.76	−16.33	7.42	−4.73	5.49	0.05

Figure 7.3
IRENE.JPG

In the first graph only the first DCT coefficient is used. In the second, the first two coefficients are used, and in the last all eight are used.

Notice that in the first graph in Figure 7.4 the IDCT function is a horizontal line while in all the other graphs it is a curve. The first DCT coefficient is known as the *DC coefficient;* all the others are called *AC coefficients.* (The names come from electrical engineering. DC current has a constant voltage while AC voltage varies according to a sinusoidal curve.) In JPEG compression, DC and AC coefficients are encoded differently. In Chapter 5 you saw references to DC and AC Huffman tables in the DQT and SOS markers. This is where the DC and AC come from.

As you move from the first graph to the last, the IDCT function gets closer and closer to the original data. In the first graph the IDCT passes through the middle of the general area containing the data points, hitting none of them. In the last graph the IDCT function goes right through the middle of all the data points. The interesting thing here is that on the third graph the IDCT is pretty close to all of the data points. From the fourth graph onward, the subsequent improvement is almost imperceptible.

This is the key to JPEG compression. Since the higher-order DCT coefficients tend to contribute less information to the image, they can be discarded while still producing a very close approximation to the original. Using the data in Table 7.1 we could get rid of half the DCT data and still achieve a good result.

Does this work all the time? For any data set, can we throw away high-order coefficients and retain a close approximation of the original data? If only things were that easy.

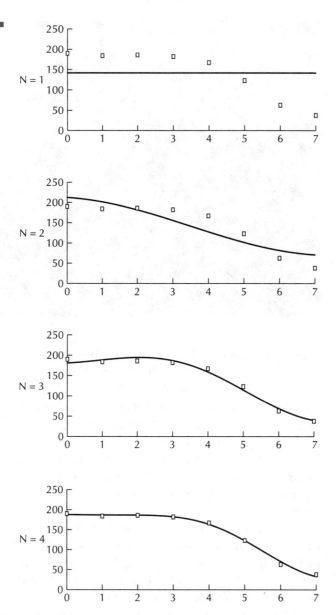

Figure 7.4
IDCT Values for the
Set of Samples in
`IRENE.JPG`

Table 7.2 on page 84 shows a set of input values and the DCT values calculated from them. Figure 7.5 on page 84 shows these values plotted against the IDCT function using seven and eight DCT coefficients. You can see that if we use this input data we cannot throw out any DCT coefficients and get a good result.

Is the data in Table 7.1 or Table 7.2 more typical in real images? That depends upon the image. In a photographic image sharp changes in data, as in

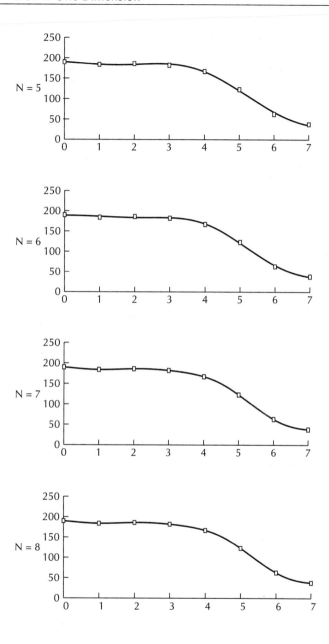

Table 7.2, are not normal. In a drawing sharp changes like this can occur frequently. This is one of the reasons that JPEG compresses photographs better than drawings. With drawings the tradeoff between compression and image quality is a greater concern, so you are generally better off using another image format, such as PNG.

Table 7.2	Input	0	0	255	255	255	0	0	0
DCT Values									
Calculated from an	n	0	1	2	3	4	5	6	7
Arbitrary Data Set	DCT coefficients	-91.57	70.84	-384.4	-125.1	90.1	24.87	20.21	106.0

Figure 7.5
Data from Table 7.2
Plotted against the
IDCT Function

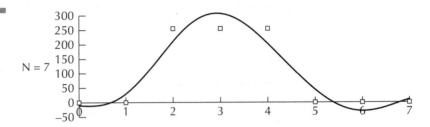

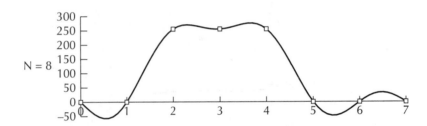

DCT in Two Dimensions

Not surprisingly, it turns out that you can get better compression using the DCT if you take into account the horizontal and vertical correlation between pixels simultaneously. In Chapter 4 we described how JPEG breaks images to 8   8 square blocks called data units. The first step in compressing a data unit is to perform a 2-dimensional DCT, which for a square matrix of size N is defined as

Equation 7.3
2-Dimensional DCT

$$T[i, j] = c(i, j) \sum_{x=0}^{N-1} \sum_{y=0}^{N-1} V[y, x] \cos \frac{(2y+1)i\pi}{2N} \cos \frac{(2x+1)j\pi}{2N}$$

where

$$c(i, j) = \frac{2}{N}, i \text{ and } j \neq 0$$

$$c(i, j) = \frac{1}{N}, i \text{ or } j = 0$$

The 2-dimensional IDCT is

Equation 7.4
2-Dimensional IDCT

$$V[y, x] = \sum_{i=0}^{N-1} \sum_{j=0}^{N-1} c(i, j) T[i, j] \cos \frac{(2y+1)i\pi}{2N} \cos \frac{(2x+1)j\pi}{2N}$$

In JPEG compression the value for N is always 8.

A more convenient method for expressing the 2-dimensional DCT is with matrix products. The forward DCT is

Equation 7.5
2-Dimensional DCT

$$T = MVM^T$$

and the inverse DCT is

Equation 7.6
2-Dimensional IDCT

$$V = M^TTM$$

where V is an 8×8 data unit matrix and M is the matrix shown in Equation 7.7.

Equation 7.7
The Discrete Cosine Transform Matrix

$$M = \begin{bmatrix} \frac{1}{\sqrt{8}} & \frac{1}{\sqrt{8}} & \frac{1}{\sqrt{8}} & \frac{1}{\sqrt{8}} & \frac{1}{\sqrt{8}} & \frac{1}{\sqrt{8}} & \frac{1}{\sqrt{8}} & \frac{1}{\sqrt{8}} \\ \frac{1}{2}\cos\frac{1}{16}\pi & \frac{1}{2}\cos\frac{3}{16}\pi & \frac{1}{2}\cos\frac{5}{16}\pi & \frac{1}{2}\cos\frac{7}{16}\pi & \frac{1}{2}\cos\frac{9}{16}\pi & \frac{1}{2}\cos\frac{11}{16}\pi & \frac{1}{2}\cos\frac{13}{16}\pi & \frac{1}{2}\cos\frac{15}{16}\pi \\ \frac{1}{2}\cos\frac{2}{16}\pi & \frac{1}{2}\cos\frac{6}{16}\pi & \frac{1}{2}\cos\frac{10}{16}\pi & \frac{1}{2}\cos\frac{14}{16}\pi & \frac{1}{2}\cos\frac{18}{16}\pi & \frac{1}{2}\cos\frac{22}{16}\pi & \frac{1}{2}\cos\frac{26}{16}\pi & \frac{1}{2}\cos\frac{30}{16}\pi \\ \frac{1}{2}\cos\frac{3}{16}\pi & \frac{1}{2}\cos\frac{9}{16}\pi & \frac{1}{2}\cos\frac{15}{16}\pi & \frac{1}{2}\cos\frac{21}{16}\pi & \frac{1}{2}\cos\frac{27}{16}\pi & \frac{1}{2}\cos\frac{33}{16}\pi & \frac{1}{2}\cos\frac{39}{16}\pi & \frac{1}{2}\cos\frac{45}{16}\pi \\ \frac{1}{2}\cos\frac{4}{16}\pi & \frac{1}{2}\cos\frac{12}{16}\pi & \frac{1}{2}\cos\frac{20}{16}\pi & \frac{1}{2}\cos\frac{28}{16}\pi & \frac{1}{2}\cos\frac{36}{16}\pi & \frac{1}{2}\cos\frac{44}{16}\pi & \frac{1}{2}\cos\frac{52}{16}\pi & \frac{1}{2}\cos\frac{60}{16}\pi \\ \frac{1}{2}\cos\frac{5}{16}\pi & \frac{1}{2}\cos\frac{15}{16}\pi & \frac{1}{2}\cos\frac{25}{16}\pi & \frac{1}{2}\cos\frac{35}{16}\pi & \frac{1}{2}\cos\frac{45}{16}\pi & \frac{1}{2}\cos\frac{55}{16}\pi & \frac{1}{2}\cos\frac{65}{16}\pi & \frac{1}{2}\cos\frac{75}{16}\pi \\ \frac{1}{2}\cos\frac{6}{16}\pi & \frac{1}{2}\cos\frac{18}{16}\pi & \frac{1}{2}\cos\frac{30}{16}\pi & \frac{1}{2}\cos\frac{42}{16}\pi & \frac{1}{2}\cos\frac{54}{16}\pi & \frac{1}{2}\cos\frac{66}{16}\pi & \frac{1}{2}\cos\frac{78}{16}\pi & \frac{1}{2}\cos\frac{90}{16}\pi \\ \frac{1}{2}\cos\frac{7}{16}\pi & \frac{1}{2}\cos\frac{21}{16}\pi & \frac{1}{2}\cos\frac{35}{16}\pi & \frac{1}{2}\cos\frac{49}{16}\pi & \frac{1}{2}\cos\frac{63}{16}\pi & \frac{1}{2}\cos\frac{77}{16}\pi & \frac{1}{2}\cos\frac{91}{16}\pi & \frac{1}{2}\cos\frac{105}{16}\pi \end{bmatrix}$$

Basic Matrix Operations

For those of you who are unfamiliar with matrices we provide a brief introduction. For more information you should find an introductory textbook on linear algebra. A *matrix* is simply an array of numbers. Generally, when we refer to a matrix we mean a two-dimensional array. In giving the dimensions of a matrix, the number of rows is traditionally specified first. An $N \times M$ matrix is a matrix with N rows and M columns. Elements within a matrix are specified using subscripts. Thus, A_{MN} refers to the element in row N and column M in matrix A.

A one-dimensional array of numbers is known as a *vector,* on which a frequently used operation is the *dot product*. The dot product operation takes two vectors with the same dimension as input and produces a number. To generate the dot product from two vectors you multiply the corresponding entries in the two vectors together and add all the products. This is an example of taking the dot product of two vectors A and B:

$$A = [2\ 2\ 4]$$

$$B = [3\ 1\ 2]$$

$$A \cdot B = 2 \times 3 + 2 \times 1 + 4 \times 2 = 16$$

Matrices can be multiplied only when they are compatible. Two matrices are compatible if the number of columns in the first matrix is equal to the number of rows in the second. All of the matrices we will be dealing with are square with the dimensions 8×8, so compatibility is not an issue. Matrix multiplication is performed by separating each matrix into a set of vectors. Each row in the first matrix forms a vector; each column in the second does also. To create the element in the Nth row and Mth column of the destination matrix we take the dot product of the vectors in the Nth row of first matrix and the Mth column of the second matrix. This is an example of multiplying the 2×2 matrices A and B:

$$A = \begin{bmatrix} 1 & 4 \\ 2 & -3 \end{bmatrix}$$

$$B = \begin{bmatrix} -1 & -2 \\ 0 & 3 \end{bmatrix}$$

$$AB = \begin{bmatrix} [1\ \ 4] \cdot [-1\ 0] & [1\ \ 4] \cdot [-2\ 3] \\ [2\ -3] \cdot [-1\ 0] & [2\ -3] \cdot [-2\ 3] \end{bmatrix} = \begin{bmatrix} -1 & 10 \\ -2 & -13 \end{bmatrix}$$

Matrix multiplication is not commutative. If A and B are matrices, we cannot say that $AB = BA$.

$$BA = \begin{bmatrix} [-1\ -2] \cdot [1\ 2] & [-1\ -2] \cdot [4\ -3] \\ [\ 0\ \ \ 3] \cdot [1\ 2] & [\ 0\ \ \ 3] \cdot [4\ -3] \end{bmatrix} = \begin{bmatrix} -5 & 2 \\ 6 & -9 \end{bmatrix}$$

Matrix multiplication is associative. If A, B, and C are matrices, then

$$(AB)C = A(BC)$$

The *matrix transpose* operation is denoted by A^T. If $B = A^T$, then for every element in B, $B_{NM} = A_{MN}$ as in the following example.

$$A = \begin{bmatrix} 1 & 2 & 3 \\ 4 & 5 & 6 \\ 7 & 8 & 9 \end{bmatrix}$$

$$A^T = \begin{bmatrix} 1 & 4 & 7 \\ 2 & 5 & 8 \\ 3 & 6 & 9 \end{bmatrix}$$

A matrix is multiplied by a number by multiplying each element in the matrix by the number.

$$A = \begin{bmatrix} 1 & 3 \\ 2 & 4 \end{bmatrix}$$

$$10 \times A = \begin{bmatrix} 10 & 30 \\ 20 & 40 \end{bmatrix}$$

That is all the linear algebra we need to get through the rest of the chapter. However, before we move on I would like to point out an interesting property of the DCT matrix M shown previously. M is what is known as an *orthogonal matrix*. If you take the dot product of any row or column with itself the result is 1. If you take the dot product of any row with any other row or any column and any other column the result is 0. If you multiply M by its transpose you get

$$MM^T = \begin{bmatrix} 1 & 0 & 0 & 0 & 0 & 0 & 0 & 0 \\ 0 & 1 & 0 & 0 & 0 & 0 & 0 & 0 \\ 0 & 0 & 1 & 0 & 0 & 0 & 0 & 0 \\ 0 & 0 & 0 & 1 & 0 & 0 & 0 & 0 \\ 0 & 0 & 0 & 0 & 1 & 0 & 0 & 0 \\ 0 & 0 & 0 & 0 & 0 & 1 & 0 & 0 \\ 0 & 0 & 0 & 0 & 0 & 0 & 1 & 0 \\ 0 & 0 & 0 & 0 & 0 & 0 & 0 & 1 \end{bmatrix}$$

Any square matrix with values of 1 on the diagonal running from the upper left to the bottom right and values of 0 everywhere else is known as an *identity matrix*. Multiplying any matrix A by the identity matrix results in A.

Using the 2-D Forward DCT

Now we return to the image IRENE.JPG to show what happens to an image using the 2-dimensional DCT. Figure 7.6 contains an 8   8 block of Y component samples from the area around Irene's eye and the 2-dimensional DCT coefficients generated from them.

In the figure the larger coefficient values are concentrated in the upper left corner. The trend is that the farther you get from the DC coefficient in the upper left corner, the smaller the values become. The DC coefficient is nearly three times as large as any of the AC coefficients.

Figure 7.6
Sample Data Unit
from IRENE.JPG
and Its DCT
Coefficients

Y Component Samples from IRENE.BMP

58	45	29	27	24	19	17	20
62	52	42	41	38	30	22	18
48	47	49	44	40	36	31	25
59	78	49	32	28	31	31	31
98	138	116	78	39	24	25	27
115	160	143	97	48	27	24	21
99	137	127	84	42	25	24	20
74	95	82	67	40	25	25	19

DCT Coefficients

−603	203	11	45	−30	−14	−14	−7
−108	−93	10	49	27	6	8	2
−42	−20	−6	16	17	9	3	3
56	69	7	−25	−10	−5	−2	−2
−33	−21	17	8	3	−4	−5	−3
−16	−14	8	2	−4	−2	1	1
0	−5	−6	−1	2	3	1	1
8	5	−6	−9	0	3	3	2

Quantization

We saw with the 1-dimensional DCT that you do not always need to use all the of the DCT coefficients with the Inverse DCT to reconstruct a close approximation of the original data. We also saw that there are situations when we need to use most, if not all, of the coefficients to reproduce something that is close. The same is true with the 2-dimensional DCT. After calculating the DCT, the next step is to find and discard the coefficients that contribute the least to the image.

The JPEG standard defines a simple mechanism for doing this known as *quantization,* which is a fancy name for division. To quantize the DCT coefficients we simply divide them by another value and round to the nearest integer.

$$Quantized\ Value\ =\ Round\left(\frac{Coefficient}{Quantum\ Value}\right)$$

To reverse the process multiply

$$Coefficient\ =\ Quantized\ Value\ \times\ Quantum\ value$$

Choosing a quantum value as small as 20 would convert over half the coefficients in Figure 7.6 to zeros.

JPEG uses a 64-element array called a *quantization table* to define quantum values for an image. Quantization tables are defined in the DQT marker described in Chapter 5. It is possible to use multiple quantization tables so that not all components need be quantized using the same values. Each value in a quantization table is used to quantize the corresponding DCT coefficient.

The JPEG standard does not specify the quantization values to be used. This is left up to the application. However, it does provide a pair of sample quantization tables that it says have been tested empirically and found to generate good results. These tables are shown in Figure 7.7.

Figure 7.7
Sample
Quantization Tables
from the JPEG
Standard

Y Component Quantization Table							
16	11	10	16	24	40	51	61
12	12	14	19	26	58	60	55
14	13	16	24	40	57	69	56
14	17	22	29	51	87	80	62
18	22	37	56	68	109	103	77
24	35	55	64	81	104	113	92
49	64	78	87	103	121	120	101
72	92	95	98	112	100	103	99

Cb and Cr Component Quantization Table							
17	18	24	47	99	99	99	99
18	21	26	66	99	99	99	99
24	26	56	99	99	99	99	99
47	66	99	99	99	99	99	99
99	99	99	99	99	99	99	99
99	99	99	99	99	99	99	99
99	99	99	99	99	99	99	99
99	99	99	99	99	99	99	99

Figure 7.8
Quantized DCT
Coefficients from
Figure 7.6

-38	18	1	-3	-1	0	0	0
-9	-8	1	3	1	0	0	0
-3	-2	0	1	0	0	0	0
4	4	0	-1	0	0	0	0
-2	-1	0	0	0	0	0	0
-1	0	0	0	0	0	0	0
0	0	0	0	0	0	0	0
0	0	0	0	0	0	0	0

The result from quantizing sample values from Figure 7.6 with the sample Y quantization table in Figure 7.7 is shown in Figure 7.8. After quantization only 19 out of 64 DCT coefficients values are nonzero. Chapter 8 covers how JPEG compresses runs of zero AC coefficient values.

Zigzag Ordering

In order to group as many of the quantized zero-value coefficients together to produce the longest runs of zero values, AC coefficients in a data unit are encoded using a zigzag path.

Figure 7.9 shows the zigzag order defined by the JPEG standard. This was briefly mentioned in Chapter 5 in the section on the DQT marker. Quantization values within quantization tables are stored in JPEG files using this zigzag ordering also. This is the ordering of the quantized AC coefficients in Figure 7.8:

18 −9 −3 −8 1 −3 1 −2 4 −2 4 0 3 −1 0 1 1 0 −1 −1 0 0 0 −1   (39 Zeros)

Figure 7.9
Zigzag Order for AC
Coefficients

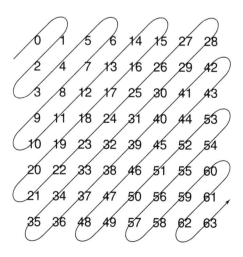

Conclusion

In this chapter we described the Discrete Cosine Transform (DCT) and quantization. The DCT is used to represent an 8×8 block of sample values as a sum of cosine functions. The DCT coefficient in the upper left corner represents a constant value and is known as the DC coefficient. All other coefficients are AC coefficients.

We used matrix operations to calculate the DCT and its inverse. In Chapter 10 we will take another look at the DCT and show how it is possible to make it faster.

More information on the DCT can be found in Rao and Yip (1990), an entire book devoted to the subject. Nelson (1992) presents a simplified, JPEG-like version of DCT compression. The sample quantization tables in this chapter come from JPEG (1994). Any introductory book on linear algebra, such as Anton (1981), will contain more information on basic matrix operations.

The source code for this chapter consists of classes for representing quantization tables and data units during compression. These classes use matrix operations to implement the DCT.

Chapter 8

Decoding Sequential- Mode JPEG Images

We dealt with most of the JPEG preliminaries in previous chapters. This chapter puts the pieces together and shows how to implement a sequential-mode JPEG decoder.

We will cover SOF_0 (baseline DCT) frames and a subset of SOF_1 (extended sequential DCT) frames. These are identical except that extended sequential frames can use 12-bit or 8-bit samples and up to four DC or AC Huffman tables, whereas baseline DCT JPEG supports only 8-bit samples and up to two DC and AC Huffman tables. If we limit ourselves to 8-bit samples and permit up to four DC or AC Huffman tables, these two frame types are decoded in exactly the same manner.

MCU Dimensions

JPEG compressed data consists of a sequence of encoded MCUs arranged from top to bottom, left to right. The first step in decoding scan data is to determine the number of data units from each scan that make up each MCU and the number of MCUs required to encode the scan.

For any component, the number of pixels a data unit spans is

$$Pixels_x = 8 \times \frac{F_{x\,max}}{F_x}$$
$$Pixels_y = 8 \times \frac{F_{y\,max}}{F_y}$$

where

$$F_x = \text{Component horizontal sampling frequency}$$

$$F_{x\,max} = \text{Maximum of all component horizontal sampling frequencies}$$

$$F_y = \text{Component vertical sampling frequency}$$

$$F_{y\,max} = \text{Maximum of all component vertical sampling frequencies}$$

If the scan is noninterleaved (i.e., it has only one component), each MCU in the scan consists of 1 data unit. The number of MCUs in the scan is $MCUs_x \times MCUs_y$ where

$$MCUs_x = \frac{ImageWidth + Pixels_x - 1}{Pixels_x}$$

$$MCUs_y = \frac{ImageHeight + Pixels_y - 1}{Pixels_y}$$

If the scan is interleaved, $MCUs_x$ and $MCUs_y$ are

$$MCUs_x = \frac{ImageWidth + 8 \times F_{x\,max} - 1}{8 \times F_{x\,max}}$$

$$MCUs_y = \frac{ImageHeight + 8 \times F_{x\,max} - 1}{8 \times F_{x\,max}}$$

Keep in mind that for an interleaved scan, $F_{x\,max}$ and $F_{y\,max}$ are the maximum sampling frequencies of all the components in the image rather than the maximum frequencies of the components in the scan.

In an interleaved scan the number of data units each component contributes to an MCU is the product of the component's sampling frequencies. Suppose you have a color image with the Y component having vertical and horizontal sampling frequencies of 2 and the Cb and Cr components having vertical and horizontal frequencies of 1. If an interleaved scan contains all three components, there are a total of 6 data units in each MCU.

The JPEG standard imposes a rather low limit of 10 data units per MCU. This places restrictions on the sampling frequencies and on the placement of components within scans. Suppose the Y component had horizontal and vertical sampling frequencies of 4. In an interleaved scan it alone would contribute 16 data units to each MCU, thereby exceeding JPEG's limit. Using such a sampling, the Y component would have to be in a noninterleaved scan.

Within a scan there are no partial MCUs or data units. If the image's dimensions are not an exact multiple of the MCU size, the compressed data includes padding to round up to the next complete MCU.

Figure 8.1 illustrates the positional relationship between the MCUs and an image. It shows an image whose dimensions are 50×50 pixels, with the Y component sampled with a horizontal and vertical frequency of 2 and the other components sampled with frequencies of 1. When the Y component is in a noninterleaved scan, the scan is composed of 7 MCU rows and 7 MCU columns, each MCU consisting of 1 data unit. The image area covered by each MCU is outlined in white.

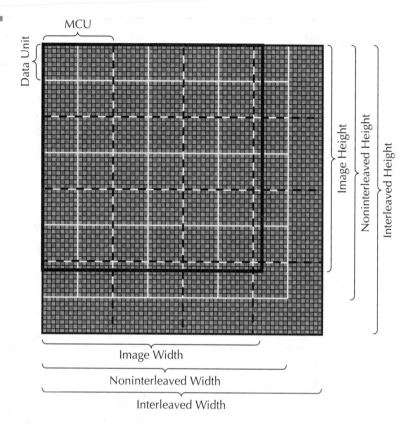

Figure 8.1
*Relationship of
MCU Size to Image
Size*

MCU

Data Unit

Image Height

Noninterleaved Height

Interleaved Height

Image Width

Noninterleaved Width

Interleaved Width

In an interleaved scan there are 4 rows and columns of MCUs. The area of the image covered by each MCU is outlined with a thin black line. In this example, the last MCU row and column represent mostly dead space.

Each MCU is encoded as a sequence of data units. Its components are encoded in the order they are listed in the SOS marker and are not interleaved. The data units from each component are ordered from top to bottom, left to right.

Algorithm 8.1 shows the procedure for decoding the MCUs within a scan.

Algorithm 8.1
MCU Decoding

```
For Each MCU In The Scan
    Begin
    For Each Component In the Scan
        Begin
        For I = 1 To Component Vertical Sampling Frequency
            Begin
            For J = 1 To Component Horizontal Sampling Frequency
                Begin
                Decode Data Unit
                End
            End
        End
    End
```

Decoding Data Units

After determining the number of MCUs and data units within each scan, the next step is to decode the individual data units. What is actually encoded for each data unit are quantized DCT coefficients. Thus, the first step is to create the DCT coefficient values. The DC coefficient is encoded first using Huffman coding. Then the AC coefficients are encoded as a group using Huffman and run-length encoding. The DC and AC coefficients are encoded with different Huffman tables, as specified on the SOS marker.

Decoding DC Coefficients

DC coefficients are stored in a JPEG file as the difference between the previous DC value encoded for the component and the current DC coefficient value. The advantage of using the difference is that it takes fewer bits to encode smaller values. Unless there are dramatic shifts in a component's DC coefficient value from one data unit to the next, the magnitudes of the differences between adjacent DC values will generally be smaller than the magnitude of the DC values themselves.

For each component the last DC value is initialized to zero at the start of a scan and reset to zero whenever a restart marker is read. This means that the first DC value in a scan and the first value following a restart marker are absolute DC values.

DC coefficients are encoded in two parts. The first part is a 1-byte Huffman encoded value that specifies the magnitude of the DC difference. Table 8.1 lists the DC magnitude code values and the corresponding coefficient values.

To convert the magnitude value to an actual DC difference value the decoder has to read a number of unencoded, literal bits from the input stream. The number of literal bits is the same as the magnitude value. When the magnitude value is zero, there are no additional bits.

	Encoded Value	DC Value Range
Table 8.1		
DC Difference	0	0
Magnitude Codes	1	–1, 1
and Ranges	2	–3, –2, 2, 3
	3	–7 . . –4, 4 . . 7
	4	–15 . . –8, 8 . . 15
	5	–31 . . –16, 16 . . 31
	6	–63 . . –32, 32 . . 63
	7	–127 . . –64, 64 . . 127
	8	–255 . . –128, 128 . . 255
	9	–511 . . –256, 256 . . 511
	10	–1023 . . –512, 512 . . 1023
	11	–2047 . . –1024, 1024 . . 2047

The first bit following the magnitude specifies the sign of the difference value. A sign bit of zero means a negative difference; a sign bit of one, a positive difference. Algorithm 8.2 defines a function for converting a magnitude value and additional bits to the difference value. This function is translated directly from the JPEG standard.

The overall procedure for decoding DC coefficients is shown in Algorithm 8.3.

Algorithm 8.2
Extend() Function

```
Function Extend (ADDITIONAL, MAGNITUDE)
    Begin
    vt = 1 LeftShift (MAGNITUDE - 1)
    If ADDITIONAL < vt Then
        return ADDITIONAL + (-1 LeftShift MAGNITUDE) + 1
    Else
        return ADDITIONAL
    End
```

Algorithm 8.3
DC Coefficient
Decoding

```
Global LASTDC
Function DecodeDC
    Begin
    CODE = HuffmanDecode ()
    BITS = ReadBits (code)
    DIFFERENCE = Extend (BITS, CODE)
    DC = DIFFERENCE + LASTDC
    LASTDC = DC
    Return DC
    End
```

Decoding AC Coefficients

Decoding AC coefficient values is a little more complicated than decoding DC coefficients. The AC coefficients in each data unit are stored in the zigzag order defined in Chapter 7. The decoder uses the AC Huffman table to decode a 1-byte value. Unlike with DC differences, this value is divided into two 4-bit fields. The 4 low-order bits contain the magnitude value, and the 4 high-order bits contain the number of zero-valued coefficients to skip before writing this coefficient. For example, the Huffman-encoded value 56_{16} specifies that the next five AC coefficients are zero and they are followed by a nonzero coefficient with a magnitude of 6 bits.

Table 8.2 lists the possible AC magnitude values and their corresponding coefficient ranges. Notice that for AC coefficients there is no entry for magnitude 0. This is because zero-valued AC coefficients are encoded using zero runs. AC magnitude values are converted to coefficient values by reading raw bits and using the Extend(), just as DC coefficients are. The only difference is that for AC coefficients the actual value, not a difference, is encoded.

	Magnitude Value	AC Value Range
Table 8.2 *AC Magnitude* *Codes and Ranges*	1	−1, 1
	2	−3, −2, 2, 3
	3	−7 . . −4, 4 . . 7
	4	−15 . . −8, 8 . . 15
	5	−31 . . −16, 16 . . 31
	6	−63 . . −32, 32 . . 63
	7	−127 . . −64, 64 . . 127
	8	−255 . . −128, 128 . . 255
	9	−511 . . −256, 256 . . 511
	10	−1023 . . −512, 512 . . 1023

Two special codes are used for encoding AC coefficient values. The code 00_{16} is used when all remaining AC coefficients in the data unit are zero. The code $F0_{16}$ represents a run of 16 zero AC coefficients. Neither of these codes is followed by any raw bits.

For each data unit, the AC coefficient decoding process is repeated until all AC coefficients have been decoded. A data unit is complete when either an end-of-block code is decoded or the last AC coefficient is expanded. Algorithm 8.4 shows the process for decoding the AC coefficients of a data unit.

Algorithm 8.4
AC Coefficient
Decoding

```
For II = 1 To 63 Do
    COEFFICIENTS [II] = 0

II = 1
While II <=63 Do
    Begin
    VALUE = DecodeUsingACTable ()
    LOBITS = VALUE And 0F₁₆
    HIBITS = (VALUE And F0₁₆) RightShift 4

    If LOBITS <> 0 Then
        Begin
        EXTRABITS = ReadRawBits (LOBITS)
        II = II + HIGHBITS
        COEFFICIENTS [II] = Extend (EXTRABITS, LOBITS)
        II = II + 1
        End
    Else
        Begin
        If HIGHBITS = F₁₆ Then
            II = II + 16 // Run of 16 Zeros
        Else If HIGHBITS = 0 Then
            II = 64 // All Done
        End
    End
```

Decoding Example

Figure 8.2 and Figure 8.3 are examples of the decoding of the first two data units for a component within a scan. In Figure 8.2, which shows the decoding of the first data unit, the last DC value for the scan is initialized with 0. First we decode the DC coefficient. Using the DC Huffman table for the component we find that the next Huffman-encoded value is 04_{16}. This magnitude value tells us that we need to read 4 raw bits (1010_2) from the input stream. The DC coefficient value is the sum of the result of the Extend() function (10) and the last DC coefficient value (0).

Now we decode the AC coefficients using the AC Huffman table for the component. The next Huffman-encoded value is 03_{16}. The four high-order bits specify the zero run (0); the low-order bits specify the magnitude value (3). We then read the next three raw bits from the input stream (010_2) and call the Extend() function, which gives −3 as the value for the first AC coefficient.

The decoding of the second AC coefficient is nearly identical to that of the first. The third Huffman decoding returns the value $E3_{16}$, which means a zero run of 14 is followed by a coefficient with a magnitude of 3 bits. We read the next 3 raw bits from the input stream (100_2) and call the Extend() function, which returns 8. We set the next 14 AC coefficients to zero followed by a coefficient with the value 8.

The next two values decoded using the AC Huffman table are the special code $F0_{16}$. No additional bits follow this code. Each time we read it we set the next 16 AC coefficients to 0.

The next code in the input stream and the raw bits that follow tell us to set the next 12 AC coefficients to zero, then set the next coefficient to 1. This is

Figure 8.2
Decoding a Component's First Data Unit in a Scan

DC Coefficients

Block	DC Table Decode	Raw Bits	DC Difference	Last DC Value	New DC Value
A	04_{16}	1010_2	10	0	10

AC Coefficients

Block	AC Table Decode	Zero Run	Raw Bits	Coefficient Value
B	03_{16}	0	010_2	−1
C	04_{16}	0	1001_2	9
D	$E3_{16}$	14	100_2	8
E	$F0_{16}$	16	None	None
F	$F0_{16}$	16	None	None
G	$C1_{16}$	12	1_2	1
H	01_{16}	0	0_2	−1

Figure 8.3
Decoding a
Component's
Second Data Unit in
a Scan

DC Coefficients

Block	DC Table Decode	Raw Bits	DC Difference	Last DC Value	New DC Value
A	00_{16}	None	0	10	10

AC Coefficients

Block	AC Table Decode	Zero Run	Raw Bits	Coefficient Value
B	02_{16}	0	10_2	2
C	01_{16}	0	0_2	−1
D	00_{16}	End of block	None	None

followed by a sequence that tells us to set the next AC coefficient to −1. Since this is AC coefficient 63 the decoding of the data unit is complete.

Figure 8.3 shows the decoding of the next data unit for the component. If this were an interleaved scan, then, depending upon the component sampling frequencies, data units for other components would be decoded before this one. First we decode the DC coefficient for the data unit. Using the DC Huffman table we find that the next magnitude value is zero, which means that are no additional raw bits. The DC difference value is simply zero. We add the difference value to the last DC value (10), which gives 10 for the coefficient value. The last DC value remains 10.

The first two AC coefficients are decoded as before. When we use the AC table to decode the magnitude value for the next coefficient we read the special code 00_{16}, which tells us to set the remaining AC coefficients to zero. The data unit is now complete.

Processing DCT Coefficients

After all of the DCT coefficients for the data unit have been read, we have to perform dequantization and the IDCT on the data unit, as described in Chapter 7. For dequantization we simply multiply each coefficient value by the corresponding entry in the quantization table. After that we perform the IDCT on the coefficients which gives the sample values.

Up-Sampling

At this stage we have down-sampled YCbCr values. From these we need to create an RGB image. For a grayscale image we are finished, since the Y value corresponds to an index into a color palette where red = green = blue. For a color image the first thing we need to do is up-sampling.

If any component has been sampled, either vertically or horizontally, at less than 1:1 (in other words, either sampling frequency is less than the maximum value of all the components in the image), the component needs to be *up-sampled,* by which we mean increasing the resolution of the component data.

Suppose we have a JPEG compressed color image where the Y component has a horizontal and vertical sampling frequency of 2 while the Cb and Cr components have a frequency of 1 in both dimensions. When the image was compressed one Y component sample was taken for each pixel, but for the Cb and Cr components one sample was taken for every 4 pixels. After the image is decompressed we need to spread the Cb and Cr component values across multiple pixels.

There are several ways to do this. The easiest method and the one we are going to use in the sample code, is to simply duplicate the Cb and Cr component values so that the sample gets stretched to a number of adjacent pixels. The drawback with this method is that it produces blocking effects. An alternative is to apply a filtering algorithm during the up-sampling process.

After up-sampling we have a Y, Cb, and Cr sample value for each pixel of a color image. The last step is to convert the YCbCr components to RGB using the conversions shown in Chapter 1.

Restart Marker Processing

One small step we omitted in the preceding discussion is the handling of restart markers. If the last DRI (Define Restart Interval) marker in the input stream before the SOS defined a nonzero value for the restart interval, the scan data should have restart markers (RST_0–RST_7) embedded within it. The restart interval specifies the number of MCUs between restart markers.

A JPEG decoder needs to maintain a counter of MCUs processed between restart markers. Whenever the counter reaches the restart interval the decoder needs to read a restart marker from the input stream.

Restart markers are placed on byte boundaries. Any fractional bits in the input stream that have not been used are discarded before the restart marker is read. The only processing that takes place after the reading of a restart marker is resetting the DC difference values for each component in the scan to zero.

If the decoder does not find a restart marker at the specified restart interval, the stream is corrupt. The decoder should ensure that the restart markers are in the order RST_0, RST_1, ... RST_7, RST_0, RST_1, ... RST_7.

Overview of JPEG Decoding

We have covered the process for decoding individual data units from start to finish. Now we are going to take a step back and look at the overall process for decoding a sequential-mode JPEG image. Keep in mind that since we are not supporting JPEG hierarchical mode, we make no distinction between a frame and an image. The overall decoding process for JPEG file is

1. Read the SOI and JFIF APP_0 markers to ensure that we have a valid JPEG file.
2. Read the DRI, DQT, and DHT markers and use them to define the restart interval, quantization tables, and Huffman tables.
3. Read a SOF marker and use it to define the image dimensions.
4. Read all the SOS markers and process the scan data following them.
5. Read the EOI marker.

This overall plan needs to be able to handle variations. The SOI and JFIF APP_0 marker must be at the beginning of the file and the EOI marker must be at the end. SOS markers must occur after the SOF marker, but DRI, DQT, and DHT markers can occur anywhere in the file before the EOI marker.

Conclusion

In this chapter we covered the representation of compressed image data within the SOS markers of a sequential-mode JPEG file. JPEG (1994), the JPEG standard, is the official source for the JPEG format. The JPEG source code contains extensive references to this document, so you can match the section numbers in the source code to the corresponding section in the standard.

The code example for this chapter is a functional JPEG decoder that can read baseline sequential and extended sequential JPEG files and convert them to Windows BMP files. Some of the components of this decoder were presented in previous chapters, so they will not be repeated here.

This application has two restrictions in the types of sequential JPEG files it can process, but neither should present much of a problem. First of all, DNL markers are not supported. Since they are not in common use, however this is a minor limitation. Second, fractional data sampling is not supported. If a color image is encoded with a component having a horizontal or vertical sampling frequency of 3 and any other component having a corresponding frequency other than 1, this will cause fractions of bits to be sampled. Fractional sampling is not used in the real world, so, again, this is not a major problem.

Component Class

The decoder uses `JpegDecoderComponent` to represent a single component. This class maintains an array (`data_units`) that contains the component's decoded data units. It is possible to implement a sequential decoder without buffering all the data units. However, this buffering is required for progressive decodings. In order to have the maximum commonality between the progressive decoder presented in Chapter 11 the sequential decoder buffers the data units as well.

DecodeSequential

The `DecodeSequential` member function decodes the next data unit within the input stream and stores the value in the `data_units` array. This function follows the decoding process presented earlier in this chapter.

Upsample

The `Upsample` function stretches the component's sample data by duplicating values. The amount of stretching is based upon the component's sampling frequencies relative to the maximum sampling frequencies for the image. There are two execution paths. One handles the simplest case where the horizontal and vertical sampling frequencies are equal to the maximum values for the image. The other path handles the stretching of components.

Color Conversion

The `RGBConvert` function converts YCbCr sample values from three components to the equivalent RGB values and stores them in a `BitmapImage` object. Since RGB conversion requires three separate components, the `RGBConvert` function is static. The `GrayscaleConvert` function does the same for grayscale conversion. For consistency this function is static as well, even though it uses only one component.

Decoder Class

The JpegDecoder class is the JPEG decoder. It reads a JPEG image from an input stream and then stores it in a BitmapImage object.

ReadImage

The `ReadImage` function reads a JPEG image from an input stream. It calls the `ReadMarker` repeatedly to process markers with the input stream until the EOI marker is read. `ReadMarker` determines the marker type and then calls functions that decode specific markers.

ReadQuantization

The `ReadQuantization` function processes a DQT marker. The `JpegDecoderQuantizationTable` objects read the actual quantization tables from the input stream. A DQT marker may define multiple quantization tables, so this function determines how many tables the marker contains and the identity of each one.

ReadHuffmanTable

This function is very similar to `ReadQuantization` except that it reads DHT markers. The actual Huffman table data is read by the `JpegHuffmanDecoder` objects. This function reads Huffman tables until no more remain in the marker data.

ReadStartOfFrame

The `ReadStartOfFrame` function reads SOF_n markers. All SOF_n markers have the same format, so the same function is used to read all types. The decoder relies upon the `ReadMarker` function to determine if the SOF_n marker is one supported by the decoder.

ReadStartOfScan

The `ReadStartOfScan` reads an SOS marker from the input stream. It determines the components that make up the scan and then stores a list of pointers to the corresponding `JpegDecoderComponent` objects within the `scan_components` array.

ReadSequentialInterleavedScan and ReadSequentialNonInterleavedScan

The `ReadSequentialInterleavedScan` and `ReadSequentialNonInterleavedScan` functions control the reading of data units from the input stream. The former is used when the current scan contains more than one component; the latter is used when there is only one component in the scan. The individual component objects read the DCT coefficients into the data units. However, this function determines the ordering of the components and which data unit is read for each component. They also keep track of the number of data units read and compare this to the restart interval in order to determine when a restart marker must be read.

Using the Decoder Class

The JpegDecoder class is used in the same manner as the other decoder classes presented in this book. The following fragment illustrates how to use it to convert a JPEG file to a Windows BMP file.

```
#include "jpgdecod.h"
#include "bmpencod.h"

ifstream input ("INPUT.JPG", ios::binary)
ofstream output ("OUTPUT.BMP", ios::binary) ;
BitmapImage image ;
JpegDecoder decoder ;
decoder.ReadImage (input, image) ;
BmpEncoder encoder ;
encoder.WriteImage (output, image) ;
```

Decoding Application

The DECODER application converts a JPEG image to BMP format. The command-line format for this application is

```
DECODER input.jpg output.bmp
```

DECODER creates a JpegDecoder object and then calls its ReadImage function to read the input file into a BitmapImage object. It creates the BMP file by calling the WriteImage function of a BmpEncoder object.

Chapter 9

Creating Sequential JPEG Files

In this chapter we cover the implementation of sequential-mode JPEG encoders. In general, the process for creating a JPEG file is the reverse of the decoding process. A major difference between encoding and decoding is that encoding requires several choices to be made while in decoding you take what you get. The endcoding choices include compression parameters, Huffman code generation, and block ordering.

Compression Parameters

In compressing an image using sequential-mode JPEG compression, we have several choices. These include

- The composition and number of quantization tables and the assignment of tables to components
- The number of Huffman tables, their assignment to components, and the method for their creation
- The number of scans and the components in each
- The frequency of restart markers
- Component sampling frequencies
- Whether to create a color or grayscale image
- Whether to use baseline or extended frames

An encoder can make these choices either on a per-image basis or globally.

Two frame types can be used for sequential JPEG with Huffman encoding: baseline sequential (SOF_0) or extended sequential (SOF_1). The only difference between the two is that baseline sequential supports only 8-bit samples and a maximum of two DC and two AC Huffman tables; extended sequential supports 8-bit and 12-bit samples and up to four DC and four AC Huffman tables. Baseline sequential is the JPEG mode implemented by most JPEG decoders; thus, for the greatest compatibility, an encoder should use it when possible. The encoder at the end of this chapter encodes only 8-bit sample data and, since there is no need to for more than two of each type of Huffman table, it uses baseline sequential.

Extended sequential is upwardly compatible with baseline sequential JPEG. If an encoder were to simply replace the SOF_0 marker with an SOF_1 marker, it would create a perfectly valid extended sequential file.

Huffman Tables

Since color images have three components and baseline mode allows only two Huffman tables of each type, an encoder has to share its Huffman tables among components or split the components among multiple scans. Our encoder always uses the Huffman tables with the identifier 0 to encode the Y component and the table with the identifier 1 to encode the Cb and Cr components. If the Cb and Cr components are encoded within the same scan, they share a Huffman table.

If an image is divided into two or more scans it is possible for the encoder to assign a different Huffman table for each scan. Our encoder only assigns the Cb and Cr components different Huffman tables when they are encoded in different scans. If they are encoded within the same scan, even if the Y component is not part of the scan, they share Huffman tables.

Quantization Tables

Both baseline and extended sequential modes allow up to four quantization tables defined for an image. Our sample encoder is only going to use two. One table (ID=0) is used for the Y component and the other (ID=1) is used for the Cb and Cr components. These table assignments are an arbitrary choice.

The next problem is how to create the quantization tables. We could allow a user to specify all the elements of the quantization table, but this would make using the decoder a little tedious, especially for people who do not know the inner workings of JPEG. Having a fixed set of quantization values would not be a good idea, either, since different types of images require different quantization values in order to decompress without noticeable defects.

Our solution originates with the Independent JPEG Group's JPEG library. We start with the sample quantization values from the JPEG standard (Figure 7.7), then scale these values down for higher quality and up for lower quality. The caller selects a quality value that ranges from 1 to 100. Quality level 50 uses the unmodified quanitization values from the JPEG standard. Quality values below 25 produce quantization values so large that the resulting compressed image will be all black. Using quantization values near 100 produces quantization values close to 1, resulting in extremely poor compression.

The sample encoding uses this formula to calculate a scaling factor for quantization values:

$$scale\ factor\ =\ e^{\log\left(2\ \times\ \frac{6 \cdot (50 - quality)}{50}\right)}$$

There is no derivation behind this formula. It is simply one that that gives a scale factor of 1 when the quality value is 50 and gives a decent scaling across the range 1–100. If you are implementing a JPEG encoder you can come up with your own scaling or use any other method you want for generating quantization values. For example, you may have quality values ranging from 1 to 4 and select from among four sets of predefined quantization tables.

An important point to take from this discussion is that quality values are all relative. The concept of a quality value does not exist within the JPEG standard but rather was developed with the implementation of JPEG encoders. The same quality value will more likely than not produce different results among different encoders even when the quality value range is the same.

Scans

In sequential JPEG the data for each component is stored in a single scan. For a color image one to three scans can be used. The five possible component groupings are shown in Figure 9.1. The individual scans can be encoded in any order, which means that there are actually thirteen different ways to group and order the components in a sequential image. A grayscale image will naturally only have one scan.

Figure 9.1
Possible
Component
Groupings for a
Color Image

		A	B	C	D	E
Scans	1	Y Cb Cr	Y	Y Cb	Y Cr	Y
	2		Cb Cr	Cr	Cb	Cb
	3					Cr

There are few reasons why an encoder would divide the image into multiple scans. If the image is being transmitted over a network and displayed on the fly, encoding the Y component by itself in the first scan allows the user to view a grayscale version of it before all the data is received. This gives some of the benefits of progressive JPEG without the implementation difficulties.

Separate scans can overcome the limitations in the number of Huffman tables allowed. Baseline JPEG allows only two Huffman tables of each type. If for some reason a separate table were needed for each component, multiple scans could be used. Figure 9.2 shows a marker ordering that would allow a color baseline JPEG image to use a different Huffman table for each component.

An encoder can allow the user to specify the component grouping into scans, or it can use a predefined grouping. The decision on which to use depends on whether flexibility or ease of use is desired. If the user is not allowed to specify the component grouping, the encoder needs to automatically divide components into multiple scans when this is required by the sampling frequencies.

Figure 9.2
Baseline Marker
Ordering That Gives
Each Component
Different Huffman
Tables

.
.
.

DHT	Defines Table 0
SOS	Y Component Uses Table 0
DHT	Redefines Table 0
DHT	Defines Table 1
SOS	Cb Component Uses Table 0, Cr Component Uses Table 1

.
.
.

Sampling Frequencies

The sample encoder allows the user to assign horizontal and vertical sampling frequencies (1–4) to each component, but this is not a requirement. A simpler method that almost always produces good results is for an encoder to allow the user to specify the sampling frequencies for the Y component while always using the value 1 for the Cb and Cr components.

If the user is permitted to specify any possible sampling frequency for any component, the encoder must then deal with the problem of fractional sampling. If all of the sampling frequencies are powers of 2 (1, 2, 4), during the down-sampling process entire pixels (1, 2, 4, 8, or 16) will be mapped to a single sample value. If, on the other hand, any component has a horizontal or vertical sampling frequency of 3 and any other component has a corresponding sampling frequency of 2 or 4, the down-sampling process will map fractional pixels to sample values. While this is legal in the JPEG standard, it is not widely supported. If you create images that use fractional sampling, very likely they will not be readable by many other applications. The sample JPEG encoder generates an exception during the compression process if the user has specified fractional sampling.

The JPEG standard (Section B.2.3) specifies that an MCU within a scan may contain a maximum of 10 data units:

$$HF_Y \times VH_Y + HF_{Cb} \times VH_{Cb} + HF_{Cr} \times VH_{Cr} \leq 10$$

This is an arbitrary limit, but it is easy to overlook. The encoder must therefore ensure that this limit is not exceeded, or else the files it produces will not be readable by decoders that conform to the JPEG standard. Suppose that the Y component has horizontal and vertical sampling frequencies of 4. Since the Y component would contribute 16 data units to an MCU in an interleaved scan, with these sampling frequencies the Y component would have to be encoded by itself in a noninterleaved scan.

The sample encoder throws an exception if the user tries to create scans with more than 10 data units per MCU. An alternative would be for the encoder to limit the user's options to sampling frequencies that will not exceed this limit. For instance, the encoder could give the user a choice of making all the sampling frequencies 1 (3 data units per MCU) or allow the Y component to have sampling frequencies of 2 and the other components to have sampling frequencies of 1 (6 data units per MCU). Yet another possibility would be for the encoder to automatically assign components to separate scans if the number of data units in an MCU is too large.

Restart Markers

Restart markers are used to create independently encoded blocks of MCUs. In a sequential JPEG file the DC coefficient is encoded as a difference value rather than as an absolute value. When an image contains no restart markers, every MCU, except for the first, depends upon the previous MCU being decoded correctly.[1] If the encoded data for an MCU gets corrupted (e.g., while the file is being transmitted over a telephone line), each subsequent MCU will be incorrectly decoded.

If an image contains restart markers, a decoder can use them to recover from corrupt compressed data. Since restart markers are placed in the output stream in sequence, decoders can compare the last one read before the corrupt data was encountered to the current one and use the restart interval to determine where in the image the decoding should resume. This works as long as the corruption in the compressed stream does not span eight restart markers. If it does, the decoder will not be able to match the remaining compressed data to its correct location within the image.

---

[1] In progressive JPEG there can be dependencies among the data units from the AC coefficients as well.

Obviously, the smaller the restart interval, the sooner the decoder can recover from an error. Having a restart interval so large that only one or two restart markers get written in the scan is usually of little value. Having too small a restart interval is not a good idea, either. Each restart marker adds two bytes of overhead to the compressed stream and can reduce the amount of data compression, especially in progressive-mode JPEG. A tiny restart interval also makes it more likely that corruption will extend past eight restart markers.

When creating JPEG files that are used on a single system or a reliable network, restart markers are rarely necessary. If you need them for error recovery, a good restart interval is the number of MCUs that make up a row.

Color or Grayscale

The JFIF standard allows either three-component color images or one-component (Y) grayscale images. A JPEG encoder can be written so that it always uses three components, but the drawback is that the grayscale images will be a bit larger and the processing required to decode them significantly more than necessary. In the RGB colorspace, shades of gray are represented with component values where $R = G = B$. If you look closely at the RGB-to-YCbCr conversion functions in Chapter 1 you will see that, with 8-bit samples, for any grayscale color ($R = X$, $G = X$, $B = X$), the corresponding YCbCr color representation is $Y = X$, $Cb = 128$, $Cr = 128$. Since 128 is subtracted from the component values before the DCT is performed, the coefficients for the Cb and Cr components in a grayscale image will all be zero. In a grayscale image the Cb and Cr components obtain outstanding compression since each data unit requires only 2-bits to encode, not counting the overhead from markers. While the amount of compressed data from the Cb and Cr components is relatively small, it is still completely useless.

An encoder can automatically determine if the incoming image is in grayscale by checking to see if the RGB color value for each pixel is such that $R = G = B$. This causes a problem if an image contains RGB values where the component's values are very close but not exactly equal—an RGB value of (101, 100, 102), for example, would look gray on the screen. An encoder could use a small delta value instead of equality to make the test:

$$abs(R - B) < \Delta$$
$$abs(R - G) < \Delta$$
$$abs(G - B) < \Delta$$

However, this raises the question of how large to make the delta and, more important, whether or not the user wants images with colors close to pure gray to be converted to grayscale. Probably the safest way to deal with grayscale images is to have the user specify to the encoder whether to compress the image using grayscale or color.

Output File Structure

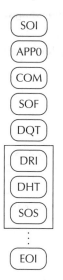

The JPEG standard is fairly flexible when it comes to the ordering of markers within an output stream. Three major marker ordering restrictions must be followed:

- The file must start with an SOI marker, follow with a JFIF APP_0 marker, and end with an EOI marker.

- For the JPEG modes we are using there can be only one SOF marker and it must occur before any SOS markers.

- All Huffman and quantization tables used by a scan must be defined by DHT and DQT markers that come before the SOS marker.

Figure 9.3 shows a block ordering for a JPEG file that will work in most situations. The sample JPEG encoder follows this scheme. Encoders that need to store application-specific information need to insert APPn blocks containing this data into the output file.

Figure 9.3
Encoder Block
Ordering

Doing the Encoding

Validations

The first step in creating a JPEG file is to validate the compression parameters. The encoder should ensure that

- The sampling frequencies do not result in scans with MCUs containing more than 10 data units.

- The sampling frequencies do not result in fractional sampling.

- All of the components in the image will be written in some scan.

Outputting the Blocks

With the exception of the compressed data that follows the SOS marker and the generation of Huffman tables for the DHT markers, creating the markers is a simple matter of filling in the values for the fields shown in Chapter 5. The only difficult part is creating the compressed data, which will be dealt with in the next few sections.

Down-Sampling

The first step in the compression process is down-sampling. That is, if a component has either a horizontal or a vertical sampling frequency of less than the maximum value of all the components, it is shrunk. Suppose we have a color image whose components have the following sampling frequencies:

	Y	Cb	Cr
Horizontal	2	1	1
Vertical	2	1	1

This means that for every two samples taken for the Y component in each direction, one sample is taken for the Cb and Cr components. Another way to look at this is to convert the sampling frequencies to intervals where each interval is the maximum frequency value divided by a component's frequency value. For the previous example the horizontal and vertical intervals are

	Y	Cb	Cr
Horizontal	1	2	2
Vertical	1	2	2

Conceptually, the down-sampling process for a component would be

```
For II = 0 To IMAGEHEIGHT - 1 Step VERTICALINTERVAL
    Begin
    For JJ = 0 To IMAGEWIDTH - 1 Step HORIZONTALINTERVAL
        Begin
        COMPONENTDOWNSAMPLE [II/VERTICALINTERVAL]
            [JJ/HORIZONTALINTERVAL] = COMPONENTPIXELDATA [II][JJ]
        End
    End
```

This process divides the component's pixel data into blocks whose dimensions are the sampling intervals, and takes one sample from each block. While this method works, a better one is to take the average sample value for each block rather than the value from one pixel.

The preceding example shows all of the component's data being down-sampled into a buffer, which in reality need not be anything other than 8×8. If the down-sampling process is organized to produce one data unit at a time, the DCT and quantization processes shown in Chapter 7 can be performed immediately, eliminating the need to buffer a component's down-sampled data.

At this point in the encoding process, an encoder can take one of two paths. It can be structured so that as soon as it has performed the DCT and quantization it immediately encodes the data unit. Or it can store in a buffer all of the DCT coefficients for the components within a scan, then handle the interleaving and data unit encoding in a separate pass.

The first option has the advantage of requiring significantly less memory than the second. The second option makes sense only if the encoder is going to support progressive JPEG (Chapter 10). Then it has to maintain a buffer containing all of the DCT coefficients for a component; otherwise, it must repeatedly down-sample and perform the DCT on the same data. If the encoder is to share as much of the same code as possible for sequential and progressive JPEG, buffering all of the component's DCT coefficients makes a lot of sense. Buffering the scan's DCT coefficients also makes it possible to generate Huffman tables from usage frequencies.

The rest of this discussion assumes that the encoder buffers the DCT coefficients. If it maintains a two-dimensional array of 8×8 DCT coefficient buffers, the size of the array will be

$$Buffer\ Width\ =\ \frac{Image\ Width + 8 \times Horizontal\ Sampling\ Interval - 1}{8 \times Horizontal\ Sampling\ Interval}$$

$$Buffer\ Height\ =\ \frac{Image\ Height + 8 \times Vertical\ Sampling\ Interval - 1}{8 \times Vertical\ Sampling\ Interval}$$

Interleaving

At this point the encoder has created buffers containing the DCT coefficients for the components in the scan. The next step is to determine the order in which the data units within the buffers are encoded. If the scan is noninterleaved (i.e., it contains one component), the ordering is simple as shown in Algorithm 9.1.

```
Global RESTARTINTERVAL
Procedure EncodeNonInterleaved
    Begin
    RESTARTCOUNTER = 0
    For II = 0 To BUFFERHEIGHT - 1 Do
        Begin
        For JJ = 0 To BUFFERWIDTH - 1 Do
            Begin
            If RESTARTINTERVAL <> 0 And RESTARTCOUNTER = RESTARTINTERVAL Then
                Begin
                OutputRestartMarker ()
                RESTARTCOUNTER = 0
                End
            EncodeDataUnit (BUFFER [II][JJ])
            RESTARTCOUNTER = RESTARTCOUNTER + 1
            End
        End
    End
End
```

Algorithm 9.1
Noninterleaved
Scan Encoding

If the scan is interleaved, the decoder needs to determine the number of MCU rows and columns that make up the image. The process is almost the same as that used for decoding JPEG images in Chapter 8. The only difference is that in decoding the sampling frequencies are read from the JPEG file whereas in encoding the sampling frequencies are input parameters. The number of MCU rows and columns is determined using the sampling frequencies for all components that make up the image, not just the components in the current scan.

The ordering of data units within an interleaved scan was illustrated in Chapter 5. Algorithm 9.2 illustrates how the ordering is implemented within an encoder. The order of components within the scan is the order in which they are listed in the SOS marker.

```
Global RESTARTINTERVAL
Procedure EncodeInterleaved (COMPONENTCOUNT, COMPONENTS [1..COMPONENTCOUNT])
    Begin
    RESTARTCOUNT = 0
    For II = 0 To MCUROWS - 1 Do
        Begin
        For JJ = 0 To MCUCOLUMNS - 1 Do
            Begin
            // This block processes a single MCU
            If RESTARTINTERVAL <> 0
                And RESTARTCOUNT = RESTARTINTERVAL Then
                Begin
                OutputRestartMarker ()
                RESTARTCOUNT = 0
                End
            For KK = 0 To COMPONENTCOUNT - 1 DO
                Begin
                For LL = 0 To COMPONENTS [KK].VERTICALFREQUENCY - 1 Do
                    Begin
                    For MM = 0 To COMPONENTS [KK].HORIZONTALFREQUENCY - 1 DO
                        Begin
                        ROW = II * COMPONENTS [KK].VERTICALFREQUENCY + LL
                        COLUMN = JJ * COMPONENTS [KK].HORIZONTALFREQUENCY + MM
                        EncodeDataUnit (COMPONENTS [KK].BUFFER [ROW][COLUMN])
                        End
                    End
                End
            RESTARTCOUNT = RESTARTCOUNT + 1
            End
        End
    End
```

───────────────

Algorithm 9.2
Noninterleaved
MCU Encoding

Data Unit Encoding

The encoding of data units is essentially the reverse of the decoding process shown in Chapter 8. There the Extend() function converted a magnitude value and extra bits into a coefficient value. ReverseExtend() does the opposite, converting a coefficient value into a magnitude and extra bits.

```
void ReverseExtend (int value,
                    unsigned int &magnitude,
                    unsigned int &bits)
{
  if (value >= 0)
  {
    bits = value ;
  }
  else
  {
    value = -value ;
    bits = ~value
  }
  magnitude = 0 ;
  while (value != 0)
  {
    value >>= 1 ;
    ++ magnitude ;
  }
  return ;
}
```

For each data unit, the DC coefficient is encoded first, followed by the AC coefficients in zigzag order. The encoded DC value is actually the difference between the DC coefficient value in the current data unit and the DC value from the last data unit processed for the same component. The DC coefficient is encoded as a Huffman-encoded magnitude value (Table 9.1) followed by a string of unencoded bits. The magnitude value specifies the number of literal bits to follow.

Only nonzero AC coefficients are encoded. They are stored as a Huffman-encoded byte value followed by a number of literal bits. The encoded byte is divided into two 4-bit fields, with the 4 low-order bits giving the coefficient magnitude value (Table 9.2) and the 4 high-order bits giving the number of zero-valued coefficients to skip. Both bit fields are set to zero when all the remaining AC coefficients are zero. The code $F0_{16}$ is used to represent a run of 16 zero-valued coefficients and is not followed by any literal bits.

Algorithm 9.3 shows how a data unit is encoded using sequential JPEG. The input parameter is an array of quantized DCT coefficients arranged in the JPEG zigzag order.

Encoded Value	DC Difference Range
0	0
1	–1, 1
2	–3, –2, 2, 3
3	–7 . . –4, 4 . . 7
4	–15 . . –8, 8 . . 15
5	–31 . . –16, 16 . . 31
6	–63 . . –32, 32 . . 63
7	–127 . . –64, 64 . . 127
8	–255 . . –128, 128 . . 255
9	–512 . . –256, 256 . . 511
10	–1023 . . –512, 512 . . 1023
11	–2047 . . –1024, 1024 . . 2047

Table 9.1
DC Difference
Magnitude Codes
and Ranges

Algorithm 9.3
Sequential-Mode
Data Unit Encoding

```
Global LAST_DC_VALUE
Procedure EncodeDataUnit (DATAUNIT [0..63])
  Begin
  DIFFERENCE = DATAUNIT [0] - LAST_DC_VALUE
  LAST_DC_VALUE = DATAUNIT [0]
  ReverseExtend (DIFFERENCE, MAGNITUDE, BITS)
  HuffmanEncodeUsingDCTable (MAGNITUDE)
  WriteRawBits (MAGNITUDE, BITS)

  ZERORUN = 0
  II = 1
  While II < 64 Do
    Begin
    If DATAUNIT [II] <> 0 Then
      Begin
      While ZERORUN >= 16 Do
        Begin
        HuffmanEncodeUsingACTable (F0₁₆)
        ZERORUN = ZERORUN - 16
        End
      ReverseExtend (DATAUNIT [II], MAGNITUDE, BITS)
      HuffmanEncodeUsingACTable ((ZERORUN LeftShift 4) Or MAGNITUDE)
      WriteRawBits (MAGNITUDE, BITS)
      End
    Else
      Begin
      ZERORUN = ZERORUN + 1
      End
    End
  If ZERORUN <> 0 Then
    Begin
    HuffmanEncodeUsingACTable (00₁₆)
    End
  End
```

Table 9.2	Encoded Value	AC Difference Value Range
AC Magnitude	1	–1, 1
Codes and Ranges	2	–3, –2, 2, 3
	3	–7 . . –4, 4 . . 7
	4	–15 . . –8, 8 . . 15
	5	–31 . . –16, 16 . . 31
	6	–63 . . –32, 32 . . 63
	7	–127 . . –64, 64 . . 127
	8	–255 . . –128, 128 . . 255
	9	–511 . . –256, 256 . . 511
	10	–1023 . . –512, 512 . . 1023

Huffman Table Generation

The code in the previous section makes use of Huffman coding, but where do we get the Huffman tables used to encode the coefficients? The JPEG standard does not specify how Huffman codes are generated. Any set of Huffman codes, where no code is longer than 16-bits and no code consists of all 1-bits, can be used. There is no requirement that the codes be assigned to values based upon usage frequencies. Thus, the simplest method for Huffman encoding is to use a predefined Huffman table. The JPEG standard includes two sets of sample Huffman codes for use with DC and AC coefficients,[2] and an encoder can be implemented so that it uses these or any other set of predefined tables. Nevertheless, while this method has the advantage of being fast and easy to implement, it obviously does not compress as well as using Huffman codes based upon usage frequencies.

Unless compression speed is a major issue, it makes sense to create the Huffman tables from usage frequencies, which requires the encoder to make two passes over the DCT coefficients in a scan. The obvious implementation method is to have separate functions for gathering statistics and outputting codes. The problem with this method is that this requires two sets of nearly identical functions that must be kept in strict synchronization. The slightest implementation change made to one set of functions would have to be made to the other, creating a maintenance nightmare.

A better solution is to use separate functions for processing individual codes. An encoder could implement two pairs of procedures similar to those shown in Algorithm 9.4.

---

[2]Section K.3 in the JPEG standard.

*Algorithm 9.4
AC and DC
Coefficient
Functions*

```
Procedure GatherDC (VALUE, EXTRABITS)
    Begin
    // EXTRABITS is not used
    IncrementFrequency (VALUE)
    End

Procedure PrintDC (VALUE, EXTRABITS)
    Begin
    FindHuffmanEncode (VALUE, CODE, CODELENGTH)
    WriteRawBits (CODELENGTH, CODE)
    If VALUE <> 0 Then
        WriteRawBits (VALUE, EXTRABITS)
    End

Procedure GatherAC (VALUE, EXTRABITS)
    Begin
    // EXTRABITS is not used
    IncrementFrequency (VALUE)
    End

Procedure PrintAC (VALUE, EXTRABITS)
    Begin
    FindHuffmanEncode (VALUE, CODE, CODELENGTH)
    WriteRawBits (CODELENGTH, CODE)
    If (VALUE And 0F_16) <> 0 Then
        WriteRawBits (VALUE And 0F_16, EXTRABITS)
    End
```

Each procedure has an identical interface, so the encoding process code can be modified to look the procedures in Algorithm 9.5, where DCPROCEDURE is a pointer to either GatherDC or PrintDC and ACPROCEDURE is a pointer to either GatherAC or PrintAC.

Using pointers to procedures allows the same function to be used both for gathering Huffman usage statistics and for encoding the actual data.

```
Global LAST_DC_VALUE
Procedure EncodeDataUnit (DATAUNIT [0..63], DCPROCEDURE, ACPROCEDURE)
    Begin
    DIFFERENCE = DATAUNIT [0] - LAST_DC_VALUE
    LAST_DC_VALUE = DATAUNIT [0]
    ReverseExtend (DIFFERENCE, MAGNITUDE, BITS)
    DCPROCEDURE (MAGNITUDE, BITS)

    ZERORUN = 0
    II = 1
    While II < 64 Do
        Begin
        If DATAUNIT [II] <> 0 Then
            Begin
            While ZERORUN >= 16 Do
                Begin
                ACPROCEDURE (F0₁₆, 0)
                ZERORUN = ZERORUN - 16
                End
            ReverseExtend (DATAUNIT [II], MAGNITUDE, BITS)
            ACPROCEDURE ((ZERORUN LEFTSHIFT 4) Or MAGNITUDE), BITS)
            End
        Else
            Begin
            ZERORUN = ZERORUN + 1
            End
        End
    If ZERORUN <> 0 Then
        Begin
        ACPROCEDURE (00₁₆)
        End
    End
```

Algorithm 9.5
Data Unit Encoding
Using Function
Pointers

Conclusion

This chapter covered the process for encoding sequential-mode JPEG images. The process for encoding baseline sequential and extended sequential files is basically the same for 8-bit images, except for restrictions on the number of tables that can be defined. The JPEG standard (JPEG 1994) contains sample Huffman and quantization tables.

The source code example for this chapter is an encoder for sequential JPEG images. The encoder application is a simple one for converting a Windows BMP file to a sequential JPEG file. The command format is

```
ENCODER input.bmp output.jpg
```

to create a color JPEG file or

```
ENCODER -g input.bmp output.jpg
```

to create a grayscale file.

Component Class

The `JpegEncoderComponent` class represents a single component during the encoding process. Its main functions are sampling and data unit encoding.

The `EncodeSequential` member function encodes data units. Two of its parameters are pointers to member functions that process codes generated from the image. This allows the same function to be used both for gathering value usage statistics for Huffman code generation and for Huffman encoding the data. These parameters will be pointers to either the `GatherDcData` and `GatherAcData` functions or the `PrintDcData` and `PrintAcData` functions. The first pair gathers statistics; the second writes Huffman-encoded values to the output stream.

Encoder Class

The encoder class is `JpegEncoder`. Two of its member functions control image compression. The compression-versus-quality tradeoff is specified using `SetQuality`. The quality value can be in the range 1–100 and determines the amount to scale the sample quantization table values. `SetSamplingFrequency` sets the horizontal and vertical sampling frequency (1–4) for a component.

By default the encoder places all components in a single scan. The `SetScanAttributes` member function can be used to place components in different scans. The last two parameters to this function are used only for progressive JPEG (Chapter 10). For now they should always be 0.

The `InterleavedPass` and `NoninterleavedPass` functions are the heart of the encoder. They control the order in which data units are encoded and when restart markers are written. These functions use pointers to member functions; thus, they can be used for both gathering Huffman usage statistics and Huffman encoding.

Chapter 10

Optimizing the DCT

At the start of the book we stated that we would strive for clarity rather than programming efficiency. This is the only chapter that deals with execution efficiency. Calculating the IDCT is the most time-consuming part of decoding a JPEG image file. Therefore, this is the best place to optimize for speed. The techniques for optimizing the IDCT work for the DCT as well. However, speed is generally more of an issue when decoding JPEG files than when encoding them.

To optimize the IDCT and DCT calculations we are going to use mathematics, not programming tricks. A basic knowledge of linear algebra and trigonometry will be very useful in getting through the derivations. Many people find it frustrating when explanations of mathematical processes leave out just enough steps to get you lost, so the explanations are rather detailed. If you have no interest in the mathematics or find this tedious, you can simply skip to the end of the chapter to find the end result.

Factoring the DCT Matrix

In Chapter 6 we explained that two matrices are multiplied by taking the dot product of the rows of the first matrix with the columns of the second matrix. When we use a matrix to calculate the IDCT we use Equation 10.1, where M is the transform matrix and T is the input data to the transform.

Equation 10.1
Inverse DCT
$$V = M^T T M$$

Since matrix multiplication is associative, we can perform the two multiplication operations in either order. For consistency, in this chapter we are going to perform the multiplication as $V = M^T(TM)$. In other words, we are going to multiply the rows of T by the columns of M to create a temporary matrix. Then we are going to multiply the columns of the temporary matrix by the rows of M^T.

When we multiply $T \times M$ each output row depends only on the corresponding row in T so we can treat the calculation of each row separately. Similarly, when we multiply M^T and the temporary matrix, each column in the output depends only on the corresponding column in the temporary matrix.

The DCT transform matrix as originally presented in Chapter 7 is repeated with the substitution $\frac{1}{2} = \sqrt{\frac{2}{8}}$ in Equation 10.2. Each row/column dot product requires 8 multiplication operations and 7 additions; therefore, transforming each row requires 64 multiplication operations and 56 additions.

Equation 10.2

$$M = \begin{bmatrix} \frac{1}{\sqrt{8}} & \frac{1}{\sqrt{8}} & \frac{1}{\sqrt{8}} & \frac{1}{\sqrt{8}} & \frac{1}{\sqrt{8}} & \frac{1}{\sqrt{8}} & \frac{1}{\sqrt{8}} & \frac{1}{\sqrt{8}} \\ \sqrt{\frac{2}{8}}\cos\frac{1}{16}\pi & \sqrt{\frac{2}{8}}\cos\frac{3}{16}\pi & \sqrt{\frac{2}{8}}\cos\frac{5}{16}\pi & \sqrt{\frac{2}{8}}\cos\frac{7}{16}\pi & \sqrt{\frac{2}{8}}\cos\frac{9}{16}\pi & \sqrt{\frac{2}{8}}\cos\frac{11}{16}\pi & \sqrt{\frac{2}{8}}\cos\frac{13}{16}\pi & \sqrt{\frac{2}{8}}\cos\frac{15}{16}\pi \\ \sqrt{\frac{2}{8}}\cos\frac{2}{16}\pi & \sqrt{\frac{2}{8}}\cos\frac{6}{16}\pi & \sqrt{\frac{2}{8}}\cos\frac{10}{16}\pi & \sqrt{\frac{2}{8}}\cos\frac{14}{16}\pi & \sqrt{\frac{2}{8}}\cos\frac{18}{16}\pi & \sqrt{\frac{2}{8}}\cos\frac{22}{16}\pi & \sqrt{\frac{2}{8}}\cos\frac{26}{16}\pi & \sqrt{\frac{2}{8}}\cos\frac{30}{16}\pi \\ \sqrt{\frac{2}{8}}\cos\frac{3}{16}\pi & \sqrt{\frac{2}{8}}\cos\frac{9}{16}\pi & \sqrt{\frac{2}{8}}\cos\frac{15}{16}\pi & \sqrt{\frac{2}{8}}\cos\frac{21}{16}\pi & \sqrt{\frac{2}{8}}\cos\frac{27}{16}\pi & \sqrt{\frac{2}{8}}\cos\frac{33}{16}\pi & \sqrt{\frac{2}{8}}\cos\frac{39}{16}\pi & \sqrt{\frac{2}{8}}\cos\frac{45}{16}\pi \\ \sqrt{\frac{2}{8}}\cos\frac{4}{16}\pi & \sqrt{\frac{2}{8}}\cos\frac{12}{16}\pi & \sqrt{\frac{2}{8}}\cos\frac{20}{16}\pi & \sqrt{\frac{2}{8}}\cos\frac{28}{16}\pi & \sqrt{\frac{2}{8}}\cos\frac{36}{16}\pi & \sqrt{\frac{2}{8}}\cos\frac{44}{16}\pi & \sqrt{\frac{2}{8}}\cos\frac{52}{16}\pi & \sqrt{\frac{2}{8}}\cos\frac{60}{16}\pi \\ \sqrt{\frac{2}{8}}\cos\frac{5}{16}\pi & \sqrt{\frac{2}{8}}\cos\frac{15}{16}\pi & \sqrt{\frac{2}{8}}\cos\frac{25}{16}\pi & \sqrt{\frac{2}{8}}\cos\frac{35}{16}\pi & \sqrt{\frac{2}{8}}\cos\frac{45}{16}\pi & \sqrt{\frac{2}{8}}\cos\frac{55}{16}\pi & \sqrt{\frac{2}{8}}\cos\frac{65}{16}\pi & \sqrt{\frac{2}{8}}\cos\frac{75}{16}\pi \\ \sqrt{\frac{2}{8}}\cos\frac{6}{16}\pi & \sqrt{\frac{2}{8}}\cos\frac{18}{16}\pi & \sqrt{\frac{2}{8}}\cos\frac{30}{16}\pi & \sqrt{\frac{2}{8}}\cos\frac{42}{16}\pi & \sqrt{\frac{2}{8}}\cos\frac{54}{16}\pi & \sqrt{\frac{2}{8}}\cos\frac{66}{16}\pi & \sqrt{\frac{2}{8}}\cos\frac{78}{16}\pi & \sqrt{\frac{2}{8}}\cos\frac{90}{16}\pi \\ \sqrt{\frac{2}{8}}\cos\frac{7}{16}\pi & \sqrt{\frac{2}{8}}\cos\frac{21}{16}\pi & \sqrt{\frac{2}{8}}\cos\frac{35}{16}\pi & \sqrt{\frac{2}{8}}\cos\frac{49}{16}\pi & \sqrt{\frac{2}{8}}\cos\frac{63}{16}\pi & \sqrt{\frac{2}{8}}\cos\frac{77}{16}\pi & \sqrt{\frac{2}{8}}\cos\frac{91}{16}\pi & \sqrt{\frac{2}{8}}\cos\frac{105}{16}\pi \end{bmatrix}$$

Notice that there is much symmetry in the matrix. We will exploit these symmetries by factoring the DCT transform matrix into the product of several sparse matrices.

The first transformation we are going to make is to factor out the constant value $\frac{1}{\sqrt{8}}$ from each element in the matrix and redefine the IDCT using the equivalent definition shown in Equation 10.3.

Equation 10.3

$$V = \frac{1}{8}M^T T M$$

For now we will ignore the $\frac{1}{8}$ factor and simply work with the matrix shown in Equation 10.4.

Equation 10.4

$$M = \begin{bmatrix} 1 & 1 & 1 & 1 & 1 & 1 & 1 & 1 \\ \sqrt{2}\cos\frac{1}{16}\pi & \sqrt{2}\cos\frac{3}{16}\pi & \sqrt{2}\cos\frac{5}{16}\pi & \sqrt{2}\cos\frac{7}{16}\pi & \sqrt{2}\cos\frac{9}{16}\pi & \sqrt{2}\cos\frac{11}{16}\pi & \sqrt{2}\cos\frac{13}{16}\pi & \sqrt{2}\cos\frac{15}{16}\pi \\ \sqrt{2}\cos\frac{2}{16}\pi & \sqrt{2}\cos\frac{6}{16}\pi & \sqrt{2}\cos\frac{10}{16}\pi & \sqrt{2}\cos\frac{14}{16}\pi & \sqrt{2}\cos\frac{18}{16}\pi & \sqrt{2}\cos\frac{22}{16}\pi & \sqrt{2}\cos\frac{26}{16}\pi & \sqrt{2}\cos\frac{30}{16}\pi \\ \sqrt{2}\cos\frac{3}{16}\pi & \sqrt{2}\cos\frac{9}{16}\pi & \sqrt{2}\cos\frac{15}{16}\pi & \sqrt{2}\cos\frac{21}{16}\pi & \sqrt{2}\cos\frac{27}{16}\pi & \sqrt{2}\cos\frac{33}{16}\pi & \sqrt{2}\cos\frac{39}{16}\pi & \sqrt{2}\cos\frac{45}{16}\pi \\ \sqrt{2}\cos\frac{4}{16}\pi & \sqrt{2}\cos\frac{12}{16}\pi & \sqrt{2}\cos\frac{20}{16}\pi & \sqrt{2}\cos\frac{28}{16}\pi & \sqrt{2}\cos\frac{36}{16}\pi & \sqrt{2}\cos\frac{44}{16}\pi & \sqrt{2}\cos\frac{52}{16}\pi & \sqrt{2}\cos\frac{60}{16}\pi \\ \sqrt{2}\cos\frac{5}{16}\pi & \sqrt{2}\cos\frac{15}{16}\pi & \sqrt{2}\cos\frac{25}{16}\pi & \sqrt{2}\cos\frac{35}{16}\pi & \sqrt{2}\cos\frac{45}{16}\pi & \sqrt{2}\cos\frac{55}{16}\pi & \sqrt{2}\cos\frac{65}{16}\pi & \sqrt{2}\cos\frac{75}{16}\pi \\ \sqrt{2}\cos\frac{6}{16}\pi & \sqrt{2}\cos\frac{18}{16}\pi & \sqrt{2}\cos\frac{30}{16}\pi & \sqrt{2}\cos\frac{42}{16}\pi & \sqrt{2}\cos\frac{54}{16}\pi & \sqrt{2}\cos\frac{66}{16}\pi & \sqrt{2}\cos\frac{78}{16}\pi & \sqrt{2}\cos\frac{90}{16}\pi \\ \sqrt{2}\cos\frac{7}{16}\pi & \sqrt{2}\cos\frac{21}{16}\pi & \sqrt{2}\cos\frac{35}{16}\pi & \sqrt{2}\cos\frac{49}{16}\pi & \sqrt{2}\cos\frac{63}{16}\pi & \sqrt{2}\cos\frac{77}{16}\pi & \sqrt{2}\cos\frac{91}{16}\pi & \sqrt{2}\cos\frac{105}{16}\pi \end{bmatrix}$$

The next few simplifications take advantage of the symmetries in the values of the cosine function to reduce the number of unique values in the transform matrix. The properties of the cosine function can be found in any mathematical handbook.

If you refer to Figure 10.1 you can see that the cosine function is cyclical such that

Equation 10.5

$$\cos x = \cos (x + 2\pi)$$

Using Equation 10.5 we can replace every occurrence of $\frac{N}{16}$ in Equation 10.4 with $\frac{N \bmod 32}{16}$, giving Equation 10.6.

Figure 10.1
Cosine Function

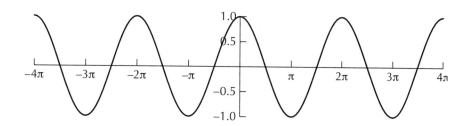

Equation 10.6

$$M = \begin{bmatrix}
1 & 1 & 1 & 1 & 1 & 1 & 1 & 1 \\
\sqrt{2}\cos\frac{1}{16}\pi & \sqrt{2}\cos\frac{3}{16}\pi & \sqrt{2}\cos\frac{5}{16}\pi & \sqrt{2}\cos\frac{7}{16}\pi & \sqrt{2}\cos\frac{9}{16}\pi & \sqrt{2}\cos\frac{11}{16}\pi & \sqrt{2}\cos\frac{13}{16}\pi & \sqrt{2}\cos\frac{15}{16}\pi \\
\sqrt{2}\cos\frac{2}{16}\pi & \sqrt{2}\cos\frac{6}{16}\pi & \sqrt{2}\cos\frac{10}{16}\pi & \sqrt{2}\cos\frac{14}{16}\pi & \sqrt{2}\cos\frac{18}{16}\pi & \sqrt{2}\cos\frac{22}{16}\pi & \sqrt{2}\cos\frac{26}{16}\pi & \sqrt{2}\cos\frac{30}{16}\pi \\
\sqrt{2}\cos\frac{3}{16}\pi & \sqrt{2}\cos\frac{9}{16}\pi & \sqrt{2}\cos\frac{15}{16}\pi & \sqrt{2}\cos\frac{21}{16}\pi & \sqrt{2}\cos\frac{27}{16}\pi & \sqrt{2}\cos\frac{1}{16}\pi & \sqrt{2}\cos\frac{7}{16}\pi & \sqrt{2}\cos\frac{13}{16}\pi \\
\sqrt{2}\cos\frac{4}{16}\pi & \sqrt{2}\cos\frac{12}{16}\pi & \sqrt{2}\cos\frac{20}{16}\pi & \sqrt{2}\cos\frac{28}{16}\pi & \sqrt{2}\cos\frac{4}{16}\pi & \sqrt{2}\cos\frac{12}{16}\pi & \sqrt{2}\cos\frac{20}{16}\pi & \sqrt{2}\cos\frac{28}{16}\pi \\
\sqrt{2}\cos\frac{5}{16}\pi & \sqrt{2}\cos\frac{15}{16}\pi & \sqrt{2}\cos\frac{25}{16}\pi & \sqrt{2}\cos\frac{3}{16}\pi & \sqrt{2}\cos\frac{13}{16}\pi & \sqrt{2}\cos\frac{23}{16}\pi & \sqrt{2}\cos\frac{1}{16}\pi & \sqrt{2}\cos\frac{11}{16}\pi \\
\sqrt{2}\cos\frac{6}{16}\pi & \sqrt{2}\cos\frac{18}{16}\pi & \sqrt{2}\cos\frac{30}{16}\pi & \sqrt{2}\cos\frac{10}{16}\pi & \sqrt{2}\cos\frac{22}{16}\pi & \sqrt{2}\cos\frac{2}{16}\pi & \sqrt{2}\cos\frac{14}{16}\pi & \sqrt{2}\cos\frac{26}{16}\pi \\
\sqrt{2}\cos\frac{7}{16}\pi & \sqrt{2}\cos\frac{21}{16}\pi & \sqrt{2}\cos\frac{3}{16}\pi & \sqrt{2}\cos\frac{17}{16}\pi & \sqrt{2}\cos\frac{31}{16}\pi & \sqrt{2}\cos\frac{13}{16}\pi & \sqrt{2}\cos\frac{27}{16}\pi & \sqrt{2}\cos\frac{19}{16}\pi
\end{bmatrix}$$

Again referring to Figure 10.1, the cosine function is symmetric along the *x*-axis such that

Equation 10.7

$$\cos \pi + x = \cos \pi - x$$

Using Equation 10.7 we can replace all the matrix elements in Equation 10.6 with arguments to the cosine function that are greater than π, giving Equation 10.8.

Equation 10.8

$$M = \begin{bmatrix}
1 & 1 & 1 & 1 & 1 & 1 & 1 & 1 \\
\sqrt{2}\cos\frac{1}{16}\pi & \sqrt{2}\cos\frac{3}{16}\pi & \sqrt{2}\cos\frac{5}{16}\pi & \sqrt{2}\cos\frac{7}{16}\pi & \sqrt{2}\cos\frac{9}{16}\pi & \sqrt{2}\cos\frac{11}{16}\pi & \sqrt{2}\cos\frac{13}{16}\pi & \sqrt{2}\cos\frac{15}{16}\pi \\
\sqrt{2}\cos\frac{2}{16}\pi & \sqrt{2}\cos\frac{6}{16}\pi & \sqrt{2}\cos\frac{10}{16}\pi & \sqrt{2}\cos\frac{14}{16}\pi & \sqrt{2}\cos\frac{14}{16}\pi & \sqrt{2}\cos\frac{10}{16}\pi & \sqrt{2}\cos\frac{6}{16}\pi & \sqrt{2}\cos\frac{2}{16}\pi \\
\sqrt{2}\cos\frac{3}{16}\pi & \sqrt{2}\cos\frac{9}{16}\pi & \sqrt{2}\cos\frac{15}{16}\pi & \sqrt{2}\cos\frac{11}{16}\pi & \sqrt{2}\cos\frac{5}{16}\pi & \sqrt{2}\cos\frac{1}{16}\pi & \sqrt{2}\cos\frac{7}{16}\pi & \sqrt{2}\cos\frac{13}{16}\pi \\
\sqrt{2}\cos\frac{4}{16}\pi & \sqrt{2}\cos\frac{12}{16}\pi & \sqrt{2}\cos\frac{12}{16}\pi & \sqrt{2}\cos\frac{4}{16}\pi & \sqrt{2}\cos\frac{4}{16}\pi & \sqrt{2}\cos\frac{12}{16}\pi & \sqrt{2}\cos\frac{12}{16}\pi & \sqrt{2}\cos\frac{4}{16}\pi \\
\sqrt{2}\cos\frac{5}{16}\pi & \sqrt{2}\cos\frac{15}{16}\pi & \sqrt{2}\cos\frac{7}{16}\pi & \sqrt{2}\cos\frac{3}{16}\pi & \sqrt{2}\cos\frac{13}{16}\pi & \sqrt{2}\cos\frac{9}{16}\pi & \sqrt{2}\cos\frac{1}{16}\pi & \sqrt{2}\cos\frac{11}{16}\pi \\
\sqrt{2}\cos\frac{6}{16}\pi & \sqrt{2}\cos\frac{14}{16}\pi & \sqrt{2}\cos\frac{2}{16}\pi & \sqrt{2}\cos\frac{10}{16}\pi & \sqrt{2}\cos\frac{10}{16}\pi & \sqrt{2}\cos\frac{2}{16}\pi & \sqrt{2}\cos\frac{14}{16}\pi & \sqrt{2}\cos\frac{6}{16}\pi \\
\sqrt{2}\cos\frac{7}{16}\pi & \sqrt{2}\cos\frac{11}{16}\pi & \sqrt{2}\cos\frac{3}{16}\pi & \sqrt{2}\cos\frac{15}{16}\pi & \sqrt{2}\cos\frac{1}{16}\pi & \sqrt{2}\cos\frac{13}{16}\pi & \sqrt{2}\cos\frac{5}{16}\pi & \sqrt{2}\cos\frac{19}{16}\pi
\end{bmatrix}$$

The cosine function is also symmetric along the *y*-axis such that

Equation 10.9

$$\cos \frac{\pi}{2} + x = -\cos \frac{\pi}{2} - x.$$

Using Equation 10.9 we can replace all arguments to the cosine function in Equation 10.8 that are greater than $\frac{\pi}{2}$, giving Equation 10.10.

Equation 10.10

$$M = \begin{bmatrix} 1 & 1 & 1 & 1 & 1 & 1 & 1 & 1 \\ \sqrt{2}\cos\frac{1}{16}\pi & \sqrt{2}\cos\frac{3}{16}\pi & \sqrt{2}\cos\frac{5}{16}\pi & \sqrt{2}\cos\frac{7}{16}\pi & -\sqrt{2}\cos\frac{7}{16}\pi & -\sqrt{2}\cos\frac{5}{16}\pi & -\sqrt{2}\cos\frac{3}{16}\pi & -\sqrt{2}\cos\frac{1}{16}\pi \\ \sqrt{2}\cos\frac{2}{16}\pi & \sqrt{2}\cos\frac{6}{16}\pi & -\sqrt{2}\cos\frac{6}{16}\pi & -\sqrt{2}\cos\frac{2}{16}\pi & -\sqrt{2}\cos\frac{2}{16}\pi & -\sqrt{2}\cos\frac{6}{16}\pi & \sqrt{2}\cos\frac{6}{16}\pi & \sqrt{2}\cos\frac{2}{16}\pi \\ \sqrt{2}\cos\frac{3}{16}\pi & -\sqrt{2}\cos\frac{7}{16}\pi & -\sqrt{2}\cos\frac{1}{16}\pi & -\sqrt{2}\cos\frac{5}{16}\pi & \sqrt{2}\cos\frac{5}{16}\pi & \sqrt{2}\cos\frac{1}{16}\pi & \sqrt{2}\cos\frac{7}{16}\pi & -\sqrt{2}\cos\frac{3}{16}\pi \\ \sqrt{2}\cos\frac{4}{16}\pi & -\sqrt{2}\cos\frac{4}{16}\pi & -\sqrt{2}\cos\frac{4}{16}\pi & \sqrt{2}\cos\frac{4}{16}\pi & \sqrt{2}\cos\frac{4}{16}\pi & -\sqrt{2}\cos\frac{4}{16}\pi & -\sqrt{2}\cos\frac{4}{16}\pi & \sqrt{2}\cos\frac{4}{16}\pi \\ \sqrt{2}\cos\frac{5}{16}\pi & -\sqrt{2}\cos\frac{1}{16}\pi & \sqrt{2}\cos\frac{7}{16}\pi & \sqrt{2}\cos\frac{3}{16}\pi & -\sqrt{2}\cos\frac{3}{16}\pi & -\sqrt{2}\cos\frac{7}{16}\pi & \sqrt{2}\cos\frac{1}{16}\pi & -\sqrt{2}\cos\frac{5}{16}\pi \\ \sqrt{2}\cos\frac{6}{16}\pi & -\sqrt{2}\cos\frac{2}{16}\pi & \sqrt{2}\cos\frac{2}{16}\pi & -\sqrt{2}\cos\frac{6}{16}\pi & -\sqrt{2}\cos\frac{6}{16}\pi & \sqrt{2}\cos\frac{2}{16}\pi & -\sqrt{2}\cos\frac{2}{16}\pi & \sqrt{2}\cos\frac{6}{16}\pi \\ \sqrt{2}\cos\frac{7}{16}\pi & -\sqrt{2}\cos\frac{5}{16}\pi & \sqrt{2}\cos\frac{3}{16}\pi & -\sqrt{2}\cos\frac{1}{16}\pi & \sqrt{2}\cos\frac{1}{16}\pi & -\sqrt{2}\cos\frac{3}{16}\pi & \sqrt{2}\cos\frac{5}{16}\pi & -\sqrt{2}\cos\frac{7}{16}\pi \end{bmatrix}$$

The value of the cosine function at $\frac{\pi}{2}$ is well known.

Equation 10.11

$$\cos\frac{\pi}{4} = \frac{\sqrt{2}}{2}$$

Substituting Equation 10.11 in to Equation 10.10 gives Equation 10.12.

Equation 10.12

$$M = \begin{bmatrix} 1 & 1 & 1 & 1 & 1 & 1 & 1 & 1 \\ \sqrt{2}\cos\frac{1}{16}\pi & \sqrt{2}\cos\frac{3}{16}\pi & \sqrt{2}\cos\frac{5}{16}\pi & \sqrt{2}\cos\frac{7}{16}\pi & -\sqrt{2}\cos\frac{7}{16}\pi & -\sqrt{2}\cos\frac{5}{16}\pi & -\sqrt{2}\cos\frac{3}{16}\pi & -\sqrt{2}\cos\frac{1}{16}\pi \\ \sqrt{2}\cos\frac{2}{16}\pi & \sqrt{2}\cos\frac{6}{16}\pi & -\sqrt{2}\cos\frac{6}{16}\pi & -\sqrt{2}\cos\frac{2}{16}\pi & -\sqrt{2}\cos\frac{2}{16}\pi & -\sqrt{2}\cos\frac{6}{16}\pi & \sqrt{2}\cos\frac{6}{16}\pi & \sqrt{2}\cos\frac{2}{16}\pi \\ \sqrt{2}\cos\frac{3}{16}\pi & -\sqrt{2}\cos\frac{7}{16}\pi & -\sqrt{2}\cos\frac{1}{16}\pi & -\sqrt{2}\cos\frac{5}{16}\pi & \sqrt{2}\cos\frac{5}{16}\pi & \sqrt{2}\cos\frac{1}{16}\pi & \sqrt{2}\cos\frac{7}{16}\pi & -\sqrt{2}\cos\frac{3}{16}\pi \\ 1 & -1 & -1 & 1 & 1 & -1 & -1 & 1 \\ \sqrt{2}\cos\frac{5}{16}\pi & -\sqrt{2}\cos\frac{1}{16}\pi & \sqrt{2}\cos\frac{7}{16}\pi & \sqrt{2}\cos\frac{3}{16}\pi & -\sqrt{2}\cos\frac{3}{16}\pi & -\sqrt{2}\cos\frac{7}{16}\pi & \sqrt{2}\cos\frac{1}{16}\pi & -\sqrt{2}\cos\frac{5}{16}\pi \\ \sqrt{2}\cos\frac{6}{16}\pi & -\sqrt{2}\cos\frac{2}{16}\pi & \sqrt{2}\cos\frac{2}{16}\pi & -\sqrt{2}\cos\frac{6}{16}\pi & -\sqrt{2}\cos\frac{6}{16}\pi & \sqrt{2}\cos\frac{2}{16}\pi & -\sqrt{2}\cos\frac{2}{16}\pi & \sqrt{2}\cos\frac{6}{16}\pi \\ \sqrt{2}\cos\frac{7}{16}\pi & -\sqrt{2}\cos\frac{5}{16}\pi & \sqrt{2}\cos\frac{3}{16}\pi & -\sqrt{2}\cos\frac{1}{16}\pi & \sqrt{2}\cos\frac{1}{16}\pi & -\sqrt{2}\cos\frac{3}{16}\pi & \sqrt{2}\cos\frac{5}{16}\pi & -\sqrt{2}\cos\frac{7}{16}\pi \end{bmatrix}$$

Disregarding the sign, only seven distinct values remain in the transform matrix. Now that the values within the transform matrix have been simplified we will factor the matrix into the product of several sparse matrices. The primary goal in the factorization of the transform matrix is to create matrix factors with as many zero values as possible. The secondary goal is to create matrices with the values +/−1. Zeros are great, ones are so-so, and everything else is bad.

The process used to factor the matrix is called *Gaussian elimination*. Gaussian elimination is beyond the scope of this book. However we have attempted to include enough steps for a reader with a basic knowledge of linear algebra to clearly see how the factors are obtained.

The following examples of matrix multiplication operations illustrate the principles of row reduction used to factor the DCT matrix.

$$\begin{bmatrix} 1 & 0 \\ 0 & 1 \end{bmatrix}\begin{bmatrix} A & B \\ C & D \end{bmatrix} = \begin{bmatrix} A & B \\ C & D \end{bmatrix}$$

$$\begin{bmatrix} 0 & 1 \\ 1 & 0 \end{bmatrix}\begin{bmatrix} A & B \\ C & D \end{bmatrix} = \begin{bmatrix} C & D \\ A & B \end{bmatrix} \quad \textit{Row Interchange}$$

$$\begin{bmatrix} 1 & 2 \\ 0 & 1 \end{bmatrix}\begin{bmatrix} A & B \\ C & D \end{bmatrix} = \begin{bmatrix} A+2C & B+2D \\ C & D \end{bmatrix} \quad \textit{Row Addition}$$

$$\begin{bmatrix} A & B \\ C & D \end{bmatrix}\begin{bmatrix} 1 & 0 \\ 0 & 1 \end{bmatrix} = \begin{bmatrix} A & B \\ C & D \end{bmatrix}$$

$$\begin{bmatrix} A & B \\ C & D \end{bmatrix}\begin{bmatrix} 0 & 1 \\ 1 & 0 \end{bmatrix} = \begin{bmatrix} B & A \\ D & C \end{bmatrix} \quad \textit{Column Interchange}$$

$$\begin{bmatrix} A & B \\ C & D \end{bmatrix}\begin{bmatrix} 1 & 2 \\ 0 & 1 \end{bmatrix} = \begin{bmatrix} A & 2A+B \\ C & 2C+D \end{bmatrix} \quad \textit{Column Addition}$$

Notice that if the matrix in Equation 10.12 is divided in half vertically, the left half of each row is either a mirror image of the right or a negative mirror image. We can factor the matrix to group the mirror image rows together and the negative mirror image rows together (Equation 10.13). This first factorization is not strictly necessary. Its only purpose is to make the remaining factorization steps clearer.

Equation 10.13

$$M = \begin{bmatrix} 1 & 0 & 0 & 0 & 0 & 0 & 0 & 0 \\ 0 & 0 & 0 & 0 & 1 & 0 & 0 & 0 \\ 0 & 0 & 1 & 0 & 0 & 0 & 0 & 0 \\ 0 & 0 & 0 & 0 & 0 & 0 & 1 & 0 \\ 0 & 1 & 0 & 0 & 0 & 0 & 0 & 0 \\ 0 & 0 & 0 & 0 & 0 & 1 & 0 & 0 \\ 0 & 0 & 0 & 1 & 0 & 0 & 0 & 0 \\ 0 & 0 & 0 & 0 & 0 & 0 & 0 & 1 \end{bmatrix}$$

$$\times \begin{bmatrix} 1 & 1 & 1 & 1 & 1 & 1 & 1 & 1 \\ 1 & -1 & -1 & 1 & 1 & -1 & -1 & 1 \\ \sqrt{1}\cos\frac{2}{16}\pi & \sqrt{1}\cos\frac{6}{16}\pi & -\sqrt{1}\cos\frac{6}{16}\pi & -\sqrt{1}\cos\frac{2}{16}\pi & -\sqrt{1}\cos\frac{2}{16}\pi & -\sqrt{1}\cos\frac{6}{16}\pi & \sqrt{1}\cos\frac{6}{16}\pi & \sqrt{1}\cos\frac{2}{16}\pi \\ \sqrt{1}\cos\frac{6}{16}\pi & -\sqrt{1}\cos\frac{2}{16}\pi & \sqrt{1}\cos\frac{2}{16}\pi & -\sqrt{1}\cos\frac{6}{16}\pi & -\sqrt{1}\cos\frac{6}{16}\pi & \sqrt{1}\cos\frac{2}{16}\pi & -\sqrt{1}\cos\frac{2}{16}\pi & \sqrt{1}\cos\frac{6}{16}\pi \\ \sqrt{1}\cos\frac{1}{16}\pi & \sqrt{1}\cos\frac{4}{16}\pi & \sqrt{1}\cos\frac{5}{16}\pi & \sqrt{1}\cos\frac{7}{16}\pi & -\sqrt{1}\cos\frac{7}{16}\pi & -\sqrt{1}\cos\frac{5}{16}\pi & -\sqrt{1}\cos\frac{3}{16}\pi & -\sqrt{1}\cos\frac{1}{16}\pi \\ \sqrt{1}\cos\frac{5}{16}\pi & -\sqrt{1}\cos\frac{1}{16}\pi & \sqrt{1}\cos\frac{7}{16}\pi & \sqrt{1}\cos\frac{3}{16}\pi & -\sqrt{1}\cos\frac{3}{16}\pi & -\sqrt{1}\cos\frac{7}{16}\pi & \sqrt{1}\cos\frac{1}{16}\pi & -\sqrt{1}\cos\frac{5}{16}\pi \\ \sqrt{1}\cos\frac{3}{16}\pi & -\sqrt{1}\cos\frac{7}{16}\pi & -\sqrt{1}\cos\frac{1}{16}\pi & -\sqrt{1}\cos\frac{5}{16}\pi & \sqrt{1}\cos\frac{5}{16}\pi & \sqrt{1}\cos\frac{1}{16}\pi & \sqrt{1}\cos\frac{7}{16}\pi & -\sqrt{1}\cos\frac{3}{16}\pi \\ \sqrt{1}\cos\frac{7}{16}\pi & -\sqrt{1}\cos\frac{5}{16}\pi & \sqrt{1}\cos\frac{3}{16}\pi & -\sqrt{1}\cos\frac{1}{16}\pi & \sqrt{1}\cos\frac{1}{16}\pi & -\sqrt{1}\cos\frac{3}{16}\pi & \sqrt{1}\cos\frac{5}{16}\pi & -\sqrt{1}\cos\frac{7}{16}\pi \end{bmatrix}$$

The factorization in Equation 10.14 removes the mirror images in Equation 10.13.

Equation 10.14

$$M = \begin{bmatrix} 1 & 0 & 0 & 0 & 0 & 0 & 0 & 0 \\ 0 & 0 & 0 & 0 & 1 & 0 & 0 & 0 \\ 0 & 0 & 1 & 0 & 0 & 0 & 0 & 0 \\ 0 & 0 & 0 & 0 & 0 & 0 & 1 & 0 \\ 0 & 1 & 0 & 0 & 0 & 0 & 0 & 0 \\ 0 & 0 & 0 & 0 & 0 & 1 & 0 & 0 \\ 0 & 0 & 0 & 1 & 0 & 0 & 0 & 0 \\ 0 & 0 & 0 & 0 & 0 & 0 & 0 & 1 \end{bmatrix}$$

$$\times \begin{bmatrix} 1 & 1 & 1 & 1 & 0 & 0 & 0 & 0 \\ 1 & -1 & -1 & 1 & 0 & 0 & 0 & 0 \\ \sqrt{2}\cos\frac{2}{16}\pi & \sqrt{2}\cos\frac{6}{16}\pi & -\sqrt{2}\cos\frac{6}{16}\pi & -\sqrt{2}\cos\frac{2}{16}\pi & 0 & 0 & 0 & 0 \\ \sqrt{2}\cos\frac{6}{16}\pi & -\sqrt{2}\cos\frac{2}{16}\pi & \sqrt{2}\cos\frac{2}{16}\pi & -\sqrt{2}\cos\frac{6}{16}\pi & 0 & 0 & 0 & 0 \\ 0 & 0 & 0 & 0 & \sqrt{2}\cos\frac{7}{16}\pi & \sqrt{2}\cos\frac{5}{16}\pi & \sqrt{2}\cos\frac{3}{16}\pi & \sqrt{2}\cos\frac{1}{16}\pi \\ 0 & 0 & 0 & 0 & \sqrt{2}\cos\frac{3}{16}\pi & \sqrt{2}\cos\frac{7}{16}\pi & -\sqrt{2}\cos\frac{1}{16}\pi & \sqrt{2}\cos\frac{5}{16}\pi \\ 0 & 0 & 0 & 0 & -\sqrt{2}\cos\frac{5}{16}\pi & -\sqrt{2}\cos\frac{1}{16}\pi & -\sqrt{2}\cos\frac{7}{16}\pi & \sqrt{2}\cos\frac{3}{16}\pi \\ 0 & 0 & 0 & 0 & -\sqrt{2}\cos\frac{1}{16}\pi & \sqrt{2}\cos\frac{3}{16}\pi & -\sqrt{2}\cos\frac{5}{16}\pi & \sqrt{2}\cos\frac{7}{16}\pi \end{bmatrix}$$

$$\times \begin{bmatrix} 1 & 0 & 0 & 0 & 0 & 0 & 0 & 1 \\ 0 & 1 & 0 & 0 & 0 & 0 & 1 & 0 \\ 0 & 0 & 1 & 0 & 0 & 1 & 0 & 0 \\ 0 & 0 & 0 & 1 & 1 & 0 & 0 & 0 \\ 0 & 0 & 0 & 1 & -1 & 0 & 0 & 0 \\ 0 & 0 & 1 & 0 & 0 & -1 & 0 & 0 \\ 0 & 1 & 0 & 0 & 0 & 0 & -1 & 0 \\ 1 & 0 & 0 & 0 & 0 & 0 & 0 & -1 \end{bmatrix}$$

In Equation 10.14, notice that the nonzero elements at the upper left corner of the center matrix form the same mirror pattern as the rows of the matrix in Equation 10.13. We factor again in a similar manner to attack that corner (Equation 10.15).

Take a look at the 4×4 submatrix at the lower right corner of the second matrix in Equation 10.15 and in Equation 10.16.

Equation 10.15

$$M = \begin{bmatrix} 1 & 0 & 0 & 0 & 0 & 0 & 0 & 0 \\ 0 & 0 & 0 & 0 & 1 & 0 & 0 & 0 \\ 0 & 0 & 1 & 0 & 0 & 0 & 0 & 0 \\ 0 & 0 & 0 & 0 & 0 & 0 & 1 & 0 \\ 0 & 1 & 0 & 0 & 0 & 0 & 0 & 0 \\ 0 & 0 & 0 & 0 & 0 & 1 & 0 & 0 \\ 0 & 0 & 0 & 1 & 0 & 0 & 0 & 0 \\ 0 & 0 & 0 & 0 & 0 & 0 & 0 & 1 \end{bmatrix}$$

$$\times \begin{bmatrix} 1 & 1 & 0 & 0 & 0 & 0 & 0 & 0 \\ 1 & -1 & 0 & 0 & 0 & 0 & 0 & 0 \\ 0 & 0 & \sqrt{2}\cos\frac{6}{16}\pi & \sqrt{2}\cos\frac{2}{16}\pi & 0 & 0 & 0 & 0 \\ 0 & 0 & -\sqrt{2}\cos\frac{2}{16}\pi & \sqrt{2}\cos\frac{6}{16}\pi & 0 & 0 & 0 & 0 \\ 0 & 0 & 0 & 0 & \sqrt{2}\cos\frac{7}{16}\pi & \sqrt{2}\cos\frac{5}{16}\pi & -\sqrt{2}\cos\frac{3}{16}\pi & \sqrt{2}\cos\frac{1}{16}\pi \\ 0 & 0 & 0 & 0 & \sqrt{2}\cos\frac{3}{16}\pi & \sqrt{2}\cos\frac{7}{16}\pi & -\sqrt{2}\cos\frac{1}{16}\pi & \sqrt{2}\cos\frac{5}{16}\pi \\ 0 & 0 & 0 & 0 & -\sqrt{2}\cos\frac{5}{16}\pi & -\sqrt{2}\cos\frac{1}{16}\pi & -\sqrt{2}\cos\frac{7}{16}\pi & \sqrt{2}\cos\frac{3}{16}\pi \\ 0 & 0 & 0 & 0 & -\sqrt{2}\cos\frac{1}{16}\pi & \sqrt{2}\cos\frac{3}{16}\pi & -\sqrt{2}\cos\frac{5}{16}\pi & \sqrt{2}\cos\frac{7}{16}\pi \end{bmatrix}$$

$$\times \begin{bmatrix} 1 & 0 & 0 & 1 & 0 & 0 & 0 & 0 \\ 0 & 1 & 1 & 0 & 0 & 0 & 0 & 0 \\ 0 & 1 & -1 & 0 & 0 & 0 & 0 & 0 \\ 1 & 0 & 0 & -1 & 0 & 0 & 0 & 0 \\ 0 & 0 & 0 & 0 & 1 & 0 & 0 & 0 \\ 0 & 0 & 0 & 0 & 0 & 0 & 1 & 0 \\ 0 & 0 & 0 & 0 & 0 & 0 & 1 & 0 \\ 0 & 0 & 0 & 0 & 0 & 0 & 0 & 1 \end{bmatrix} \times \begin{bmatrix} 1 & 0 & 0 & 0 & 0 & 0 & 0 & 1 \\ 0 & 1 & 0 & 0 & 0 & 0 & 1 & 0 \\ 0 & 0 & 1 & 0 & 0 & 1 & 0 & 0 \\ 0 & 0 & 0 & 1 & 1 & 0 & 0 & 0 \\ 0 & 0 & 0 & 1 & -1 & 0 & 0 & 0 \\ 0 & 0 & 1 & 0 & 0 & -1 & 0 & 0 \\ 0 & 1 & 0 & 0 & 0 & 0 & -1 & 0 \\ 1 & 0 & 0 & 0 & 0 & 0 & 0 & -1 \end{bmatrix}$$

Equation 10.16

$$S = \begin{bmatrix} \sqrt{2}\cos\frac{7}{16}\pi & \sqrt{2}\cos\frac{5}{16}\pi & \sqrt{2}\cos\frac{3}{16}\pi & \sqrt{2}\cos\frac{1}{16}\pi \\ \sqrt{2}\cos\frac{3}{16}\pi & \sqrt{2}\cos\frac{7}{16}\pi & -\sqrt{2}\cos\frac{1}{16}\pi & \sqrt{2}\cos\frac{5}{16}\pi \\ -\sqrt{2}\cos\frac{5}{16}\pi & -\sqrt{2}\cos\frac{1}{16}\pi & -\sqrt{2}\cos\frac{7}{16}\pi & \sqrt{2}\cos\frac{3}{16}\pi \\ -\sqrt{2}\cos\frac{1}{16}\pi & \sqrt{2}\cos\frac{3}{16}\pi & -\sqrt{2}\cos\frac{5}{16}\pi & \sqrt{2}\cos\frac{7}{16}\pi \end{bmatrix}$$

This matrix can be factored out even more if we take advantage of these relations, which can be found in any book of standard mathematical formulas.

Equation 10.17

$$\cos \alpha + \cos \beta = 2 \cos \tfrac{1}{2}(\alpha + \beta) \cos \tfrac{1}{2}(\alpha - \beta)$$

$$\cos \alpha - \cos \beta = 2 \sin \tfrac{1}{2}(\alpha + \beta) \sin \tfrac{1}{2}(\alpha - \beta)$$

Using Equation 10.17 we find that

Equation 10.18

$$\cos \tfrac{1}{16}\pi = \tfrac{1}{\sqrt{2}}\left(\cos \tfrac{3}{16}\pi + \cos \tfrac{5}{16}\pi\right)$$

$$\cos \tfrac{3}{16}\pi = \tfrac{1}{\sqrt{2}}\left(\cos \tfrac{1}{16}\pi + \cos \tfrac{7}{16}\pi\right)$$

$$\cos \tfrac{5}{16}\pi = \tfrac{1}{\sqrt{2}}\left(\cos \tfrac{1}{16}\pi - \cos \tfrac{7}{16}\pi\right)$$

$$\cos \tfrac{7}{16}\pi = \tfrac{1}{\sqrt{2}}\left(\cos \tfrac{3}{16}\pi - \cos \tfrac{5}{16}\pi\right)$$

A derivation from Equation 10.18. The other values are derived in a similar manner.

$$\tfrac{1}{2}\left(2 \cos \tfrac{3}{16}\pi + 2 \sin \tfrac{3}{16}\pi\right) = \cos \tfrac{3}{16}\pi + \sin \tfrac{3}{16}\pi$$

$$= \cos \tfrac{3}{16}\pi + \cos \tfrac{5}{16}\pi \qquad\qquad \text{Equation 7.11}$$

$$= 2 \cos \tfrac{1}{2}\left(\tfrac{3}{16}\pi + \tfrac{5}{16}\pi\right) \cos \tfrac{1}{2}\left(\tfrac{3}{16}\pi - \tfrac{5}{16}\pi\right) \qquad \text{Equation 7.20}$$

$$= 2 \cos \tfrac{\pi}{4} \cos\left(-\tfrac{\pi}{16}\right)$$

$$= 2 \cos \tfrac{\pi}{4} \cos \tfrac{\pi}{16}$$

$$= 2 \tfrac{\sqrt{2}}{2} \cos \tfrac{\pi}{16}$$

$$= 2 \cos \tfrac{1}{16}\pi$$

Substituting Equation 10.18 into Equation 10.16 gives the results in Equation 10.19.

Equation 10.19

$$
S = \begin{bmatrix}
\sqrt{2}\cos\frac{7}{16}\pi & \frac{1}{\sqrt{2}}\left(\sqrt{2}\cos\frac{1}{16}\pi - \sqrt{2}\cos\frac{7}{16}\pi\right) & \frac{1}{\sqrt{2}}\left(\sqrt{2}\cos\frac{1}{16}\pi + \sqrt{2}\cos\frac{7}{16}\pi\right) & \sqrt{2}\cos\frac{1}{16}\pi \\
\sqrt{2}\cos\frac{3}{16}\pi & \frac{1}{\sqrt{2}}\left(\sqrt{2}\cos\frac{3}{16}\pi - \sqrt{2}\cos\frac{5}{16}\pi\right) & -\frac{1}{\sqrt{2}}\left(\sqrt{2}\cos\frac{3}{16}\pi + \sqrt{2}\cos\frac{5}{16}\pi\right) & \sqrt{2}\cos\frac{5}{16}\pi \\
-\sqrt{2}\cos\frac{5}{16}\pi & -\frac{1}{\sqrt{2}}\left(\sqrt{2}\cos\frac{3}{16}\pi + \sqrt{2}\cos\frac{5}{16}\pi\right) & -\frac{1}{\sqrt{2}}\left(\sqrt{2}\cos\frac{3}{16}\pi - \sqrt{2}\cos\frac{5}{16}\pi\right) & \sqrt{2}\cos\frac{3}{16}\pi \\
-\sqrt{2}\cos\frac{1}{16}\pi & \frac{1}{\sqrt{2}}\left(\sqrt{2}\cos\frac{1}{16}\pi + \sqrt{2}\cos\frac{7}{16}\pi\right) & -\frac{1}{\sqrt{2}}\left(\sqrt{2}\cos\frac{1}{16}\pi - \sqrt{2}\cos\frac{7}{16}\pi\right) & \sqrt{2}\cos\frac{7}{16}\pi
\end{bmatrix}
$$

Equation 10.19 can be factored into Equation 10.20.

Equation 10.20

$$
S = \begin{bmatrix}
\sqrt{2}\cos\frac{7}{16}\pi & 0 & 0 & \sqrt{2}\cos\frac{1}{16}\pi \\
0 & \sqrt{2}\cos\frac{3}{16}\pi & \sqrt{2}\cos\frac{5}{16}\pi & 0 \\
0 & -\sqrt{2}\cos\frac{5}{16}\pi & \sqrt{2}\cos\frac{3}{16}\pi & 0 \\
-\sqrt{2}\cos\frac{1}{16}\pi & 0 & 0 & \sqrt{2}\cos\frac{7}{16}\pi
\end{bmatrix}
\times
\begin{bmatrix}
1 & -1 & 1 & 0 \\
1 & 1 & -1 & 0 \\
0 & -1 & -1 & 1 \\
0 & 1 & 1 & 1
\end{bmatrix}
$$

$$
\times
\begin{bmatrix}
1 & 0 & 0 & 0 \\
0 & \frac{1}{\sqrt{2}} & 0 & 0 \\
0 & 0 & \frac{1}{\sqrt{2}} & 0 \\
0 & 0 & 0 & 1
\end{bmatrix}
$$

Equation 10.20 can be still further factored as shown in Equation 10.21.

Equation 10.21

$$
S = \begin{bmatrix}
\sqrt{2}\cos\frac{7}{16}\pi & 0 & 0 & \sqrt{2}\cos\frac{1}{16}\pi \\
0 & \sqrt{2}\cos\frac{3}{16}\pi & \sqrt{2}\cos\frac{5}{16}\pi & 0 \\
0 & -\sqrt{2}\cos\frac{5}{16}\pi & \sqrt{2}\cos\frac{3}{16}\pi & 0 \\
-\sqrt{2}\cos\frac{1}{16}\pi & 0 & 0 & \sqrt{2}\cos\frac{7}{16}\pi
\end{bmatrix}
\times
\begin{bmatrix}
1 & -1 & 0 & 0 \\
1 & 1 & 0 & 0 \\
0 & 0 & -1 & 1 \\
0 & 0 & 1 & 1
\end{bmatrix}
$$

$$
\times
\begin{bmatrix}
1 & 0 & 0 & 0 \\
0 & 1 & -1 & 0 \\
0 & 1 & 1 & 0 \\
0 & 0 & 0 & 1
\end{bmatrix}
\times
\begin{bmatrix}
1 & 0 & 0 & 0 \\
0 & \frac{1}{\sqrt{2}} & 0 & 0 \\
0 & 0 & \frac{1}{\sqrt{2}} & 0 \\
0 & 0 & 0 & 1
\end{bmatrix}
$$

Putting Equation 10.21 into Equation 10.15 gives the matrix shown in Equation 10.22.

Equation 10.22

$$
M =
\begin{bmatrix}
1 & 0 & 0 & 0 & 0 & 0 & 0 & 0 \\
0 & 0 & 0 & 0 & 1 & 0 & 0 & 0 \\
0 & 0 & 1 & 0 & 0 & 0 & 0 & 0 \\
0 & 0 & 0 & 0 & 0 & 0 & 1 & 0 \\
0 & 1 & 0 & 0 & 0 & 0 & 0 & 0 \\
0 & 0 & 0 & 0 & 0 & 1 & 0 & 0 \\
0 & 0 & 0 & 1 & 0 & 0 & 0 & 0 \\
0 & 0 & 0 & 0 & 0 & 0 & 0 & 1
\end{bmatrix}
$$

$$
\times
\begin{bmatrix}
1 & 1 & 0 & 0 & 0 & 0 & 0 & 0 \\
1 & -1 & 0 & 0 & 0 & 0 & 0 & 0 \\
0 & 0 & \sqrt{2}\cos\frac{6}{16}\pi & \sqrt{2}\cos\frac{2}{16}\pi & 0 & 0 & 0 & 0 \\
0 & 0 & -\sqrt{2}\cos\frac{2}{16}\pi & \sqrt{2}\cos\frac{6}{16}\pi & 0 & 0 & 0 & 0 \\
0 & 0 & 0 & 0 & \sqrt{2}\cos\frac{7}{16}\pi & 0 & 0 & \sqrt{2}\cos\frac{1}{16}\pi \\
0 & 0 & 0 & 0 & 0 & \sqrt{2}\cos\frac{3}{16}\pi & \sqrt{2}\cos\frac{5}{16}\pi & 0 \\
0 & 0 & 0 & 0 & 0 & -\sqrt{2}\cos\frac{5}{16}\pi & \sqrt{2}\cos\frac{3}{16}\pi & 0 \\
0 & 0 & 0 & 0 & -\sqrt{2}\cos\frac{1}{16}\pi & 0 & 0 & \sqrt{2}\cos\frac{7}{16}\pi
\end{bmatrix}
$$

$$
\times
\begin{bmatrix}
1 & 0 & 0 & 0 & 0 & 0 & 0 & 0 \\
0 & 1 & 0 & 0 & 0 & 0 & 0 & 0 \\
0 & 0 & 1 & 0 & 0 & 0 & 0 & 0 \\
0 & 0 & 0 & 1 & 0 & 0 & 1 & 0 \\
0 & 0 & 0 & 0 & 1 & -1 & 0 & 0 \\
0 & 0 & 0 & 0 & 1 & 1 & 0 & 0 \\
0 & 0 & 0 & 0 & 0 & 0 & -1 & 1 \\
0 & 0 & 0 & 0 & 0 & 0 & 1 & 1
\end{bmatrix}
\times
\begin{bmatrix}
1 & 0 & 0 & 0 & 0 & 0 & 0 & 0 \\
0 & 1 & 0 & 0 & 0 & 0 & 0 & 0 \\
0 & 0 & 1 & 0 & 0 & 0 & 0 & 0 \\
0 & 0 & 0 & 1 & 0 & 0 & 0 & 0 \\
0 & 0 & 0 & 0 & 1 & 0 & 0 & 0 \\
0 & 0 & 0 & 0 & 0 & 1 & -1 & 0 \\
0 & 0 & 0 & 0 & 0 & 1 & 1 & 0 \\
0 & 0 & 0 & 0 & 0 & 0 & 0 & 1
\end{bmatrix}
\times
\begin{bmatrix}
1 & 0 & 0 & 0 & 0 & 0 & 0 & 0 \\
0 & 1 & 0 & 0 & 0 & 0 & 0 & 0 \\
0 & 0 & 1 & 0 & 0 & 0 & 0 & 0 \\
0 & 0 & 0 & 1 & 0 & 0 & 0 & 0 \\
0 & 0 & 0 & 0 & 1 & 0 & 0 & 0 \\
0 & 0 & 0 & 0 & 0 & \frac{1}{\sqrt{2}} & 0 & 0 \\
0 & 0 & 0 & 0 & 0 & 0 & \frac{1}{\sqrt{2}} & 0 \\
0 & 0 & 0 & 0 & 0 & 0 & 0 & 1
\end{bmatrix}
$$

$$
\times
\begin{bmatrix}
1 & 0 & 0 & 1 & 0 & 0 & 0 & 0 \\
0 & 1 & 1 & 0 & 0 & 0 & 0 & 0 \\
0 & 1 & -1 & 0 & 0 & 0 & 0 & 0 \\
1 & 0 & 0 & -1 & 0 & 0 & 0 & 0 \\
0 & 0 & 0 & 0 & 1 & 0 & 0 & 0 \\
0 & 0 & 0 & 0 & 0 & 1 & 0 & 0 \\
0 & 0 & 0 & 0 & 0 & 0 & 1 & 0 \\
0 & 0 & 0 & 0 & 0 & 0 & 0 & 1
\end{bmatrix}
\times
\begin{bmatrix}
1 & 0 & 0 & 0 & 0 & 0 & 0 & 1 \\
0 & 1 & 0 & 0 & 0 & 0 & 1 & 0 \\
0 & 0 & 1 & 0 & 0 & 1 & 0 & 0 \\
0 & 0 & 0 & 1 & 1 & 0 & 0 & 0 \\
0 & 0 & 0 & 1 & -1 & 0 & 0 & 0 \\
0 & 0 & 1 & 0 & 0 & -1 & 0 & 0 \\
0 & 1 & 0 & 0 & 0 & 0 & -1 & 0 \\
1 & 0 & 0 & 0 & 0 & 0 & 0 & -1
\end{bmatrix}
$$

Equation 10.22 appears to be much more complicated than the original in Equation 10.2, but it actually requires fewer steps to calculate. Multiplying a row vector and M requires 64 multiplication and 56 addition operations. In the factored matrices any nonzero value that is not equal to $+/-1$ represents a multiplication and all but one nonzero value in each column represents an addition. A zero in a factor represents no operation and almost all of the array elements are zeros. Table 10.1 shows the operations required for each matrix multiplication with the factored matrices.

Table 10.1
Operations
Required After
Factorization

Matrix	Addition	Multiplication
1	0	0
2	8	12
3	4	0
4	2	0
5	0	2
6	4	0
7	8	0
Total	26	14

Most processors take longer to execute multiplication instructions than additions. For example, on my system the speed advantage is about $4:1$ in favor of addition. Therefore, it is usually advantageous to replace multiplication operations with addition. In the factored matrix most of the multiplication operations are in groups of the form

Equation 10.23

$$X = A \cos \alpha + B \sin \alpha$$
$$Y = A \sin \alpha - B \cos \alpha$$

This form is well known in computer graphics because it represents the rotation of the point (A, B) by an angle. A rotation uses four multiplication operations and two additions, but if it is calculated as shown in Equation 10.23, it requires 3 multiplications and 3 additions. If this method is used for multiplying the matrix, the total number of operations required to multiply a row by the DCT matrix becomes 11 multiplications and 29 additions.

Equation 10.24

$$T = \cos \alpha (A + B)$$

$$X = T - (\cos \alpha - \sin \alpha) B$$

$$Y = -T + (\cos \alpha + \sin \alpha) A$$

The following code example is an implementation of an IDCT function that slavishly follows the factorization in Equation 10.22 so that you can clearly see how the factored matrix multiplications are implemented in code.

```
typedef double MATRIX [8][8] ;
const double C1 = (sqrt (2.0) * cos (M_PI/16.0)) ;
const double C2 = (sqrt (2.0) * cos (2.0*M_PI/16.0)) ;
const double C3 = (sqrt (2.0) * cos (3.0*M_PI/16.0)) ;
const double S1 = (sqrt (2.0) * sin (M_PI/16.0)) ;
const double S2 = (sqrt (2.0) * sin (2.0*M_PI/16.0)) ;
const double S3 = (sqrt (2.0) * sin (3.0*M_PI/16.0)) ;
const double SQRT2 = (1.0 / sqrt(2.0)) ;
unsigned int Limit (double input)
{
  double value = input + 128.5 ;
  if (value < 0)
    return 0 ;
  else if (value > 255)
    return 255 ;
  else
    return (unsigned int) value ;
}
  void InverseDCT (MATRIX input, MATRIX output)
  {
    double tmp[SampleWidth][SampleWidth] ;
    for (int row = 0 ; row < 8 ; ++ row)
    {
      double a0 = input[row][0] ;
      double a1 = input[row][4] ;
      double a2 = input[row][2] ;
      double a3 = input[row][6] ;
      double a4 = input[row][1] ;
      double a5 = input[row][5] ;
      double a6 = input[row][3] ;
      double a7 = input[row][7] ;

      double b0 = (a0 + a1) ;
      double b1 = (a0 - a1) ;
//       b2 = S2 * 2 - C2 * a3 ;
//       b3 = C2 * a2 + S2 * a3 ;
      double r0 = S2 * (a2 + a3) ;
      double b2 = r0 - (S2+C2) * a3 ;
      double b3 = r0 - (S2-C2) * a2 ;
//       b4 = S1 * a4 - C1 * a7 ;
//       b7 = C1 * a4 + S1 * a7 ;
```

```
        double r1 = S1 * (a4+a7) ;
        double b4 = r1 - (S1+C1) * a7 ;
        double b7 = r1 - (S1-C1) * a4 ;
//      b5 = C3 * a5 - S3 * a6 ;
//      b6 = S3 * a5 + C3 * a6 ;
        double r2 = C3 * (a5 + a6) ;
        double b5 = r2 - (C3+S3) * a6 ;
        double b6 = r2 - (C3-S3) * a5 ;

        double c0 = b0 ;
        double c1 = b1 ;
        double c2 = b2 ;
        double c3 = b3 ;
        double c4 = b4 + b5 ;
        double c5 = b5 - b4 ;
        double c6 = b7 - b6 ;
        double c7 = b7 + b6 ;

        double d0 = c0 ;
        double d1 = c1 ;
        double d2 = c2 ;
        double d3 = c3 ;
        double d4 = c4 ;
        double d5 = c6 + c5 ;
        double d6 = c6 - c5 ;
        double d7 = c7 ;

        double e0 = d0 ;
        double e1 = d1 ;
        double e2 = d2 ;
        double e3 = d3 ;
        double e4 = d4 ;
        double e5 = SQRT2 * d5 ;
        double e6 = SQRT2 * d6 ;
        double e7 = d7 ;

        double f0 = e0 + e3 ;
        double f1 = e1 + e2 ;
        double f2 = e1 - e2 ;
        double f3 = e0 - e3 ;
        double f4 = e4 ;
        double f5 = e5 ;
        double f6 = e6 ;
        double f7 = e7 ;

        tmp [row][0] = (f0 + f7) ;
        tmp [row][1] = (f1 + f6) ;
        tmp [row][2] = (f2 + f5) ;
        tmp [row][3] = (f3 + f4) ;
        tmp [row][4] = (f3 - f4) ;
```

```
         tmp [row][5] = (f2 - f5) ;
         tmp [row][6] = (f1 - f6) ;
         tmp [row][7] = (f0 - f7) ;
      }

      for (int col = 0 ; col < 8 ; ++ col)
      {
         double a0 = tmp [0][col] ;
         double a1 = tmp [4][col] ;
         double a2 = tmp [2][col] ;
         double a3 = tmp [6][col] ;
         double a4 = tmp [1][col] ;
         double a5 = tmp [5][col] ;
         double a6 = tmp [3][col] ;
         double a7 = tmp [7][col] ;

         double b0 = (a0 + a1) ;
         double b1 = (a0 - a1) ;
//       b2 = S2 * a2 - C2 * a3 ;
//       b3 = C2 * a2 + S2 * a3 ;
         double r0 = S2 * (a2 + a3) ;
         double b2 = r0 - (S2+C2) * a3 ;
         double b3 = r0 - (S2-C2) * a2 ;
//       b4 = S1 * a4 - C1 * a7 ;
//       b7 = C1 * a4 + S1 * a7 ;
         double r1 = S1 * (a4+a7) ;
         double b4 = r1 - (S1+C1) * a7 ;
         double b7 = r1 - (S1-C1) * a4 ;
//       b5 = C3 * a5 - S3 * a6 ;
//       b6 = S3 * a5 + C3 * a6 ;
         double r2 = C3 * (a5 + a6) ;
         double b5 = r2 - (C3+S3) * a6 ;
         double b6 = r2 - (C3-S3) * a5 ;

         double c0 = b0 ;
         double c1 = b1 ;
         double c2 = b2 ;
         double c3 = b3 ;
         double c4 = b4 + b5 ;
         double c5 = b5 - b4 ;
         double c6 = b7 - b6 ;
         double c7 = b7 + b6 ;

         double d0 = c0 ;
         double d1 = c1 ;
         double d2 = c2 ;
         double d3 = c3 ;
         double d4 = c4 ;
         double d5 = c6 + c5 ;
         double d6 = c6 - c5 ;
         double d7 = c7 ;
```

```
        double e0 = d0 + (128*8) ;
        double e1 = d1 + (128*8) ;
        double e2 = d2 ;
        double e3 = d3 ;
        double e4 = d4 ;
        double e5 = SQRT2 * d5 ;
        double e6 = SQRT2 * d6 ;
        double e7 = d7 ;

        double f0 = e0 + e3 ;
        double f1 = e1 + e2 ;
        double f2 = e1 - e2 ;
        double f3 = e0 - e3 ;
        double f4 = e4 ;
        double f5 = e5 ;
        double f6 = e6 ;
        double f7 = e7 ;

        double g0 = f0 + f7 ;
        double g1 = f1 + f6 ;
        double g2 = f2 + f5 ;
        double g3 = f3 + f4 ;
        double g4 = f3 - f4 ;
        double g5 = f2 - f5 ;
        double g6 = f1 - f6 ;
        double g7 = f0 - f7 ;

        output [0][col] = Limit (g0/8.0) ;
        output [1][col] = Limit (g1/8.0) ;
        output [2][col] = Limit (g2/8.0) ;
        output [3][col] = Limit (g3/8.0) ;
        output [4][col] = Limit (g4/8.0) ;
        output [5][col] = Limit (g5/8.0) ;
        output [6][col] = Limit (g6/8.0) ;
        output [7][col] = Limit (g7/8.0) ;
    }
}
```

Scaled Integer Arithmetic

On most processors, floating-point operations take much longer than integer operations. Another method for speeding up the IDCT and DCT calculations is to use only integer operations. To simulate real numbers we scale the integer values by multiplying them by a power of 2.

If we were to scale all values by the 2, then we could represent the values … $-2, -1.5, 1, -.5, 0, .5, 1, 1.5, 2$ … using integers. If we scale them by 4, we can represent … $-1.25, -1, -.75, -.5, -.25, 0, .25, .5, .75, 1, 1.25$. The more we scale the integers, the more precision we get in the calculation. Unfortunately, if we scale the integers so much that an integer overflow occurs, we get incorrect results.

The sample code below illustrates how to use scaled integers. In this example the integer values are scaled by a factor of 2^5, which is implemented using a left shift. To convert from a scaled integer to a regular integer you would use a right shift operation with the scale factor. Here we used division to convert to a floating-point value in order to preserve fractions.

```
const int scale = 5 ;
long v1 = 2 << scale ;
long v2 = 3 << scale ;
// Addition
long v3 = v1 + v2 ;
// Multiplication
long v4 = (v1 * v2) >> scale ;
// Division
long v5 = (v1 << scale) / v2 ;
cout << (double) v3 / (1 << scale) << endl ;
cout << (double) v4 / (1 << scale) << endl ;
cout << (double) v5 / (1 << scale) << endl ;
```

The problem with using scaled integers rather than floating-point values is that unless you have a system with 64-bit integers you can never get the same precision you can with floating-point numbers. Generally the difference between the two methods is very small, but a difference does exist that can produce greater rounding errors.

If you are implementing a JPEG application, you may wish to use floating-point values when you are compressing images and scaled integers when you are decompressing them. Generally speed is more important when you want to view a compressed image than when you are compressing one. This would give you more accuracy when you create an image and more speed when you are viewing one.

Merging Quantization and the DCT

Something we did not account for in the operation totals in Table 10.1 is that we factored out the value $\frac{1}{8}$ from the IDCT equation. As you can see in Equation 10.3, this means that we have another 64 multiplication operations to add in at the end. If the IDCT is implemented using scaled integers, then dividing by 8 can be done as a bit shift that can be combined with descaling the final result. Unfortunately, this does not work with floating-point numbers.

Another way to get rid of the term $\frac{1}{8}$ is to merge this value with the quantization values. In fact, if we factor the DCT matrix a little differently, it is possible to save even more than the 64 operations resulting from this term. For this factorization of the DCT matrix we are going to follow the same steps as in the previous one until we get to Equation 10.15. From there we will branch off on another path.

A formula that will play a key role in the factorization is the product of cosines formula shown in Equation 10.25.

Equation 10.25

$$\cos \alpha \cos \beta = \tfrac{1}{8}(\cos (\alpha + \beta) + \cos (\alpha - \beta))$$

In the factored matrix in Equation 10.15 the cosine terms in each row or column can be grouped into pairs

$$\left(\left(\tfrac{1}{16}\,\pi, \tfrac{7}{16}\,\pi\right), \left(\tfrac{2}{16}\,\pi, \tfrac{6}{16}\,\pi\right)\left(\tfrac{3}{16}\,\pi, \tfrac{5}{16}\,\pi\right)\right)$$

whose sum is $\frac{\pi}{2}$, where the value of the cosine function is zero.

If we extract this submatrix from Equation 10.15 (Equation 10.26) it can be factored as in Equation 10.27 using the cosine sum formula in Equation 10.25.

Equation 10.26

$$\begin{bmatrix} \sqrt{2}\,\cos \tfrac{6}{16}\pi & \sqrt{2}\,\cos \tfrac{2}{16}\pi \\ -\sqrt{2}\,\cos \tfrac{2}{16}\pi & \sqrt{2}\,\cos \tfrac{6}{16}\pi \end{bmatrix}$$

Equation 10.27

$$\begin{bmatrix} \sqrt{2}\cos\frac{6}{16}\pi & \sqrt{2}\cos\frac{2}{16}\pi \\ -\sqrt{2}\cos\frac{2}{16}\pi & \sqrt{2}\cos\frac{6}{16}\pi \end{bmatrix}$$

$$= \begin{bmatrix} \dfrac{\sqrt{2}}{\cos\frac{2}{16}\pi} & 0 \\ 0 & \dfrac{\sqrt{2}}{\cos\frac{6}{16}\pi} \end{bmatrix} \times \begin{bmatrix} 2\cos\frac{2}{16}\pi\cos\frac{6}{16}\pi & 2\cos\frac{2}{16}\pi\cos\frac{2}{16}\pi \\ -2\cos\frac{6}{16}\pi\cos\frac{2}{16}\pi & 2\cos\frac{6}{16}\pi\cos\frac{6}{16}\pi \end{bmatrix}$$

$$= \begin{bmatrix} \dfrac{\sqrt{2}}{\cos\frac{2}{16}\pi} & 0 \\ 0 & \dfrac{\sqrt{2}}{\cos\frac{6}{16}\pi} \end{bmatrix} \times \begin{bmatrix} \cos\frac{4}{16}\pi & \cos\frac{4}{16}\pi+\cos(0) \\ -\cos\frac{4}{16}\pi & -\cos\frac{4}{16}\pi+\cos(0) \end{bmatrix}$$

$$= \begin{bmatrix} \dfrac{\sqrt{2}}{\cos\frac{2}{16}\pi} & 0 \\ 0 & \dfrac{\sqrt{2}}{\cos\frac{6}{16}\pi} \end{bmatrix} \times \begin{bmatrix} \cos\frac{4}{16}\pi & \cos\frac{4}{16}\pi+1 \\ -\cos\frac{4}{16}\pi & -\cos\frac{4}{16}\pi+1 \end{bmatrix}$$

$$= \begin{bmatrix} \dfrac{\sqrt{2}}{\cos\frac{2}{16}\pi} & 0 \\ 0 & \dfrac{\sqrt{2}}{\cos\frac{6}{16}\pi} \end{bmatrix} \times \begin{bmatrix} 1 & 1 \\ -1 & 1 \end{bmatrix} \times \begin{bmatrix} \cos\frac{4}{16}\pi & \cos\frac{4}{16}\pi \\ 0 & 1 \end{bmatrix}$$

$$= \begin{bmatrix} \dfrac{\sqrt{2}}{\cos\frac{2}{16}\pi} & 0 \\ 0 & \dfrac{\sqrt{2}}{\cos\frac{6}{16}\pi} \end{bmatrix} \times \begin{bmatrix} 1 & 1 \\ -1 & 1 \end{bmatrix} \times \begin{bmatrix} \cos\frac{4}{16}\pi & 0 \\ 0 & 1 \end{bmatrix} \times \begin{bmatrix} 1 & 1 \\ 0 & 1 \end{bmatrix}$$

The trick in this factorization is to choose the cosine row scaling values in such a way that the cos (0) terms end up in the same column.

If we create another submatrix for the remaining cosine terms in Equation 10.15, we can follow a similar factorization process (Equation 10.28).

Equation 10.28

$$
\begin{bmatrix}
\sqrt{2}\cos\frac{7}{16}\pi & \sqrt{2}\cos\frac{5}{16}\pi & \sqrt{2}\cos\frac{3}{16}\pi & \sqrt{2}\cos\frac{1}{16}\pi \\
\sqrt{2}\cos\frac{3}{16}\pi & \sqrt{2}\cos\frac{7}{16}\pi & -\sqrt{2}\cos\frac{1}{16}\pi & \sqrt{2}\cos\frac{5}{16}\pi \\
-\sqrt{2}\cos\frac{5}{16}\pi & -\sqrt{2}\cos\frac{1}{16}\pi & -\sqrt{2}\cos\frac{7}{16}\pi & \sqrt{2}\cos\frac{3}{16}\pi \\
-\sqrt{2}\cos\frac{1}{16}\pi & \sqrt{2}\cos\frac{3}{16}\pi & -\sqrt{2}\cos\frac{5}{16}\pi & \sqrt{2}\cos\frac{7}{16}\pi
\end{bmatrix}
$$

$$
=
\begin{bmatrix}
\dfrac{\sqrt{2}}{2\cos\frac{1}{16}\pi} & 0 & 0 & 0 \\
0 & \dfrac{\sqrt{2}}{2\cos\frac{5}{16}\pi} & 0 & 0 \\
0 & 0 & \dfrac{\sqrt{2}}{2\cos\frac{3}{16}\pi} & 0 \\
0 & 0 & 0 & \dfrac{\sqrt{2}}{2\cos\frac{7}{16}\pi}
\end{bmatrix}
$$

$$
\times
\begin{bmatrix}
2\cos\frac{1}{16}\pi\cos\frac{7}{16}\pi & 2\cos\frac{1}{16}\pi\cos\frac{5}{16}\pi & 2\cos\frac{1}{16}\pi\cos\frac{3}{16}\pi & 2\cos\frac{1}{16}\pi\cos\frac{1}{16}\pi \\
2\cos\frac{5}{16}\pi\cos\frac{3}{16}\pi & 2\cos\frac{5}{16}\pi\cos\frac{7}{16}\pi & -2\cos\frac{5}{16}\pi\cos\frac{1}{16}\pi & 2\cos\frac{5}{16}\pi\cos\frac{5}{16}\pi \\
-2\cos\frac{3}{16}\pi\cos\frac{5}{16}\pi & -2\cos\frac{3}{16}\pi\cos\frac{1}{16}\pi & -2\cos\frac{3}{16}\pi\cos\frac{7}{16}\pi & 2\cos\frac{3}{16}\pi\cos\frac{3}{16}\pi \\
-2\cos\frac{7}{16}\pi\cos\frac{1}{16}\pi & 2\cos\frac{7}{16}\pi\cos\frac{3}{16}\pi & -2\cos\frac{7}{16}\pi\cos\frac{5}{16}\pi & 2\cos\frac{7}{16}\pi\cos\frac{7}{16}\pi
\end{bmatrix}
$$

Table 10.2
Operations
Required for the
New Factorization

Matrix	Addition	Multiplication
1	0	6
2	0	0
3	6	0
4	2	2
5	2	0
6	2	3
7	1	0
8	4	0
9	4	0
10	8	0
Total	29	11

Once again, the cosine scaling terms have been chosen so that all of the cos (0) terms end up in the same column. Equation 10.29 is the remainder of the factorization.

$$
\begin{bmatrix}
2\cos\frac{1}{16}\pi\cos\frac{7}{16}\pi & 2\cos\frac{1}{16}\pi\cos\frac{5}{16}\pi & 2\cos\frac{1}{16}\pi\cos\frac{3}{16}\pi & 2\cos\frac{1}{16}\pi\cos\frac{1}{16}\pi \\
2\cos\frac{5}{16}\pi\cos\frac{3}{16}\pi & 2\cos\frac{5}{16}\pi\cos\frac{7}{16}\pi & -2\cos\frac{5}{16}\pi\cos\frac{1}{16}\pi & 2\cos\frac{5}{16}\pi\cos\frac{5}{16}\pi \\
-2\cos\frac{3}{16}\pi\cos\frac{5}{16}\pi & -2\cos\frac{3}{16}\pi\cos\frac{1}{16}\pi & -2\cos\frac{3}{16}\pi\cos\frac{7}{16}\pi & 2\cos\frac{3}{16}\pi\cos\frac{3}{16}\pi \\
-2\cos\frac{7}{16}\pi\cos\frac{1}{16}\pi & 2\cos\frac{7}{16}\pi\cos\frac{3}{16}\pi & -2\cos\frac{7}{16}\pi\cos\frac{5}{16}\pi & 2\cos\frac{7}{16}\pi\cos\frac{7}{16}\pi
\end{bmatrix}
$$

$$
=
\begin{bmatrix}
\cos\frac{6}{16}\pi & \cos\frac{6}{16}\pi+\cos\frac{4}{16}\pi & \cos\frac{2}{16}\pi+\cos\frac{4}{16}\pi & \cos\frac{2}{16}\pi \\
\cos\frac{2}{16}\pi & \cos\frac{2}{16}\pi-\cos\frac{4}{16}\pi & -\cos\frac{6}{16}\pi-\cos\frac{4}{16}\pi & -\cos\frac{6}{16}\pi \\
-\cos\frac{2}{16}\pi & -\cos\frac{2}{16}\pi-\cos\frac{4}{16}\pi & \cos\frac{6}{16}\pi-\cos\frac{4}{16}\pi & \cos\frac{6}{16}\pi \\
-\cos\frac{6}{16}\pi & -\cos\frac{6}{16}\pi+\cos\frac{4}{16}\pi & -\cos\frac{2}{16}\pi+\cos\frac{4}{16}\pi & -\cos\frac{2}{16}\pi
\end{bmatrix}
$$

$$
=
\begin{bmatrix}
1 & 0 & 0 & 1 \\
0 & 1 & 1 & 0 \\
0 & 1 & -1 & 0 \\
-1 & 0 & 0 & 1
\end{bmatrix}
\times
\begin{bmatrix}
\cos\frac{6}{16}\pi & \cos\frac{6}{16}\pi & \cos\frac{2}{16}\pi & \cos\frac{2}{16}\pi \\
0 & -\cos\frac{4}{16}\pi & -\cos\frac{4}{16}\pi & 1 \\
\cos\frac{2}{16}\pi & \cos\frac{2}{16}\pi & -\cos\frac{6}{16}\pi & -\cos\frac{6}{16}\pi \\
0 & \cos\frac{4}{16}\pi & \cos\frac{4}{16}\pi & 1
\end{bmatrix}
$$

$$
=
\begin{bmatrix}
1 & 0 & 0 & 1 \\
0 & 1 & 1 & 0 \\
0 & 1 & -1 & 0 \\
-1 & 0 & 0 & 1
\end{bmatrix}
\times
\begin{bmatrix}
1 & 0 & 0 & 0 \\
0 & -1 & 0 & 1 \\
0 & 0 & 1 & 0 \\
0 & 1 & 0 & 1
\end{bmatrix}
\times
\begin{bmatrix}
\cos\frac{6}{16}\pi & \cos\frac{6}{16}\pi & \cos\frac{2}{16}\pi & \cos\frac{2}{16}\pi \\
0 & \cos\frac{4}{16}\pi & \cos\frac{4}{16}\pi & 0 \\
\cos\frac{2}{16}\pi & \cos\frac{2}{16}\pi & -\cos\frac{6}{16}\pi & -\cos\frac{6}{16}\pi \\
0 & 0 & 0 & 1
\end{bmatrix}
$$

$$
=
\begin{bmatrix}
1 & 0 & 0 & 1 \\
0 & 1 & 1 & 0 \\
0 & 1 & -1 & 0 \\
-1 & 0 & 0 & 1
\end{bmatrix}
\times
\begin{bmatrix}
1 & 0 & 0 & 0 \\
0 & -1 & 0 & 1 \\
0 & 0 & 1 & 0 \\
0 & 1 & 0 & 1
\end{bmatrix}
\times
\begin{bmatrix}
\cos\frac{6}{16}\pi & 0 & \cos\frac{2}{16}\pi & 0 \\
0 & \cos\frac{4}{16}\pi & 0 & 0 \\
\cos\frac{2}{16}\pi & 0 & -\cos\frac{6}{16}\pi & 0 \\
0 & 0 & 0 & 1
\end{bmatrix}
\times
\begin{bmatrix}
1 & 1 & 0 & 0 \\
0 & 1 & 1 & 0 \\
0 & 0 & 1 & 1 \\
0 & 0 & 0 & 1
\end{bmatrix}
$$

Equation 10.29

We can repeat the factorization process with the matrix with the cosine terms to give Equation 10.30.

$$
\begin{bmatrix}
\cos \frac{6}{16}\pi & 0 & \cos \frac{2}{16}\pi & 0 \\
0 & \cos \frac{4}{16}\pi & 0 & 0 \\
\cos \frac{2}{16}\pi & 0 & -\cos \frac{6}{16}\pi & 0 \\
0 & 0 & 0 & 1
\end{bmatrix}
$$

$$
=
\begin{bmatrix}
\frac{1}{2\cos\frac{2}{16}\pi} & 0 & 0 & 0 \\
0 & 1 & 0 & 0 \\
0 & 0 & \frac{1}{2\cos\frac{6}{16}\pi} & 0 \\
0 & 0 & 0 & 1
\end{bmatrix}
\times
\begin{bmatrix}
2\cos\frac{2}{16}\pi\cos\frac{6}{16}\pi & 0 & 2\cos\frac{2}{16}\pi\cos\frac{2}{16}\pi & 0 \\
0 & \cos\frac{4}{16}\pi & 0 & 0 \\
2\cos\frac{2}{16}\pi\cos\frac{6}{16}\pi & 0 & -2\cos\frac{6}{16}\pi\cos\frac{6}{16}\pi & 0 \\
0 & 0 & 0 & 1
\end{bmatrix}
$$

$$
\begin{bmatrix}
2\cos\frac{2}{16}\pi\cos\frac{6}{16}\pi & 0 & 2\cos\frac{2}{16}\pi\cos\frac{2}{16}\pi & 0 \\
0 & \cos\frac{4}{16}\pi & 0 & 0 \\
2\cos\frac{2}{16}\pi\cos\frac{6}{16}\pi & 0 & -2\cos\frac{6}{16}\pi\cos\frac{6}{16}\pi & 0 \\
0 & 0 & 0 & 1
\end{bmatrix}
=
\begin{bmatrix}
\cos\frac{8}{16}\pi+\cos\frac{4}{16}\pi & 0 & \cos\frac{4}{16}\pi+\cos(0) & 0 \\
0 & \cos\frac{4}{16}\pi & 0 & 0 \\
\cos\frac{8}{16}\pi+\cos\frac{4}{16}\pi & 0 & \cos\frac{4}{16}\pi-\cos(0) & 0 \\
0 & 0 & 0 & 1
\end{bmatrix}
$$

$$
=
\begin{bmatrix}
\cos\frac{4}{16}\pi & 0 & \cos\frac{4}{16}\pi+1 & 0 \\
0 & \cos\frac{4}{16}\pi & 0 & 0 \\
\cos\frac{4}{16}\pi & 0 & \cos\frac{4}{16}\pi-1 & 0 \\
0 & 0 & 0 & 1
\end{bmatrix}
$$

$$
=
\begin{bmatrix}
1 & 0 & 1 & 0 \\
0 & 1 & 0 & 0 \\
1 & 0 & -1 & 0 \\
0 & 0 & 0 & 1
\end{bmatrix}
\times
\begin{bmatrix}
\cos\frac{4}{16}\pi & 0 & 0 & 0 \\
0 & \cos\frac{4}{16}\pi & 0 & 0 \\
0 & 0 & 1 & 0 \\
0 & 0 & 0 & 1
\end{bmatrix}
\times
\begin{bmatrix}
1 & 0 & 1 & 0 \\
0 & 1 & 0 & 0 \\
0 & 0 & 1 & 0 \\
0 & 0 & 0 & 1
\end{bmatrix}
$$

Equation 10.30

Putting it all together by substituting Equation 10.27, Equation 10.28, and Equation 10.30 into Equation 10.15 gives Equation 10.31.

$$
M =
\begin{bmatrix}
1 & 0 & 0 & 0 & 0 & 0 & 0 & 0 \\
0 & 0 & 0 & 0 & 1 & 0 & 0 & 0 \\
0 & 0 & 1 & 0 & 0 & 0 & 0 & 0 \\
0 & 0 & 0 & 0 & 0 & 0 & 1 & 0 \\
0 & 1 & 0 & 0 & 0 & 0 & 0 & 0 \\
0 & 0 & 0 & 0 & 0 & 1 & 0 & 0 \\
0 & 0 & 0 & 1 & 0 & 0 & 0 & 0 \\
0 & 0 & 0 & 0 & 0 & 0 & 0 & 1
\end{bmatrix}
\times
\begin{bmatrix}
1 & 0 & 0 & 0 & 0 & 0 & 0 & 0 \\
0 & 1 & 0 & 0 & 0 & 0 & 0 & 0 \\
0 & 0 & \frac{\sqrt{2}}{2\cos\frac{2}{16}\pi} & 0 & 0 & 0 & 0 & 0 \\
0 & 0 & 0 & \frac{\sqrt{2}}{2\cos\frac{6}{16}\pi} & 0 & 0 & 0 & 0 \\
0 & 0 & 0 & 0 & \frac{\sqrt{2}}{2\cos\frac{1}{16}\pi} & 0 & 0 & 0 \\
0 & 0 & 0 & 0 & 0 & \frac{\sqrt{2}}{2\cos\frac{5}{16}\pi} & 0 & 0 \\
0 & 0 & 0 & 0 & 0 & 0 & \frac{\sqrt{2}}{2\cos\frac{3}{16}\pi} & 0 \\
0 & 0 & 0 & 0 & 0 & 0 & 0 & \frac{\sqrt{2}}{2\cos\frac{7}{16}\pi}
\end{bmatrix}
$$

$$
\times
\begin{bmatrix}
1 & 0 & 0 & 0 & 0 & 0 & 0 & 0 \\
0 & 0 & 0 & 0 & 1 & 0 & 0 & 0 \\
0 & 0 & 1 & 0 & 0 & 0 & 0 & 0 \\
0 & 0 & 0 & 0 & 0 & 0 & 1 & 0 \\
0 & 1 & 0 & 0 & 0 & 0 & 0 & 0 \\
0 & 0 & 0 & 0 & 0 & 1 & 0 & 0 \\
0 & 0 & 0 & 1 & 0 & 0 & 0 & 0 \\
0 & 0 & 0 & 0 & 0 & 0 & 0 & 1
\end{bmatrix}
\times
\begin{bmatrix}
1 & 0 & 0 & 0 & 0 & 0 & 0 & 0 \\
0 & 1 & 0 & 0 & 0 & 0 & 0 & 0 \\
0 & 0 & 1 & 1 & 0 & 0 & 0 & 0 \\
0 & 0 & -1 & 1 & 0 & 0 & 0 & 0 \\
0 & 0 & 0 & 0 & 1 & 0 & 0 & 1 \\
0 & 0 & 0 & 0 & 0 & 1 & 1 & 0 \\
0 & 0 & 0 & 0 & 1 & -1 & 0 & 0 \\
0 & 0 & 0 & 0 & -1 & 0 & 0 & 1
\end{bmatrix}
\times
\begin{bmatrix}
1 & 0 & 0 & 0 & 0 & 0 & 0 & 0 \\
0 & 1 & 0 & 0 & 0 & 0 & 0 & 0 \\
0 & 0 & 1 & 0 & 0 & 0 & 0 & 0 \\
0 & 0 & 0 & 1 & 0 & 0 & 0 & 0 \\
0 & 0 & 0 & 0 & \frac{1}{2\cos\frac{2}{16}\pi} & 0 & 0 & 0 \\
0 & 0 & 0 & 0 & 0 & -1 & 0 & 1 \\
0 & 0 & 0 & 0 & 0 & 0 & \frac{1}{2\cos\frac{6}{16}\pi} & 0 \\
0 & 0 & 0 & 0 & 0 & 1 & 0 & 1
\end{bmatrix}
$$

$$
\times
\begin{bmatrix}
1 & 0 & 0 & 0 & 0 & 0 & 0 & 0 \\
0 & 1 & 0 & 0 & 0 & 0 & 0 & 0 \\
0 & 0 & 1 & 0 & 0 & 0 & 0 & 0 \\
0 & 0 & 0 & 1 & 0 & 0 & 0 & 0 \\
0 & 0 & 0 & 0 & 1 & 0 & 1 & 0 \\
0 & 0 & 0 & 0 & 0 & 1 & 0 & 0 \\
0 & 0 & 0 & 0 & 1 & 0 & -1 & 0 \\
0 & 0 & 0 & 0 & 0 & 0 & 0 & 1
\end{bmatrix}
\times
\begin{bmatrix}
1 & 1 & 0 & 0 & 0 & 0 & 0 & 0 \\
1 & -1 & 0 & 0 & 0 & 0 & 0 & 0 \\
0 & 0 & \cos\frac{4}{16}\pi & 0 & 0 & 0 & 0 & 0 \\
0 & 0 & 0 & 1 & 0 & 0 & 0 & 0 \\
0 & 0 & 0 & 0 & \cos\frac{4}{16}\pi & 0 & 0 & 0 \\
0 & 0 & 0 & 0 & 0 & \cos\frac{4}{16}\pi & 0 & 0 \\
0 & 0 & 0 & 0 & 0 & 0 & 1 & 0 \\
0 & 0 & 0 & 0 & 0 & 0 & 0 & 1
\end{bmatrix}
\times
\begin{bmatrix}
1 & 0 & 0 & 0 & 0 & 0 & 0 & 0 \\
0 & 1 & 0 & 0 & 0 & 0 & 0 & 0 \\
0 & 0 & 1 & 0 & 0 & 0 & 0 & 0 \\
0 & 0 & 0 & 1 & 0 & 0 & 0 & 0 \\
0 & 0 & 0 & 0 & 1 & 0 & 1 & 0 \\
0 & 0 & 0 & 0 & 0 & 1 & 0 & 0 \\
0 & 0 & 0 & 0 & 0 & 0 & 1 & 0 \\
0 & 0 & 0 & 0 & 0 & 0 & 0 & 1
\end{bmatrix}
$$

$$
\times
\begin{bmatrix}
1 & 0 & 0 & 0 & 0 & 0 & 0 & 0 \\
0 & 1 & 0 & 0 & 0 & 0 & 0 & 0 \\
0 & 0 & 1 & 1 & 0 & 0 & 0 & 0 \\
0 & 0 & 0 & 1 & 0 & 0 & 0 & 0 \\
0 & 0 & 0 & 0 & 1 & 1 & 0 & 0 \\
0 & 0 & 0 & 0 & 0 & 1 & 1 & 0 \\
0 & 0 & 0 & 0 & 0 & 0 & 1 & 1 \\
0 & 0 & 0 & 0 & 0 & 0 & 0 & 1
\end{bmatrix}
\times
\begin{bmatrix}
1 & 0 & 0 & 1 & 0 & 0 & 0 & 0 \\
0 & 1 & 1 & 0 & 0 & 0 & 0 & 0 \\
0 & 1 & -1 & 0 & 0 & 0 & 0 & 0 \\
1 & 0 & 0 & -1 & 0 & 0 & 0 & 0 \\
0 & 0 & 0 & 0 & 1 & 0 & 0 & 0 \\
0 & 0 & 0 & 0 & 0 & 1 & 0 & 0 \\
0 & 0 & 0 & 0 & 0 & 0 & 1 & 0 \\
0 & 0 & 0 & 0 & 0 & 0 & 0 & 1
\end{bmatrix}
\times
\begin{bmatrix}
1 & 0 & 0 & 0 & 0 & 0 & 0 & 1 \\
0 & 1 & 0 & 0 & 0 & 0 & 1 & 0 \\
0 & 0 & 1 & 0 & 0 & 1 & 0 & 0 \\
0 & 0 & 0 & 1 & 1 & 0 & 0 & 0 \\
0 & 0 & 0 & 1 & -1 & 0 & 0 & 0 \\
0 & 0 & 1 & 0 & 0 & -1 & 0 & 0 \\
0 & 1 & 0 & 0 & 0 & 0 & -1 & 0 \\
1 & 0 & 0 & 0 & 0 & 0 & 0 & -1
\end{bmatrix}
$$

Equation 10.31

$$
\begin{bmatrix}
1 & 0 & 0 & 0 & 0 & 0 & 0 & 0 \\
0 & 0 & 0 & 0 & 1 & 0 & 0 & 0 \\
0 & 0 & 1 & 0 & 0 & 0 & 0 & 0 \\
0 & 0 & 0 & 0 & 0 & 0 & 1 & 0 \\
0 & 1 & 0 & 0 & 0 & 0 & 0 & 0 \\
0 & 0 & 0 & 0 & 0 & 1 & 0 & 0 \\
0 & 0 & 0 & 1 & 0 & 0 & 0 & 0 \\
0 & 0 & 0 & 0 & 0 & 0 & 0 & 1
\end{bmatrix}
\times
\begin{bmatrix}
1 & 0 & 0 & 0 & 0 & 0 & 0 & 0 \\
0 & 1 & 0 & 0 & 0 & 0 & 0 & 0 \\
0 & 0 & \dfrac{\sqrt{2}}{2\cos\frac{2}{16}\pi} & 0 & 0 & 0 & 0 & 0 \\
0 & 0 & 0 & \dfrac{\sqrt{2}}{2\cos\frac{6}{16}\pi} & 0 & 0 & 0 & 0 \\
0 & 0 & 0 & 0 & \dfrac{\sqrt{2}}{2\cos\frac{1}{16}\pi} & 0 & 0 & 0 \\
0 & 0 & 0 & 0 & 0 & \dfrac{\sqrt{2}}{2\cos\frac{5}{16}\pi} & 0 & 0 \\
0 & 0 & 0 & 0 & 0 & 0 & \dfrac{\sqrt{2}}{2\cos\frac{3}{16}\pi} & 0 \\
0 & 0 & 0 & 0 & 0 & 0 & 0 & \dfrac{\sqrt{2}}{2\cos\frac{7}{16}\pi}
\end{bmatrix}
$$

$$
\times
\begin{bmatrix}
1 & 0 & 0 & 0 & 0 & 0 & 0 & 0 \\
0 & \dfrac{\sqrt{2}}{2\cos\frac{1}{16}\pi} & 0 & 0 & 0 & 0 & 0 & 0 \\
0 & 0 & \dfrac{\sqrt{2}}{2\cos\frac{2}{16}\pi} & 0 & 0 & 0 & 0 & 0 \\
0 & 0 & 0 & \dfrac{\sqrt{2}}{2\cos\frac{3}{16}\pi} & 0 & 0 & 0 & 0 \\
0 & 0 & 0 & 0 & 1 & 0 & 0 & 0 \\
0 & 0 & 0 & 0 & 0 & \dfrac{\sqrt{2}}{2\cos\frac{5}{16}\pi} & 0 & 0 \\
0 & 0 & 0 & 0 & 0 & 0 & \dfrac{\sqrt{2}}{2\cos\frac{6}{16}\pi} & 0 \\
0 & 0 & 0 & 0 & 0 & 0 & 0 & \dfrac{\sqrt{2}}{2\cos\frac{7}{16}\pi}
\end{bmatrix}
\times
\begin{bmatrix}
1 & 0 & 0 & 0 & 0 & 0 & 0 & 0 \\
0 & 0 & 0 & 0 & 1 & 0 & 0 & 0 \\
0 & 0 & 1 & 0 & 0 & 0 & 0 & 0 \\
0 & 0 & 0 & 0 & 0 & 0 & 1 & 0 \\
0 & 1 & 0 & 0 & 0 & 0 & 0 & 0 \\
0 & 0 & 0 & 0 & 0 & 1 & 0 & 0 \\
0 & 0 & 0 & 1 & 0 & 0 & 0 & 0 \\
0 & 0 & 0 & 0 & 0 & 0 & 0 & 1
\end{bmatrix}
$$

Equation 10.32

Since Equation 10.32 holds true, the matrix multiplication operation can be reordered so that the scaling is the first step when calculating the IDCT and the last step when calculating the FDCT.

Substituting Equation 10.32 into Equation 10.31 gives Equation 10.33.

The number of operations needed to calculate each row or column using the factorization in Equation 10.33 is shown in Table 10.2 (page 141).

$$
M =
\begin{bmatrix}
1 & 0 & 0 & 0 & 0 & 0 & 0 & 0 \\
0 & \dfrac{\sqrt{2}}{2\cos\frac{1}{16}\pi} & 0 & 0 & 0 & 0 & 0 & 0 \\
0 & 0 & \dfrac{\sqrt{2}}{2\cos\frac{2}{16}\pi} & 0 & 0 & 0 & 0 & 0 \\
0 & 0 & 0 & \dfrac{\sqrt{2}}{2\cos\frac{3}{16}\pi} & 0 & 0 & 0 & 0 \\
0 & 0 & 0 & 0 & 1 & 0 & 0 & 0 \\
0 & 0 & 0 & 0 & 0 & \dfrac{\sqrt{2}}{2\cos\frac{5}{16}\pi} & 0 & 0 \\
0 & 0 & 0 & 0 & 0 & 0 & \dfrac{\sqrt{2}}{2\cos\frac{6}{16}\pi} & 0 \\
0 & 0 & 0 & 0 & 0 & 0 & 0 & \dfrac{\sqrt{2}}{2\cos\frac{7}{16}\pi}
\end{bmatrix}
$$

$$
\times
\begin{bmatrix}
1 & 0 & 0 & 0 & 0 & 0 & 0 & 0 \\
0 & 0 & 0 & 0 & 1 & 0 & 0 & 0 \\
0 & 0 & 1 & 0 & 0 & 0 & 0 & 0 \\
0 & 0 & 0 & 0 & 0 & 0 & 1 & 0 \\
0 & 1 & 0 & 0 & 0 & 0 & 0 & 0 \\
0 & 0 & 0 & 0 & 0 & 1 & 0 & 0 \\
0 & 0 & 0 & 1 & 0 & 0 & 0 & 0 \\
0 & 0 & 0 & 0 & 0 & 0 & 0 & 1
\end{bmatrix}
\times
\begin{bmatrix}
1 & 0 & 0 & 0 & 0 & 0 & 0 & 0 \\
0 & 1 & 0 & 0 & 0 & 0 & 0 & 0 \\
0 & 0 & 1 & 1 & 0 & 0 & 0 & 0 \\
0 & 0 & -1 & 1 & 0 & 0 & 0 & 0 \\
0 & 0 & 0 & 0 & 1 & 0 & 0 & 1 \\
0 & 0 & 0 & 0 & 0 & 1 & 1 & 0 \\
0 & 0 & 0 & 0 & 0 & 1 & -1 & 0 \\
0 & 0 & 0 & 0 & -1 & 0 & 0 & 1
\end{bmatrix}
\times
\begin{bmatrix}
1 & 0 & 0 & 0 & 0 & 0 & 0 & 0 \\
0 & 1 & 0 & 0 & 0 & 0 & 0 & 0 \\
0 & 0 & 1 & 0 & 0 & 0 & 0 & 0 \\
0 & 0 & 0 & 1 & 0 & 0 & 0 & 0 \\
0 & 0 & 0 & 0 & \dfrac{1}{2\cos\frac{2}{16}\pi} & 0 & 0 & 0 \\
0 & 0 & 0 & 0 & 0 & -1 & 0 & 1 \\
0 & 0 & 0 & 0 & 0 & 0 & \dfrac{1}{2\cos\frac{6}{16}\pi} & 0 \\
0 & 0 & 0 & 0 & 0 & 1 & 0 & 1
\end{bmatrix}
$$

$$
\times
\begin{bmatrix}
1 & 0 & 0 & 0 & 0 & 0 & 0 & 0 \\
0 & 1 & 0 & 0 & 0 & 0 & 0 & 0 \\
0 & 0 & 1 & 0 & 0 & 0 & 0 & 0 \\
0 & 0 & 0 & 1 & 0 & 0 & 0 & 0 \\
0 & 0 & 0 & 0 & 1 & 0 & 1 & 0 \\
0 & 0 & 0 & 0 & 0 & 1 & 0 & 0 \\
0 & 0 & 0 & 0 & 1 & 0 & -1 & 0 \\
0 & 0 & 0 & 0 & 0 & 0 & 0 & -1
\end{bmatrix}
\times
\begin{bmatrix}
1 & 1 & 0 & 0 & 0 & 0 & 0 & 0 \\
1 & -1 & 0 & 0 & 0 & 0 & 0 & 0 \\
0 & 0 & \cos\frac{4}{16}\pi & 0 & 0 & 0 & 0 & 0 \\
0 & 0 & 0 & 1 & 0 & 0 & 0 & 0 \\
0 & 0 & 0 & 0 & \cos\frac{4}{16}\pi & 0 & 0 & 0 \\
0 & 0 & 0 & 0 & 0 & \cos\frac{4}{16}\pi & 0 & 0 \\
0 & 0 & 0 & 0 & 0 & 0 & 1 & 0 \\
0 & 0 & 0 & 0 & 0 & 0 & 0 & 1
\end{bmatrix}
\times
\begin{bmatrix}
1 & 0 & 0 & 0 & 0 & 0 & 0 & 0 \\
0 & 1 & 0 & 0 & 0 & 0 & 0 & 0 \\
0 & 0 & 1 & 0 & 0 & 0 & 0 & 0 \\
0 & 0 & 0 & 1 & 0 & 0 & 0 & 0 \\
0 & 0 & 0 & 0 & 1 & 0 & 1 & 0 \\
0 & 0 & 0 & 0 & 0 & 1 & 0 & 0 \\
0 & 0 & 0 & 0 & 0 & 0 & 1 & 0 \\
0 & 0 & 0 & 0 & 0 & 0 & 0 & 1
\end{bmatrix}
$$

$$
\times
\begin{bmatrix}
1 & 0 & 0 & 0 & 0 & 0 & 0 & 0 \\
0 & 1 & 0 & 0 & 0 & 0 & 0 & 0 \\
0 & 0 & 1 & 1 & 0 & 0 & 0 & 0 \\
0 & 0 & 0 & 1 & 0 & 0 & 0 & 0 \\
0 & 0 & 0 & 0 & 1 & 1 & 0 & 0 \\
0 & 0 & 0 & 0 & 0 & 1 & 1 & 0 \\
0 & 0 & 0 & 0 & 0 & 0 & 1 & 1 \\
0 & 0 & 0 & 0 & 0 & 0 & 0 & 1
\end{bmatrix}
\times
\begin{bmatrix}
1 & 0 & 0 & 1 & 0 & 0 & 0 & 0 \\
0 & 1 & 1 & 0 & 0 & 0 & 0 & 0 \\
0 & 1 & -1 & 0 & 0 & 0 & 0 & 0 \\
1 & 0 & 0 & -1 & 0 & 0 & 0 & 0 \\
0 & 0 & 0 & 0 & 1 & 0 & 0 & 0 \\
0 & 0 & 0 & 0 & 0 & 1 & 0 & 0 \\
0 & 0 & 0 & 0 & 0 & 0 & 1 & 0 \\
0 & 0 & 0 & 0 & 0 & 0 & 0 & 1
\end{bmatrix}
\times
\begin{bmatrix}
1 & 0 & 0 & 0 & 0 & 0 & 0 & 1 \\
0 & 1 & 0 & 0 & 0 & 0 & 1 & 0 \\
0 & 0 & 1 & 0 & 0 & 1 & 0 & 0 \\
0 & 0 & 0 & 1 & 1 & 0 & 0 & 0 \\
0 & 0 & 1 & 0 & 0 & -1 & 0 & 0 \\
0 & 1 & 0 & 0 & 0 & 0 & -1 & 0 \\
1 & 0 & 0 & 0 & 0 & 0 & 0 & -1
\end{bmatrix}
$$

Equation 10.33

The additional benefit in this factorization is that we can eliminate the six multiplication operations in the first matrix by merging them with the quantization or dequantization processes. Matrix multiplication is associative and matrix multiplication by a scalar is commutative. Therefore, if M is factored as shown in Equation 9.31, the matrix operations in the IDCT calculation (Equation 10.34) can be ordered so that these three operations take place first (Equation 10.35).

Equation 10.34

$$V = \tfrac{1}{8}M^T T M \qquad \text{IDCT}$$

$$T = \tfrac{1}{8}M V M^T \qquad \text{FDCT}$$

Equation 10.35

$$\tfrac{1}{8} \times \begin{bmatrix} 1 & 0 & 0 & 0 & 0 & 0 & 0 & 0 \\ 0 & \dfrac{\sqrt{2}}{2\cos\frac{1}{16}\pi} & 0 & 0 & 0 & 0 & 0 & 0 \\ 0 & 0 & \dfrac{\sqrt{2}}{2\cos\frac{2}{16}\pi} & 0 & 0 & 0 & 0 & 0 \\ 0 & 0 & 0 & \dfrac{\sqrt{2}}{2\cos\frac{3}{16}\pi} & 0 & 0 & 0 & 0 \\ 0 & 0 & 0 & 0 & 1 & 0 & 0 & 0 \\ 0 & 0 & 0 & 0 & 0 & \dfrac{\sqrt{2}}{2\cos\frac{5}{16}\pi} & 0 & 0 \\ 0 & 0 & 0 & 0 & 0 & 0 & \dfrac{\sqrt{2}}{2\cos\frac{6}{16}\pi} & 0 \\ 0 & 0 & 0 & 0 & 0 & 0 & 0 & \dfrac{\sqrt{2}}{2\cos\frac{7}{16}\pi} \end{bmatrix} \times T$$

$$\times \begin{bmatrix} 1 & 0 & 0 & 0 & 0 & 0 & 0 & 0 \\ 0 & \dfrac{\sqrt{2}}{2\cos\frac{1}{16}\pi} & 0 & 0 & 0 & 0 & 0 & 0 \\ 0 & 0 & \dfrac{\sqrt{2}}{2\cos\frac{2}{16}\pi} & 0 & 0 & 0 & 0 & 0 \\ 0 & 0 & 0 & \dfrac{\sqrt{2}}{2\cos\frac{3}{16}\pi} & 0 & 0 & 0 & 0 \\ 0 & 0 & 0 & 0 & 1 & 0 & 0 & 0 \\ 0 & 0 & 0 & 0 & 0 & \dfrac{\sqrt{2}}{2\cos\frac{5}{16}\pi} & 0 & 0 \\ 0 & 0 & 0 & 0 & 0 & 0 & \dfrac{\sqrt{2}}{2\cos\frac{6}{16}\pi} & 0 \\ 0 & 0 & 0 & 0 & 0 & 0 & 0 & \dfrac{\sqrt{2}}{2\cos\frac{7}{16}\pi} \end{bmatrix}$$

The effect of this expression is to multiply each element in the matrix V by the constant value S_{ij}, where

Equation 10.36

$$S_{ij} = \tfrac{1}{8}F(i)F(j)$$

$$F(0) = 1$$

$$F(n) = \frac{\sqrt{2}}{2\cos\frac{n}{16}\pi}, \; n = 1, 2, 3, 4, 5, 6, 7$$

In JPEG decoding, the IDCT is immediately preceded by dequantization which multiplies each of the elements in T by a constant value. If we merge the IDCT and dequantization processes by scaling each quantization value by S_{ij}, then the steps in Equation 10.35 can be eliminated. In the FDCT the operations in Equation 10.35 become the final step before quantization. If each element in the quantization table used for encoding is divided by S_{ij}, then these operations can be eliminated from the DCT as well. This leaves 29 addition operations and 5 multiplication operations per data unit.

Conclusion

In this chapter you have seen how matrix factorization can be used to dramatically reduce the number of operations required to implement the DCT and IDCT. Efficiency is a product of design; not a result of coding. Before cluttering up your code with performance enhancements, be sure to do measurements to ensure that the performance benefit, if any, is worth the lack of clarity.

The code examples for this chapter are new implementations of the JpegEncoderDataUnit, JpegDecoderDataUnit, JpegEncoderQuantizationTable, and JpegDecoderQuantizationTable classes that were originally presented in Chapter 7. The new classes merge the DCT and IDCT with quantization using the process described in this chapter.

These new classes are structured so that they can replace the previous versions in the JpegDecoder (Chapter 8) and JpegEncoder (Chapter 9) classes with few modifications. JpegDecoder needs no modifications to use the new classes. JpegEncoder needs to add a call to the BuildScaledTables member function of the quantization table class before performing the DCT.

Chapter 11

Progressive JPEG

This chapter covers the encoding and decoding of progressive JPEG images, which, while infrequently used, are becoming more common. One driving force behind the use of progressive JPEG is the World Wide Web, an ideal use for progressive JPEG images. Using progressive images in Web pages makes it possible for users to get a good idea of the contents of a Web page before the images are completely downloaded. The other major force behind progressive JPEG is the increasing availability of software and libraries (notably the IJG's library) that support it.

Component Division in Progressive JPEG

A sequential JPEG file may contain a single scan, or the data may be organized into multiple scans, each containing one or more components. However, in sequential JPEG, each component is completely encoded within one scan. In progressive JPEG, components are encoded across multiple scans. Each component is contained in at least two scans and possibly in as many as 896.[1]

Components are divided across scans in two distinct ways. One of these is known as spectral selection. *Spectral selection* refers to the division of the component into bands of DCT coefficients. Each band is a continuous range of DCT coefficients using the zigzag order. The only restriction on the coefficients in a band, other than that the band must contain a continuous range, is that the DC component must be in a band by itself. At a minimum, a component will be divided into two scans: one containing the DC coefficient and the other the AC

---

[1] In practice the number of scans is never anywhere near the high end of this range.

coefficients. At the most extreme the component can be divided into 64 bands with one coefficient in each.

The first scan for a component must contain the DC coefficients. The bands containing the AC coefficients may be encoded in any order. Progressive scans containing the DC coefficient may be interleaved while scans containing AC coefficients must be noninterleaved. Figure 11.1 shows an example of a data unit divided into four bands.

The other component division in progressive scans is known as *successive approximation,* which is used in conjunction with spectral selection to divide individual bands into a number of scans. Unlike spectral selection, successive approximation in a progressive image is completely optional. When it is used, the precision of the initial band is reduced by a number of bits. Subsequent scans for the band increase the precision one bit at a time.

The conversion function used with successive approximation is called the *point transform* in the JPEG standard. For DC coefficients the point transform is simply a right shift by the number of bits specified by the successive approximation value. For AC coefficients the point transform is

$$Output = \frac{Input}{2^{Successive\ Approximation}}$$

At first glance it may appear that the AC and DC point transforms are the same, but this is not the case. Table 11.1 shows the AC and DC point transforms with a successive approximation value of 1. Notice that the AC and DC point

Figure 11.1
Example of a Data Unit Divided into Spectral Selection Bands

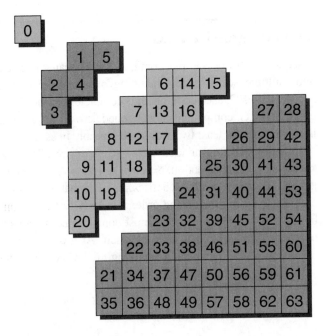

Table 11.1	Input	DC	AC
DC and AC Values	5	2	2
with a Successive	4	2	2
Approximation	3	1	1
Value of 1	2	1	1
	1	0	0
	0	0	0
	−1	−1	0
	−2	−1	−1
	−3	−2	−1
	−4	−2	−2
	−5	−3	−2

Figure 11.2
Sample Scan
Division by Spectral
Selection and
Successive
Approximation

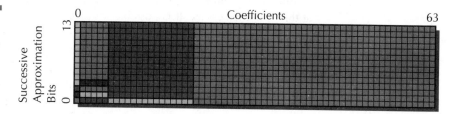

transform values may be different for negative values and, for the AC point transform, $F(X) = -F(-X)$.

Figure 11.2 is an example of a component divided into 12 scans using a combination of spectral selection and successive approximation. The spectral selection division is the same as that shown in Figure 11.1. The first scan in this example contains the DC coefficient with a successive approximation of 3. The
remaining three spectral selection bands can be output in any order. However,
within each band, the scans that refine coefficients using successive approximation must be in strict order.

Processing Progressive JPEG Files

The overall processing of Progressive JPEG files can be implemented in the
same manner that is commonly used for sequential files. The major difference is
in the processing of the scans. Figure 11.3 illustrates the difference between the
processing of sequential files and progressive files.

It should be apparent that displaying progressive JPEG files on the fly
requires significantly more processing than displaying sequential files or even
displaying progressive files only after they have been completely decoded. This
is why displaying progressive JPEG files on the fly only makes sense if the data

Figure 11.3
Sequential and
Progressive JPEG
Processing

Sequential Process

```
While MORESCANS Do
  Begin
  ReadScanData
  End
PerformIDCT
ColorConvert
DisplayImage
```

Progressive Process

```
While MORESCANS Do
  Begin
  ReadScanData
  PerformIDCT
  ColorConvert
  DisplayImage
  End
```

is being received over a network at a relatively slow rate compared to the speed of the processor.

Figure 11.3 shows progressive JPEG images being updated after every scan but this is not necessary. It is possible for a decoder to be implemented so that it updates and displays the image only when the decoder determines that it has received enough new data for updating. When displaying the image on the fly, the process for updating is the same as for a sequential file. If a progressive image is not displayed on the fly, the overall decoding process is basically the same as for sequential JPEG and there is little difference in the amount of processing required.

Processing Progressive Scans

The first step in decoding a progressive scan is to determine which of these types the scan is. There are four types of progressive scans and each is processed in a different manner.

	DC	AC
First scan for a band	1. First DC scan	3. First AC scan
Refining scan for a band	2. Refining DC scan	4. Refining AC scan

All of the information needed to determine the scan type is stored in the SOS marker,[2] where the spectral selection start and end fields specify the coefficients in the band. If both of these values are zero, the scan is a DC scan. If both values are nonzero, then it is an AC scan.

The successive approximation value is stored in two 4-bit fields packed into 1 byte. If the 4 high-order bits are zero, the scan is the first scan for the band. Otherwise, when this field is nonzero it is a refining scan. If both of these bit fields are zero, then successive approximation is not used for the band.

---

[2]See Chapter 5.

The processing of the first scan for a band is identical whether or not successive approximation is used.

The validations on these fields that decoders should perform include the following:

- If the spectral selection start is zero, the spectral selection end must be zero.
- If the spectral selection end is zero, the spectral selection start must be zero.
- The spectral selection start must not be greater than the spectral selection end.
- If the spectral selection start is not zero, the scan may contain only one component.
- The spectral selection end may not be greater than 63.
- The low-order and high-order successive approximation bit fields may not be greater than 13.
- The high-order successive approximation bits must be either zero or one greater than the low-order bits.

MCUs in Progressive Scans

Data in progressive scans is organized into MCUs in exactly the same manner as in sequential scans. DC progressive scans can be interleaved or noninterleaved. AC scans are always noninterleaved so there will always be one data unit per MCU. For progressive scans containing AC data, the number and position of the data units are the same as for a noninterleaved sequential scan.

Progressive scans may include restart markers. The restart interval specifies the number of MCUs between restart markers just as in sequential scans. In DC scans, restart marker processing is the same as in sequential scans. For AC scans, the end-of-band runs may not cross restart markers. *End-of-band* runs will be explained shortly.

Huffman Table Usage In Progressive Scans

The SOS marker specifies the numeric identifier of the Huffman tables used by each component in the scan. The JPEG standard requires that all of the Huffman tables required by a scan be defined before the SOS marker. When a decoder is handling progressive scans it must validate the existence of the Huffman tables used by the scan differently from the way it does with a sequential scan.

Each component in a sequential scan requires two Huffman tables (DC and AC). In progressive JPEG a scan will use either DC tables or AC tables, but not both. In fact, a refining progressive DC scan does not use Huffman tables at all. It is entirely possible for a progressive DC scan to occur in a JPEG file before any AC Huffman tables have been defined, something that is illegal in sequential JPEG.

Data Unit Decoding

First DC Scans

The process for decoding the first scan for DC coefficients is nearly identical to that for DC coefficients in a sequential scan (see Chapter 8). The only difference is that the point transform is applied to the decoded DC value (left-shifted by the successive approximation value) before being stored as a coefficient value. Algorithm 11.1 illustrates the decoding of a data unit.

Algorithm 11.1
Decoding
Progressive DC
Coefficients

```
GLOBAL SUCCESSIVEAPPROXIMATION
GLOBAL LAST_DC_VALUE

Procedure FirstDCDataunit (COEFFICIENTS [0..63])
    Begin
    BITCOUNT = DecodeUsingDCHuffmanTable ()
    BITS = ReadLiteralBits (BITCOUNT)
    DCDIFFERENCE = Extent (BITS, BITCOUNT)
    DCVALUE = DCDIFFERENCE + LAST_DC_VALUE
    LAST_DC_VALUE = DCVALUE
    COEFFICIENTS [II] = DCVALUE LeftShift SUCCESSIVEAPPROXIMATION
    End
```

Refining DC Scans

Refining DC scans are the simplest of all JPEG scans to handle. The scan's compressed data consists entirely of raw data bits, one bit per data unit. Algorithm 11.2 shows all the processing required to process a data unit in this type of scan.

Algorithm 11.2
Refining DC
Coefficients

```
GLOBAL SUCCESSIVEAPPROXIMATION

Procedure RefineDCDataUnit (COEFFICIENTS [0..63])
    Begin
    BIT = ReadLiteralBits (1)
    DCCOEFFICIENTS [0] = DCCOEFFICIENTS [0]
                    Or (BIT LeftShift SUCCESSIVEAPPROXIMATION)
    End
```

First AC Scans

The simplicity of decoding DC coefficients is more than compensated for by the complexity of decoding AC coefficients. For the first scan of an AC band the encoding is similar to sequential with some additions.

Progressive JPEG adds the concept of an *end-of-band* (EOB) run. This is a run of data units where the AC coefficients within the band are all zero. In sequential JPEG each data unit is encoded independently from every other. Because of EOB runs, data units are not independent in AC scans.

In sequential JPEG the Huffman-encoded value 00_{16} is used to set the remaining coefficients in a data unit to zero. This is equivalent to an EOB run of 1. Progressive scans can contain much longer EOB runs. Table 11.2 lists the EOB codes and the possible EOB run lengths associated with them.

Raw bits following the Huffman-encoded byte are used to specify EOB runs just as they are with literal values. The 4 high-order bits specify the number of additional bits when used as part of an EOB code. Since EOB runs are always positive, the Extend() function is not used. Instead, the conversion from raw bits to the EOB run length is

EOBRUN = (1 LeftShift HIGHBITS) + ReadRawBits (HIGHBITS)

If an EOB code occurs in the compressed stream when a band has been partially processed, the current band becomes the first data unit in the EOB run and the remaining coefficients are set to zero. Be sure to count the current band when processing an EOB run.

Table 11.2
AC Codes and Corresponding EOB Run Length

Code Value	EOB Run Length
00_{16}	1
10_{16}	2–3
20_{16}	4–7
30_{16}	8–15
40_{16}	16–31
50_{16}	32–63
60_{16}	64–127
70_{16}	128–127
80_{16}	256–511
90_{16}	512–1023
$A0_{16}$	1,024–2047
$B0_{16}$	2,048–4095
$C0_{16}$	4,096–8191
$D0_{16}$	8,192–16,383
$E0_{16}$	16,384–32,767

Algorithm 11.3 shows how the first scan for an AC band is decoded. The main differences between sequential and progressive processing are:

- Only coefficients within the spectral selection band are updated.
- Coefficient values are left-shifted by the successive approximation value.
- EOB run processing

Refining AC Scans

Refining AC scans is the nightmare of progressive JPEG decoding. The implementation problem is that these scans contain data to refine all previously nonzero coefficients that are skipped as a result of a zero run or EOB run.

In a refining AC scan, the 4 low-order bits of the Huffman-encoded values can be only 1 or zero. This should make sense since a refining scan only adds 1 bit per coefficient. If a coefficient needed more than 1 bit it would have been encoded in earlier scans.

The processing of refining AC scans is nearly identical to that of initial scans. Whenever the value of the 4 low-order bits of the Huffman-encoded value is 1, a coefficient is being made nonzero for the first time. This value is immediately followed in the input stream by 1 raw sign bit. The new coefficient value is

```
If SignBit = 1 Then
    CoefficientValue = 1 LeftShift ScanSuccessiveApproximation
Else If SignBit = 0 Then
    CoefficientValue = -1 LeftShift ScanSuccessiveApproximation
```

This is essentially the same as using the Extend function.

The major difference in refining scans is the processing of zero and EOB runs. Zero runs in a refining scan only count zero-valued coefficients. This sequence of coefficients would be skipped by a zero run of 4 (not 6):

```
0 0 4 0 2 0
```

Whenever a nonzero coefficient is skipped, as a result of a zero or EOB run, the input stream contains 1 raw bit to refine that coefficient.

In our previous example, suppose that the Huffman-encoded value were 41_{16}. Three raw bits would follow this code: The first bit would be the sign bit for the coefficient being made nonzero; the next bit would refine the coefficient with the value 4, and the last would refine the coefficient with the value 2.

Algorithm 11.4 shows the process for refining a previously nonzero coefficient.

Once the correct number of zero-valued coefficients has been skipped, the next coefficient is assigned the value found at the start of the procedure. Notice that the data for coefficients is not stored strictly in order. The data for the last coefficient comes first in the input stream.

```
Global EOBRUN
Global SSS // Spectral Selection Start
Global SSE // Spectral Selection End
Global SUCCESSIVEAPPROXIMATION
Global EOBRUN

Procedure ACFirstDataUnit (COEFFICIENTS [0..63])
    Begin

    For II = SSS To SSE Do
        COEFFICIENTS [II] = 0

    If EOBRUN > 0 Then
        Begin
        EOBRUN = EOBRUN - 1
        Return
        End

    II = SSS
    While II <= SSE Do
        Begin
        VALUE = DecodeUsingACTable
        LOBITS = VALUE And 0F16
        HIBITS = (VALUE And F016) RightShift 4

        If LOBITS <> 0 Then
            Begin
            EXTRABITS = ReadRawBits (LOBITS)
            II = II + HIGHBITS
            COEFFICIENTS [II]
                = Extend (EXTRABITS, LOBITS) LeftShift SUCCESSIVEAPPROXIMATION
            II = II + 1
            End
        Else
            Begin
            If HIGHBITS = F16 Then
                II = II + 16 // Run of 16 Zeros
            Else If HIGHBITS = 0 Then
                II = SSE + 1
            Else
                // We subtract one to account for ending the current block.
                EOBRUN = (1 LeftShift HIGHBITS) + ReadRawBits (HIGHBITS) - 1
            Return
            End
        End
    End
```

Algorithm 11.3
Decoding
Progressive AC
Coefficients

Algorithm 11.4
Refining AC
Coefficient Values

```
Procedure RefineAC (COEFFICIENT)
    Begin
    If COEFFICIENT > 0 Then
        Begin
        If ReadRawBits (1) <> 0 Then
            Begin
            COEFFICIENT = COEFFICIENT
                        + (1 LeftShift SUCCESSIVEAPPROXIMATION)
            End
        End
    Else if COEFFICIENT < 0 Then
        Begin
        If ReadRawBits (1) <> 0 Then
            Begin
            COEFFICIENT = COEFFICIENT
                        + (-1 LeftShift SUCCESSIVEAPPROXIMATION)
        End
    End
End
```

If the 4 low-order bits of the Huffman-encoded byte are zero, the code does not create any new nonzero coefficients. However, the process of updating existing nonzero coefficients still takes place. When the value of the Huffman-encoded byte is $F0_{16}$ the next 16 zero-valued coefficients are skipped but all intervening nonzero-valued coefficients are updated using the previous procedure.

As with initial scans, the code values 00_{16}, 10_{16}, ... $E0_{16}$ instruct the decoder to skip to the end of a number of bands. The 4 high-order bits specify the number of additional bits to read and the EOB count is calculated in the same way as before. All nonzero-valued coefficients that are skipped as a result of an EOB skip are refined using raw bits.

An important thing to remember when skipping zero-valued coefficients is that the decoder should end up either at the end of a band or on a zero valued coefficient.

Suppose a band contained 20 coefficients with these values

```
0 0 0 0 0 8 0 0 0 8 0 8 0 0 0 0 0 0 8 8
↑
```

at the start of a scan. If the first byte decoded for this band were the value 81_{16}, this would instruct the decoder to skip 8 zero-values. After skipping 5 coefficients the decoder would read 1 raw bit to refine the first value of 8.

```
      Refined
        ↓
0 0 0 0 0 8 0 0 0 8 0 8 0 0 0 0 0 0 8 8
              ↑
```

The decoder would skip the next 3 zero-valued coefficients (for a total of 8), at which point it would be positioned here.

0 0 0 0 0 8 0 0 0 8 0 8 0 0 0 0 0 0 8 8
$\uparrow$

Since this coefficient is already nonzero, all we can do is refine it. The decoder should advance to the next zero-valued coefficient while refining the nonzero coefficients it skips.

Refined   New Coefficient
＼ ↓

0 0 0 0 0 8 0 0 0 8 4 8 0 0 0 0 0 0 8 8
$\uparrow$

Algorithm 11.5 illustrates the process for refining AC coefficients in a progressive scan.

Algorithm 11.5
Refining AC
Progressive AC
Coefficients

```
Global SSS // Spectral Selection Start
Global SSE // Spectral Selection End
Global SUCCESSIVEAPPROXIMATION
Global EOBRUN

Procedure ACRefineDataUnit (COEFFICIENTS [0..63])
  Begin
  II = SSS
  While II <= SSE Do
    Begin
    If EOBRUN > 0 Then
      Begin
      While II <= SSE Do
        Begin
        If COEFFICIENT [II] <> 0 Then
          RefineAC (COEFFICIENT (II)
        II = II + 1
        End
      EOBRUN = EOBRUN - 1
      Return
      End
    VALUE = DecodeUsingACTable
    LOBITS = VALUE AND 0F₁₆
    HIBITS = (VALUE AND F0₁₆) RightShift 4

    If LOBITS = 1 Then
      Begin
      EXTRABIT = ReadRawBits (1)
      While HIGHBITS > 0 OR COEFFICIENTS [II] <> 0 Do
        Begin
        If COEFFICIENTS [II] <> 0 Then
          RefineAC (COEFFICIENTS [II])
```

(continued)

Algorithm 11.5
Continued

```
            Else
              HIGHBITS = HIGHBITS - 1
          II = II + 1
          End
      If EXTRABIT <> 0
          COEFFICIENTS [II] = 1 LeftShift SUCCESSIVEAPPROXIMATION
      Else
          COEFFICIENTS [II] = -1 LeftShift SUCCESSIVEAPPROXIMATION
      II = II + 1
      End
    Else If LOBITS = 0 Then
      Begin
      If HIGHBITS = F16 Then // Run of 16 Zeros
        Begin
        While HIGHBITS >= 0 Do
          Begin
          If COEFFICIENTS [II] <> 0 Then
            RefineAC (COEFFICENTS [II])
          Else
            HIGHBITS = HIGHBITS - 1
          End
        End
      Else If HIGHBITS = 0 Then
        EOBRUN = 1
      Else
        EOBRUN = (1 LeftShift HIGHBITS) + ReadRawBits (HIGHBITS)
      End
    End
End
```

Preparing to Create Progressive JPEG Files

The biggest issue in implementing a progressive JPEG encoder is figuring out how to specify what goes into each scan. For each scan, the encoder needs to identify:

- The components to include (multiple components in DC bands only)

- The spectral range

- The successive approximation

Requiring the user to specify all the parameters for each scan would be tedious and error prone. A possible approach would be to predefine a set of scan sequences that the user could select from. A method that we have found works well is to define a default scan sequence for progressive scans and allow the user to make modifications if desired. For each scan, the user can assign the components, the last value in the spectral range, and the initial successive approximation value. At the start of the encoding process, the spectral range of the earlier scans is used to determine the initial spectral range of later scans. If the user has defined the scans for a component with the last values in the spectral range set to

    0 5 20 63

then the encoder automatically assigns these ranges

    0-0 1-5 6-20 21-63

as the spectral bands for the scan.

The encoder processes the scans in the order defined by the user. If spectral selection is specified for any of the scans, the decoder repeats the scan list and reduces the spectral selection by 1. It then outputs all the scans that contain spectral bands that still have to be refined. This process is intermediate in complexity. It gives the user many options for outputting progressive scans, but it does not allow the user to have complete control over scan content and ordering.

An encoder should not be overzealous when it comes to breaking image data into scans. Each scan in a progressive image should contribute meaningful data to it. Since the last AC coefficient is almost always zero, creating scans with a spectral range of 63 to 63 or even 61 to 63 is not very useful. The deeper into the zigzag order you go, the more coefficients should be included in a scan. As a general guideline, the larger the quantization values, the larger the number of coefficients per band.

Successive approximation has even greater potential for abuse. Using spectral selection, a band can be divided into up to 14 bands, where the last 13 scans contribute 1 bit to each coefficient in the band. With 8-bit sample data, DC coefficients require no more than 11 bits to encode (for 12-bit samples this number is 15). Using a successive approximation value of 13 to encode 8-bit data makes no sense since many scans will contribute no data to the image.

Because the magnitude of AC coefficients is generally much smaller than that of DC coefficients, using successive approximation to divide AC coefficients into a large number of scans makes even less sense. Reasonable successive approximation values are determined by the magnitude of the quantization values and how far the band is into the zigzag order.

If the encoder allows the user to specify the contents of the scans, it needs to perform several validations to ensure that the output file will contain a valid JPEG image. In addition to the sequential validations, a progressive encoder should ensure that:

- The scans contain the entire spectral range for each component.

- The spectral bands for a component do not overlap.

- Spectral bands containing the DC coefficient do not contain any AC coefficients.

- The sucessive approximation value is in the range 0–13.

Encoding Progressive Scans

Encoding a progressive JPEG image is very similar to encoding a sequential image using multiple scans. As with progressive decoding, the significant differences are in the encoding of data units.

As you saw earlier in this chapter, there are four distinct types of scans within a progressive JPEG file. The JPEG encoder in Chapter 9 used `InterleavedPass()` and `Noninterleaved()` to drive the creation of scans. These functions handled division of the image into MCUs and the processing of restart markers. They were implemented so that they took pointers to member functions to do the actual data unit encoding. This may have looked odd with sequential images, but this same function is used to control progressive DC scans once integrated with progressive JPEG code, thus allowing the same code to drive a total of three types of scans.

Huffman Coding

Progressive images may have up to four DC and four AC Huffman tables defined at any time. The progressive JPEG source code at the end of this chapter only uses a maximum of two of each type, just like the baseline sequential code presented earlier. As before, two passes are made to encode each scan: the first is used to gather Huffman frequency statistics, and the second is used to encode and output the data. The same driver code is used for each pass, with pointers to functions controlling which of these two operations is performed for a given pass.

Data Unit Encoding

DC First Scans

With the exception of applying the point transform to the coefficient value, the encoding of DC coefficients in the first scan of a band is identical to the encoding of DC coefficients in a sequential scan. DC coefficients are encoded as the difference between the current coefficient and the value of the last encoded value for the same component. The difference is encoded as a Huffman-encoded magnitude value followed by a number of literal bits.

For simplicity, the example below shows only one last-DC-value variable. An actual implementation requires a separate variable for each component. Just as with sequential JPEG, the last DC coefficient value for each component should be set to zero at the start of the scan and whenever a restart marker is processed.

Algorithm 11.6 illustrates the process for encoding a data unit in a first DC scan.

Algorithm 11.6
Encoding DC
Coefficients in
Initial Scans

```
Global SUCCESSIVEAPPROXIMATION
Global LAST_DC_VALUE

Function CountBits (VALUE)
    Begin
    COUNT = 0
    While VALUE <> 0 Do
        Begin
        COUNT = COUNT + 1
        VALUE = VALUE RightShift 1
        End
    End

Procedure EncodeDCFirst (COEFFICIENTS [0..63])
    Begin
    // Point Transform
    VALUE = COEFFICIENTS [0] RightShift SUCCESSIVEAPPROXIMATION
    DIFFERENCE = VALUE - LAST_DC_VALUE
    LAST_DC_VALUE = DIFFERENCE
    If DIFFERENCE >= 0 Then
        Begin
        BITCOUNT = CountBits (DIFFERENCE)
        HuffmanEncode (BITCOUNT)
        OuputLiteralBits (BITCOUNT, DIFFERENCE)
        End
    Else
        Begin
        BITCOUNT = CountBits (-DIFFERENCE)
        HuffmanEncodeDC (BITCOUNT)
        OuputLiteralBits (BITCOUNT, DIFFERENCE Xor FFFFFFFF₁₆)
        End
    End
```

Refining DC Scans

Encoding refining DC coefficients for a data unit is trivial as shown in Algorithm 11.7. A scan contains a single bit for refining a DC coefficient. No Huffman coding is required.

Algorithm 11.7
Encoding DC
Coefficients in
Refining Scans

```
Global SUCCESSIVEAPPROXIMATION

Procedure EncodeDCRefine (COEFFICIENTS [0..63])
    Begin
    VALUE = (COEFFICIENTS [0] RightShift SUCCESSIVEAPPROXIMATION) And 1
    OutputLiteralBits (1, VALUE)
    End
```

AC First Scans

AC coefficients are encoded using a sequence of Huffman-encoded bytes followed by a string of literal bits. The Huffman-encoded byte is divided into two 4-bit fields. If the 4 low-order bits are not zero, the code represents a nonzero literal coefficient. The low-order bits are the magnitude of the code and specify the number of literal bits that follow. The 4 high-order bits specify the number of zero-valued coefficients to skip before writing the nonzero coefficient.

The byte code $F0_{16}$ means that the next 16 coefficient values are zero. Any other value with the 4 low-order bits set to zero represents the magnitude of a run of bands that are all zero (see Table 11.2). The 4 high-order bits specify the number of raw bits written to the output stream used to specify the exact EOB run length.

An encoder processes a data unit by starting at the first coefficient in the band and working to the last coefficient, proceeding in zigzag order. Only nonzero coefficients are processed in AC encoding. The encoder needs to maintain a count of the number of consecutive zero-valued coefficients within the data unit and a count of blocks where all the coefficients are zero.

Algorithm 11.8 illustrates how to encode a data unit in a progressive AC first scan. The EncodeACRefine procedure calls the PrintEOBRun procedure to output any outstanding EOB runs right before encoding a literal coefficient. What is not shown in this example is that PrintEOBRun must be called whenever a restart marker is output. EOB runs may not cross restart markers. PrintEOBRun must also be called at the end of the data unit encoding to ensure that all EOB runs have been flushed to the output stream.

Algorithm 11.8
Encoding AC Initial
AC Scans

```
Global SUCCESSIVEAPPROXIMATION
Global SSS
Global SSE
Global EOBRUN

Procedure PrintEOBRun
    Begin
    If EOBRUN = 0 Then
        Return
    BITCOUNT = CountBits (EOBRUN RightShift 1)
    HuffmanEncodeAC (BITCOUNT LeftShift 4)
    OutputLiteralBits (BITCOUNT, EOBRUN)
    End

Procedure EncodeACFirst (COEFFICIENTS [0..63])
    Begin
    ZERORUN = 0 // Number of sequential zero coefficients
```

(continued)

```
For II = SSS To SSE)
    Begin
    // Point Transform
    VALUE = COEFFICIENTS [II] / (1 LeftShift SUCCESSIVEAPPROXIMATION)
    If Value = 0 Then
        ZERORUN = ZERORUN + 1
    Else
        Begin
        // We have literal value so any EOB run started with a
        // previous block is over as well as a zero run within
        // this block.
        PrintEOBRun
        // The longest zero run we can put out with a literal
        // is 15. If we have a longer run then we need to
        // output the code for 16 zeros before we write
        // the literal
        While ZERORUN >= 16 Do
            Begin
            HuffmanEncodeAC (F016)
            ZERORUN = ZERORUN - 16
            End
        If VALUE > 0 Then
            Begin
            BITCOUNT = CountBits (VALUE)
            HuffmanEncodeAC ((ZERORUN LeftShift 4) Or BITCOUNT)
            OutputLiteralBits (BITCOUNT, VALUE)
            End
        Else
            Begin
            BITCOUNT = CountBits (-VALUE)
            HuffmanEncodeAC ((ZERORUN LeftShift 4) Or BITCOUNT)
            OutputLiteralBits (BITCOUNT, VALUE Xor FFFFFFFF₁₆)
            End
        ZERORUN = 0
        End
    End

// If the band ended in a run of zero then convert them
// into an EOB run.
If ZERORUN <> 0 Then
    Begin
    EOBRUN = EOBRUN + 1
    // Make sure we do not exceed the maximum EOB run.
    If EOBRUN = 7FFF₁₆ Then
        PrintEOBRun
    End
End
```

Algorithm 11.8
Continued

Refining AC Scans

Refining AC scans is one of the most complex processes in JPEG encoding. The encoding process for refining AC scans follows the basic pattern used by the first scan for a band. An important issue with refining scans is that Huffman-encoded value/literal bits sequences are used only to encode coefficients that the current scan will make nonzero for the first time. Coefficients that were made nonzero in a previous scan are not included in zero runs. Instead, any code that causes zero values to be skipped is followed by a refining bit for each of the intervening nonzero values.

Algorithm 11.9 illustrates the process for encoding refining AC scans. The `RefineBand` procedure contains most of the logic specific to refining scans. It outputs a refining bit for each nonzero code that is skipped.

The codes used to encode the scans are identical to those used with the first AC scan for a band. The only difference in the encoded data is that Huffman-encoded value/literal bits pairs are followed by a series of bits that refine each coefficient value skipped. If a zero or EOB run causes the coefficients from M to N to be skipped, `RefineBand (M,N)` outputs the refining bits.

The `RefineEOBRun` procedure for refining scans is slightly different than that for first scans because it has to refine all of the nonzero coefficients that are skipped. The skipping of coefficients because of EOB runs requires additional global data. The example uses the variables RUNSTARTDATAUNIT and RUNSTARTCOEFFICIENT to mark the data unit and coefficient where the EOB run began. (An EOB run can start in the middle of a data unit)

The encoding of data units is also more complicated. Since the zero run is the count of zero-valued coefficients, not the number of coefficients skipped in the zero run, the code for processing zero runs of greater than 16 is a bit more complicated as well.

```
Global DATAUNITS [0..*][0..63]
Global CURRENTDATAUNIT // Index of the current data unit in DATAUNITS
Global EOBRUN
Global RUNSTARTDATAUNIT
Global RUNSTARTCOEFFICIENT
Global SSS        // Spectral Selection Start
Global SSE        // Spectral Selection End
Global SUCCESSIVEAPPROXIMATION
```

(continued)

Algorithm 11.9
Encoding Refining
AC Scans

```
Procedure RefineBand (COEFFICIENTS [0..63], START, END)
    Begin
    For II = START To END
        Begin
        VALUE = COEFFICIENTS [II] / (1 LeftShift SUCCESSIVEAPPROXIMATION)
        If VALUE <> 0 Then
            Begin
            If VALUE < 0 Then
                VALUE = - VALUE
            OutputLiteralBits (1, VALUE And 1)
            End
        End
    End

Procedure PrintEOBRun
    Begin
    If EOBRUN = 0 Then
        Return
    BITCOUNT = CountBits (EOBRUN RightShift 1)
    HuffmanEncodeAC (BITCOUT LeftShift 4)
    OutputLiteralBits (BITCOUNT, EOBRUN)

    For II = 1 To EOBRUN DO
        Begin
        RefineBand (DATAUNITS [RUNSTARTDATAUNIT + II - 1],
                    RUNSTARTCOEFFICIENT, SSE)
        RUNSTARTCOEFFICIENT = SSS
        End
    EOBRUN = 0
    End

Procedure EncodeACRefine (COEFFICIENTS [0..63])
    Begin
    ZERORUN = 0
    For II = SSS To SSE DO
        Begin
        VALUE = COEFFICIENTS [II] / (1 LeftShift SUCCESSIVEAPPROXIMATION)
        If VALUE = 0 Then
            Begin
            If ZERORUN = 0 Then
                ZEROSTART = II
            ZERORUN = ZERORUN + 1
            End
        Else If Value = 1 Or Value = -1 Then
            Begin
            PrintEOBRun
```

(continued

Algorithm 11.9
Continued

```
        While ZERORUN >= 16 Do
            Begin
            ZEROLIMIT = ZEROSTART
            ZEROCOUNT = 0
            While ZEROCOUNT < 16 Do
                Begin
                OLDVALUE = COEFFICIENTS [ZEROLIMIT]
                        / (1 LeftShift SUCCESSIVEAPPROXIMATION)
                If OLDVALUE = 0 Then
                    ZEROCOUNT = ZEROCOUNT + 1
                ZEROLIMIT = ZEROLIMIT + 1
                End
            HuffmanEncodeAC (F0₁₆)
            RefineBand (COEFFICIENTS, ZEROSTART, ZEROLIMIT - 1)
            ZEROSTART = ZEROLIMIT
            ZERORUN = ZERORUN - 16
            End
        If VALUE > 0 Then
            Begin
            BITCOUNT = CountBits (VALUE)
            HuffmanEncodeAC ((ZERORUN LEFTSHIFT 4) Or BITCOUNT)
            OutputLiteralBits (BITCOUNT, VALUE)
            End
        Else
            Begin
            BITCOUNT = CountBits (-VALUE)
            HuffmanEncodeAC ((ZERORUN LEFTSHIFT 4) Or BITCOUNT)
            OutputLiteralBits (BITCOUNT, VALUE Xor FFFFFFFF₁₆)
            End
        RefineBand (COEFFICIENTS, ZEROSTART, II - 1)
        ZERORUN = 0
        End
    End

If ZERORUN <> 0 Then
    Begin
    If EOBRUN = 0 Then
        Begin
        RUNSTARTDATAUNIT = CURRENTDATAUNIT
        RUNSTARTCOEFFICIENT = ZEROSTART
        End
    EOBRUN = EOBRUN + 1
    If EOBRUN = 7FFF₁₆ Then
        PrintEOBRun
    End
End
```

Algorithm 11.9
Continued

Conclusion

This chapter on progressive mode brings to a close our coverage of JPEG. In this and preceding chapters, we have discussed all of the JPEG features that are in common use. The material presented covers all of the JPEG modes that you are likely to encounter in JPEG files on the Internet.

The source code for this chapter is not a complete example, but rather the additional code required to expand the sample applications from Chapters 8 and 9 to include progressive encoding and decoding.

Chapter 12

GIF

Format: GIF
Origin: Compuserve
Definition: Graphics Interchange Format
            Specification Version 89a

This chapter describes the Compuserve GIF format and the LZW compression method used to compress image data in this format. Until recently, Compuserve GIF (Graphics Interchange Format) was the most widely used format for image storage.

In 1987 Compuserve published the first GIF specification called GIF87a. This specification was freely distributed, and the format was adopted by practically every image processing application. Compuserve later released an enhanced, upwardly compatible version of the standard known as GIF89a. However, most GIF images use only the features in GIF87a.

The main features of GIF are:

- Up to 256 colors using 1 to 8 bits per pixel
- Multiple images per file

Because of its better compression and greater color depth, JPEG has generally replaced GIF for photographic images. GIF continues to be used for other applications, but legal entanglements have certainly condemned it to obsolescence.

Byte Ordering

The GIF format stores multi-byte integers with the least significant byte first (little-endian). Bit strings are read from the least significant bit to the most significant bit. In bit strings that cross byte boundaries, the bits in the second byte are more significant than the bits in the first byte.

File Structure

| Header |
| Global Screen Descriptor |
| Global Color Table |
| Image 1 |
| Image 2 |
| Image 3 |
| ⋮ |
| Image *n* |
| Trailer |

Figure 12.1
GIF File Structure

A GIF file consists of a fixed area at the start of the file, followed by a variable number of blocks and ending with an image trailer. In the GIF87a format the variable area consists solely of image definitions. In the GIF89a format these can be either images or extension blocks. The general format of a GIF file is shown in Figure 12.1.

GIF Header

The GIF header is required and must occur at the very start of the file. The header allows an application to identify the format as GIF and determine the version. Table 12.1 shows the structure of the GIF header. It is still common for applications that do not use the features added in GIF89a to create GIF87a headers in order to insure the image is compatible with older decoders.

Logical Screen Descriptor

The *global screen* description defines the logical screen area in which the individual images in the GIF file are displayed. It specifies the dimensions of the area as well as the background color (selected from the global color table). The individual image descriptors specify where the image is to be placed within the logical screen. The screen descriptor structure is 7 bytes and is shown in Table 12.2.

Figure 12.2 illustrates the relationship between the logical screen and the individual images in a GIF file.

Global Color Table

The individual images within the file can either use the global color table or define a color table of their own. Having the images in a file share the global

Table 12.1
GIF Header Structure

Field Name	Size	Description
Signature	3 bytes	Must be the ASCII string GIF.
Version	3 bytes	Must be the ASCII string 87a or 89b.

Table 12.2
Logical Screen
Descriptor Format

Field Name	Size	Description
Logical Screen Width	2 bytes	
Logical Screen Height	2 bytes	
Bit Fields	1 byte	
Global Color Table Size	Bits 0–2	$2^{(N+1)}$ gives the number of entries in the global color table.
Color Table Sort Flag	Bit 3	Set when the colors in the global color table are sorted in order of importance.
Bits Per Pixel	Bits 4–6	Bits per pixel minus 1.
Global Color Table Flag	Bit 7	Set when there is a global color table.
Background Color	1 byte	Index into the global color table.
Pixel Aspect Ratio	1 byte	If this value is nonzero, the pixel width and height are not equal. $(N+15)/64$ is the pixel width divided by the pixel height.

Figure 12.2
Logical
Screen/Image
Relationship

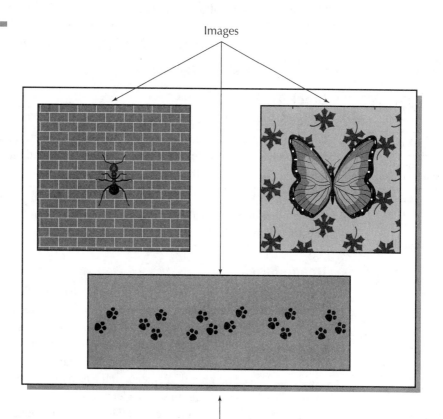

Images

Logical Screen

Table 12.3 Color Table Entry Format	Field Name	Size	Description
	Red	1 byte	Red component value
	Green	1 byte	Green component value
	Blue	1 byte	Blue component value

Table 12.4 Block Codes	Code	Type
	21_{16}	Extension
	$2C_{16}$	Image block
	$3B_{16}$	GIF terminator

color table reduces the file size and makes it easier for systems that can display a limited number of colors. In addition, the global color table specifies the background color for the logical screen.

If the global color table bit is set in the screen descriptor, the global color table immediately follows the screen descriptor. The global color table is an array of structures whose format is shown in Table 12.3. The number of entries in the array is determined from the Global Color Table Size field in the screen descriptor.

Block Types

After the global color table, the variable part of the GIF file begins. The file contains a sequence of blocks that are identified by a 1-byte code at the start of the block. Table 12.4 lists the block types and the associated block code.

Terminator

The terminator block marks the end of the GIF file. This block is 1 byte long and consists solely of the block code.

Image Block

An image block defines an image within the GIF file. The image starts with an image header structure that defines its size and placement. The format of this structure is given in Table 12.5. If the Local Color Table flag in the image header is set, the image uses a local color table rather than the global color table. Just like the global color table, the local color table is an array of color entries (Table 12.3). The number of elements in the array is determined from the Local Color Table Size field in the header.

Figure 12.3 shows the general layout of an image definition within a GIF file.

Image Header

Local Color Table

Minimum Code Size

Data Block 1

Data Block 2

Data Block 3

⋮

Data Block *n*

Terminator

Figure 12.3
Image Definition
Structure

Table 12.5
Image Header
Structure

Field Name	Size	Description
Left Position	2 bytes	Left offset of the image within the logical screen.
Right Position	2 bytes	Top offset of the image within the logical screen.
Image Width	2 bytes	
Image Height	2 bytes	
Bit Field	1 byte	
Local Color Table Size	Bits 0–2	$(N+1)^2$ is the number of entries in the local color table.
Reserved	Bits 3–4	Unused.
Sort Flag	Bit 5	If set, the colors in the local color table are sorted in order of importance.
Interlace Flag	Bit 6	If set, the image data is interlaced.
Local Color Table Flag	Bit 7	If set the image uses a local color table.

The color table (or the image header if there is no color table) is followed by one byte that contains the initial code size used in the compressed data. The value in this field is usually 8.

Data Blocks

The code size byte is immediately followed by an uninterrupted series of data blocks that contain the compressed image data. A data block consists of a 1-byte count field, followed by 1 to 255 data bytes.

The chain of data blocks for an image is always terminated by a data block with zero data bytes—in other words, a single zero-valued byte. We will postpone the discussion of the compressed block format until later in the chapter.

Extension Blocks

Extension blocks were added to GIF in the GIF89a specification. The layout of an extension block is shown in Figure 12.4. The first byte in the extension block contains the code 21_{16}. This is followed by a second byte that contains a code that specifies the extension type. The extension type codes are listed in Table 12.6.

The format of the extension header is specific to the extension type. The first byte in the header gives the size of the header not including the size byte. The header is followed by a list of data blocks. Each block consists of a count byte followed by 1 to 255 data bytes. The list of data blocks is terminated by a zero byte (data block with zero data bytes).

The structure of the extension blocks is such that an application can skip over them without having to understand the structure of each individual extension type. Algorithm 12.1 illustrates how to skip over an extension.

Figure 12.4
Extension Block
Format

Code	Type
1	Plain text extension
F9	Graphic control extension
FE	Comment extension
FF	Application extension

*Algorithm 12.1
Skipping GIF
Extension Blocks*

```
DATA = ReadByte () // Extension Type
DATA = ReadByte () // Count
While DATA <> 0
    Begin
    For II = 1 To DATA
        ReadByte ()
    End
```

Plain Text Extension

The *plain text extension* block is used to draw a grid of fixed-spaced text on the logical screen. This extension consists of a header followed by a series of data blocks containing the text to draw. The data blocks following the header contain the text to display. The format of the plain text extension header is shown in Table 12.7.

Graphic Control Extension

The *graphic control extension* affects how the next image in the GIF file is to be drawn. Graphic control extensions are commonly used to specify how the

*Table 12.7
Plain Text Extension
Format*

Field Name	Size	Description
Block Size	1 byte	The value 12
Text Grid Left	2 bytes	Text position in the logical screen
Text Grid Right	2 bytes	Text position in the logical screen
Text Grid Width	2 bytes	Size of the text block in pixels
Text Grid Height	2 bytes	Size of the text block in pixels
Character Cell Width	1 byte	Width in pixels of each character
Character Cell Height	1 byte	Height in pixels of each character
Text Foreground Color	1 byte	Index into the global color table for the text color
Text Background Color	1 byte	Index into the global color table for the background color

Field Name	Size	Description
Block Size	1 byte	Must be 4.
Bit Fields	1 byte	
Transparent Color Flag	Bit 0	Set when the Transparent Color Index is used.
User Input Flag	Bit 1	When set, the application should wait for user input before displaying the next image.
Disposal Method	Bits 2–4	Specifies what the decoder is to do after the image is displayed. 0—No action. 1—Leave the image In place. 2—Restore the background color. 3—Restore what was in place before the image was drawn.
Reserved	Bits 5–7	
Delay Time	2 bytes	The amount of time the decoder should wait before continuing to process the stream in 1/100ths of a second.
Transparent Color Index	1 byte	If Transparent Color Flag is set, pixels with this color value are not written to the display.

Table 12.8
Graphic Control
Extension Header

individual frames in a GIF animation are drawn. There can only be one graphic control extension per image. This GIF extension block has no data, so a terminating data byte with a value of zero immediately follows the header. The graphic control extension header is shown in Table 12.8.

Comment Extension

The *comment extension* allows an encoder to store information of any type within a GIF file. An application should not use a comment extension to store data that it uses to control how the GIF stream is to be processed. The comment extension has no header, not even a count byte. The data blocks containing the comment text immediately follow the extension type code.

Application Extension

An encoder can use an *application extension* block to store data within a GIF stream that is specific to the application. Its purpose is similar to that of a comment extension except that it may be used to hold data that affects the decoding processes. The application-specific data is stored within the data blocks that follow the header. The format of the application header is shown in Table 12.9.

Field Name	Size	Description
Block Size	1 byte	11
Application ID	8 bytes	An ASCII string that identifies the application that created the block
Authentication Code	3 bytes	Three bytes an application may use to authenticate the block

Table 12.9
Application
Extension Header

Interlacing

In general, GIF images are stored from top to bottom, left to right. However, if the interlace flag in the image header is set, the rows of pixel data are not transmitted in strict top-to-bottom order. Instead, the image is transmitted in four passes. The first pass contains the pixel data for every eighth row starting with the topmost row (row zero). The remaining passes fill in the rows omitted in the previous passes. Table 12.10 shows the rows included in each pass.

The interlacing process serves the same function as progressive JPEG. When an image is transmitted across a network it allows the user to get an idea of what it contains before all the image data is downloaded. Applications that display interlaced GIFs on the fly will usually fill in the missing rows in a pass with copies of the rows already received. On the first pass it will copy each row eight times, four times on the second pass, and once on the third pass. This gives the effect of having the image fading in rather than having disconnected rows on the screen.

Pass	Starting Row	Interval
1	0 (Top row)	8
2	4	8
3	2	4
4	1	2

Table 12.10
Interlacing Row
Interlacing

Compressed Data Format

The pixel data within a GIF image is compressed using a process known as LZW. LZW is what is known as a *dictionary-based compression scheme.* By that, we mean a compression method that maintains a list or dictionary of sequences within the uncompressed data. During compression, when these sequences occur in the uncompressed data they are replaced by a code that references the sequence in the dictionary. The longer the dictionary sequences are and the more frequently they are repeated in the uncompressed data, the greater the compression.

The trick in dictionary-based compression is how to transmit the dictionary in the compressed data. The most common dictionary-based compression schemes in use are based upon those described by Abraham Lempel and Jacob Ziv (1977 and 1978), and known as LZ77 and LZ78, respectively. LZ77 uses a sliding window into the uncompressed data to implement the dictionary.[1] LZ78 builds a dictionary dynamically from the uncompressed data.

GIF Compression

LZW is a variant of the LZ78 process that was described in a paper by Terry Welsh of Sperry (now Unisys) in 1984. Compuserve adopted it for use in the GIF format shortly afterwards. In the LZW method, the compressed data stream consists entirely of codes that identify strings in a dictionary. The dictionary is initialized so that it contains each possible data value as a predefined string. For example, if 8-bit data is being encoded, the dictionary initially contains 256 1-byte strings containing the values 0–255.

The compression reads characters from the input stream and appends them to the current string until the current string no longer has a match in the dictionary. At that point it outputs the code for the longest matching string, adds the nonmatching string to the dictionary (the matching string plus one character), and finally starts a new string that contains the first nonmatching character. Each time a code is written to the output stream, an entry is added to the dictionary.

Algorithm 12.2 illustrates how the dictionary is created in the LZW process. Here we are assuming that 8-bit data is being used and that the function Output writes 9-bit codes to the output stream.

Figure 12.5 shows how a sample string would be compressed using the LZW process. The first column shows the string at each stage in the compression process; the second column shows the value written to the output stream at each stage; and the third column shows the new code that is created.

This input string in Figure 12.5 consists of 27 characters. Using 8 bits per character, the string requires 216 bits. The LZW process uses 20 literal values and dictionary codes to represent the string, so 9 bits are required to encode each LZW value, giving a total of 180 bits—a reduction of 17% in the compressed version. It takes only 33 codes to encode the same string repeated twice (a 31% reduction) and 42 codes to encode it repeated three times (a 41% reduction). The more repetition in the input stream, the greater the compression the LZW process gives.

---

[1]The LZ77 method will be described in greater detail in the chapters on PNG.

Algorithm 12.2
Simplified LZW
Compression

```
Global String DICTIONARY [0..511]
Global NEXTCODE = 256

Procedure Initialize
    Begin
    For I = 0 To NEXTCODE - 1 Do
    DICTIONARY [I] = CHARACTER (I)
    End

Function SearchDictionary (String SEARCH)
    Begin
    For I = 0 To NEXTCODE - 1 Do
        Begin
        If DICTIONARY [I] = SEARCH Then
            Return I
        End
    Return -1
    End

Procedure Compress (String DATA)
    Begin
    Initialize
    LASTSTRING = NULL
    For I = 1 To Length (DATA) Do
        Begin
        CurrentString = LASTSTRING + DATA [I]
        CODE = SearchDictionary (CURRENTSTRING)
        If CODE < 0 Then
            Begin
            // We now have a string with no match in the
            // dictionary. Output the code for the longest
            // string with a match.
            CODE = SearchDictionary (LASTSTRING)
            Output (CODE)
            // Add the nonmatching string to the dictionary.
            DICTIONARY [NEXTCODE] = CURRENTSTRING
            NEXTCODE = NEXTCODE + 1
            // Start a new string, beginning at the point
            // where we no longer had a match.
            LASTSTRING = DATA [I]
            End
        Else
            Begin
            // The current string has a match in the dictionary.
            // Keep adding to it until there is no match.
            LASTSTRING = CURRENTSTRING
            End
        End
    // Output what is left over.
    Output (SearchDictionary (LASTSTRING))
    End
```

Figure 12.5
LZW Compression
Example

A MAN A PLAN A CANAL PANAMA

Input	Output	New Code
A MAN A PLAN A CANAL PANAMA	A	
MAN A PLAN A CANAL PANAMA	<SPACE>	256='A<SPACE>'
MAN A PLAN A CANAL PANAMA	M	257='<SPACE>M'
AN A PLAN A CANAL PANAMA	A	258='MA'
N A PLAN A CANAL PANAMA	N	259='AN'
A PLAN A CANAL PANAMA	<SPACE>	260='N<SPACE>'
A PLAN A CANAL PANAMA	256	261='A'
PLAN A CANAL PANAMA	P	262='A<SPACE>P'
LAN A CANAL PANAMA	L	263='PL'
AN A CANAL PANAMA	259	264='LA'
A CANAL PANAMA	261	265='AN<SPACE>'
CANAL PANAMA	<SPACE>	266='<SPACE>A<SPACE>'
CANAL PANAMA	C	267='<SPACE>C'
ANAL PANAMA	259	268='CA'
AL PANAMA	A	269='ANA'
L PANAMA	L	270='AL'
PANAMA	<SPACE>	271='L<SPACE>'
PANAMA	P	272='<SPACE>P'
ANAMA	269	273='PA'
MA	258	274='ANAM'

GIF Decompression

An LZW decompressor reads one code at a time from the compressed stream while maintaining the dictionary in the same way the compressor does. Each code simply gets translated from the dictionary.

The only subtlety in decompression is that it is possible for the compressed stream to contain codes that have not been defined in the dictionary. Figure 12.6 contains a compression example that illustrates how this situation can occur. Notice that the code 259 is output at the same time the code is defined. A decoder processing this sequence would read 259 before code 259 is defined.

This situation can only occur when the new dictionary string consists of the string for the last code processed with the last character of the last code defined added. In Figure 12.6, the last code output before 259 is 256, whose value is 'AB'. The last character of the previous code (258) is 'A', so the dictionary string for 259 is 'AB' + 'A' = 'ABA'.

Algorithm 12.3 illustrates the LZW expansion process.

Figure 12.6
LZW Example with a
Code Used Before it
is Defined

ABYABABAX

Input	Output	New Code
ABYABABAX	A	
BYABABAX	B	256='AB'
YABABAX	Y	257='BY'
ABABAX	256	258='YA'
ABAX	259	259='ABA'
X	X	260='ABAX'

Algorithm 12.3
Simplified LZW
Expansion

```
Procedure Expand
  Begin
  LASTCODE = InputCode ()
  Output (LASTCODE)
  While NOT EndOfStream DO
    Begin
    CODE = InputCode ()
    If CODE < NEXTCODE Then
      Begin
      Output (Dictionary [CODE])
      Dictionary [NEXTCODE] = Dictionary [LASTCODE]
                          + Dictionary [NEXTCODE -1][1]
      NEXTCODE = NEXTCODE + 1
      LASTCODE = CODE
      End
    Else
      Begin
      // Special Case where the code is used before it is defined.
      Dictionary [NEXTCODE] = Dictionary [LASTCODE]
                          + Dictionary [LASTCODE][1]
      NEXTCODE = NEXTCODE + 1
      Output (DICTIONARY [CODE])
      LASTCODE = CODE
      End
    End
  End
```

Code Sizes

Up to now we have assumed that we are using 9 bits to represent dictionary codes and literal values in the compressed data stream. If we have an input stream larger than 256 bytes we need to use 10 bits to represent each value. Larger input streams can require even larger code sizes. Since choosing a code size that is too large gives poor compression, how would you select a code size that is suitable for most situations?

The solution to this problem in LZW compression is to use varying code sizes. At the start of the compression process, each value is stored using the smallest possible number of bits (almost always 9). When the number of codes becomes too large to be represented by the current code size, the code size is increased by 1 bit. If the initial code size is 9, codes are output using 9 bits until code 512 is created. Then the code size is automatically bumped up to 10 bits. Likewise, after reaching 1024 it is increased to 11 bits. Twelve bits is the maximum code size allowed by GIF. When the code values reach $2^{12}-1$, GIF encoders and decoders stop adding to the dictionary.

A GIF encoder can output a special *clear code* to instruct the decoder to reset the dictionary to its initial state. An encoder may wish to output a clear code whenever it detects a situation where compression would be improved by using a new dictionary. An obvious situation where this might be desirable is after the maximum code sized is reached. Repeated clear codes are legal, but wasteful.

The value for the clear code is not fixed, but rather depends upon the minimum code size that followed the image header. The minimum code size gives the number of bits used to encode the pixel data. Usually this value is 8 bits per pixel, but pixel values for images that do not use 256 colors can be compressed using fewer bits.

Table 12.11 shows the relationship of the minimum code size to the code usage within a GIF image. The *end code* is used to mark the end of a compressed stream.

Dictionary Structure

In the GIF compression and decompression examples we used an array of strings to represent the dictionary. Normally the dictionary is represented as a tree structure. Figure 12.7 shows how the strings generated from compressing the string ABABCABD can be arranged in a tree structure. A code can be translated to a string by starting at the tree node for the code and working to the tree root.

Translating the code by walking the tree from a leaf to the root produces the string in reverse order. In Figure 12.7, following the code 260 gives "DBA". A stack is used to put the string in the correct order. While walking the tree, each time a leaf node is reached, the corresponding character is pushed on the stack. When you reach the root of the tree, you pop characters off in the correct order.

The tree can be represented as an array of structures. Since the maximum code length is 12 bits, the maximum number of tree nodes is 2^{12}. The size of the stack is also 2^{12} characters.

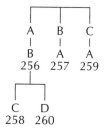

Figure 12.7
Tree Represenation of an LZW Dictionary

Table 12.11
GIF Code Usage

Encoded Value Range	Usage
$0-2^{Minimum\ Code\ Size}-1$	Literal codes
$2^{Minimum\ Code\ Size}$	Clear code
$2^{Minimum\ Code\ Size}+1$	End code
$2^{Minimum\ Code\ Size}+2-2^{12}-1$	String codes

Algorithm 12.4 illustrates how LZW decompression can be implemented using a tree structure for a dictionary and using variable length codes.

Algorithm 12.4
GIF Expansion

```
Global Structure DICTIONARYTREE Array [0..2^12-1]
    Begin
    Byte CHARACTER
    Integer PARENT
    End

Global STACK Array [1.. 2^12] Of Byte
Global STACKPOINTER
Global MINIMUMCODESIZE = 8
Global CODESIZE
Global ENDCODE
Global CLEARCODE
Global NEXTCODE
Global FIRSTCHARACTER

Procedure InitializeDictionary
    Begin
    For II = 0 To 2^CodeSize-1 Do
        Begin
        DICTIONARYTREE [II].CHARACTER = II
        DICTIONARYTREE [II].PARENT = 0
        End
    STACKPOINTER = 0
    CODESIZE = MINIMUMCODESIZE
    CLEARCODE = 2^MINIMUMCODESIZE
    ENDCODE = CLEARCODE + 1
    NEXTCODE = ENDCODE + 1
    End

Procedure OutputCode (CODE)
    Begin
    // Push the characters of the dictionary entry
    // on the stack in reverse order.
    Do
        Begin
        STACK [STACKPOINTER] = DICTIONARYTREE [CODE].CHARACTER
        STACKPOINTER = STACKPOINTER + 1
        CODE = DICTIONARYTREE [CODE].PARENT
        End
    While DICTIONARYTREE [CODE].PARENT <> 0

    // The tree structure makes it more difficult to
    // find the first character in the last code processed.
    // We remember it here.
FIRSTCHARACTER = STACK [STACKPOINTER]
```

(continued)

Algorithm 12.4
Continued

```
    // Pop the value off the stack in reverse order.
    While STACKPOINTER > 0 Do
        Begin
        Output (STACK [STACKPOINTER])
        STACKPOINTER = STACKPOINTER - 1
        End
    End

Procedure Expand (OUTPUT : String)
    Begin
    InitializeDictionary ()

    CODE = ReadBits (CODESIZE)
    While CODE = ClearCode Do
        CODE = ReadBits (CODESIZE)

    OutputCode (CODE)
    While TRUE Do
        Begin
        LASTCODE = CODE
        If NEXTCODE >= 2^CODESIZE And CODESIZE < 12 Then
            CODESIZE = CODESIZE + 1
        CODE = ReadBits (CODESIZE)
        If CODE = ENDCODE Then
            Return
        Else If CODE = CLEARCODE Then
            Begin
            InitializeDictionary ()
            CODE = ReadBits (CODESIZE)
            While CODE = CLEARCODE Do
                CODE = ReadBits (CODESIZE)
            If CODE = ENDCODE Then
                Return
            OutputCode (CODE)
            End
        Else If CODE < NEXTCODE Then
            Begin
            OutputCode (CODE)
            DICTIONARYTREE [NEXTCODE].PARENT = LASTCODE
            DICTIONARYTREE [NEXTCODE].CHARACTER = FIRSTCHARACTER
            NEXTCODE = NEXTCODE + 1
            End
        Else
            Begin
            // Special Case of an Undefined Code
            DICTIONARYTREE [NEXTCODE].PARENT = LASTCODE
            DICTIONARYTREE [NEXTCODE].CHARACTER = FIRSTCHARACTER
            NEXTCODE = NEXTCODE + 1
            OutputCode (CODE)
            End
        End
    End
```

Animated GIF

Unlike all of the other formats discussed in this book, GIF allows multiple images to be stored in a single file. Web browsers have taken advantage of this capability to store simple animations. There is no official standard that describes how multi-image GIF files should be displayed. Many image viewers will just display the first image in a GIF file. However, among the major Web browsers, there is some consistency in how GIF animations are displayed.

Figure 12.8 shows a series of four frames that compose a simple animation sequence. To store this as a GIF animation, the four images are encoded one after another in separate image blocks. Typically a Web browser will display each image in sequence as rapidly as it can. You can use a graphic control extension (Table 12.8) to control the amount of time between the individual frames. A graphic control extension only affects the image that immediately follows it, so you will probably need one for each image in the animation sequence.

Most applications will only play an animation once. To create an animation that repeats in a loop you have to include a special application extension (Table 12.9), whose format is shown in Table 12.12. Although the application ID is "NETSCAPE," this only reflects the creator of the block. Other Web browsers recognize this block format as well.

The Repeat Count field in the application extension gives the number of times the animation is played. A value of zero specifies that the animation is repeated indefinitely. Since displaying images can take up a significant amount

*Figure 12.8
Sample GIF
Animation*

*Table 12.12
Loop Application
Extension Format*

Field Name	Size	Description
Block Size	1 byte	11
Application ID	8 bytes	"NETSCAPE"
Authentication Code	3 bytes	"2.0"
Block Size	1 byte	3
Extension Type	1 byte	1
Repeat Count	2 bytes	Number of times the animation should repeat
Terminator	1 byte	0

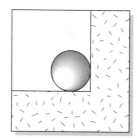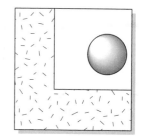

Figure 12.9
An Animation That
Partially Updates
the Logical Screen

of CPU time on home computers, especially those with no delays, it is generally not a good idea to have animations loop forever.

The *logical screen descriptor* (Table 12.2) specifies the dimensions of the animation. Each image does not have to update the entire logical screen. The dimensions and position fields in the image header (Table 12.5) can specify a region within the logical screen for an image to update. Not updating the screen in every image can reduce the size of the GIF file significantly.

Figure 12.9 shows how the previous animation can be set up so that it only updates part of the logical screen.

Legal Problems

Welsh did not mention in his 1984 paper, "IEEE Computer," that he had filed for a patent in 1983 on the process he described. The patent was subsequently granted (4,558,302) in 1985 and assigned to Sperry (now Unisys). For whatever reason (software patents were new and untested legal territory at the time), Compuserve never checked to see if LZW was patented when it issued the GIF specification.

Over time the use of GIF grew and the patent issues remained theoretical until 1994, when Unisys started to demand licensing fees for LZW from GIF users. This made the use of GIF impossible in freely distributed applications.

Solving the GIF patent issue is not simply an issue of getting a license from Unisys. There are numerous other patents related to LZ compression that an implementation could infringe upon. A notable GIF-related patent was awarded to Victor Miller and Mark Wegman of IBM in 1989 (4,814,726). Their patent describes a process that is almost identical to the LZW process. As a result of the patent situation, anyone using GIF in any type of application needs the advice of an attorney.

The fundamental problem is that the LZW process itself is a derivative of earlier work. With the patent database full of LZ derivations, it is impossible to determine what patents an innovative GIF implementation might infringe upon.

Worse than simply their numbers, these patents are written in legalese, making them difficult to understand. With the legal mess surrounding GIF, the best solution for developers is to use other formats. Unlike JPEG, the patent situation with GIF is unlikely to be satisfactorily resolved.

Uncompressed GIF

It is the LZW process, not GIF, that is covered by patents, and it is entirely possible to create GIF files that do not use LZW compression. The easiest way to implement a GIF encoder without using LZW is to simply encode each data byte using 9 bits and output a clear code after every 254 codes. While this gives negative compression, a conforming GIF decoder will correctly interpret the data.

Other GIF-compatible compression schemes have been implemented. It is possible to count runs of the same pixel value or alternating pixel values and compress them in the GIF format. What is unknown is when these methods cross the bounds of any of the various patents.

Conclusion

The GIF format was the first image format to be universally accepted. Unfortunately, legal problems have ended GIF development. Unlike other major graphics formats, no enhancements to GIF are under way. This, coupled with inherent limitations compared to other formats, has made it essentially dead.

Nelson (1992) gives a excellent introduction to the LZ compression methods and their general implementation. The LZ77, LZ78, and LZW algorithms were originally described in Ziv (1977, 1978) and Welsh (1984).

We can tell you how GIF works. Unfortunately, we cannot show you as well. Because of the patent issue, there is no GIF source code on the accompanying CD. Simply writing about GIF in a book requires involving lawyers in the process. Shakespeare was right.

Chapter 13

PNG

Format: Portable Network Graphics
Origin: PNG Development Group
Definition: PNG Specification V1.0 (RFC 2083)
ZLIB Data Format V3.3 (RFC 1950)
DEFLATE Compressed Data Format
Specification V1.3 (RFC 1951)

Portable Network Graphics (PNG) is the newest graphics format in this book. It is just now starting to receive widespread use by the Internet community, and is already supported by any image viewing application worth using.

The PNG format uses a lossless compression process and supports the following:

- Up to 48 bits per pixel in color images
- 1-, 2-, 4-, 8-, and 16-bit sample precision
- Alpha channel for full control of transparency
- Sophisticated color matching

Because of the legal issues surrounding the use of GIF, PNG should now be used instead of GIF in those applications where JPEG is not a suitable alternative. In situations where you need lossless compression for 24-bit images, such as the intermediate format for images that are repeatedly edited, PNG is much better suited than JPEG.

189

In this chapter we are going to cover the structure of PNG files and the format of the individual chunks that are defined by the PNG standard. In the two following chapters we will cover the format of the compressed data and how to read and write PNG files.

History

When Unisys began demanding license fees from users of GIF it became impossible to use GIF in many situations, notably in free software. After Unisys's action, the JPEG format quickly replaced GIF for photographic images. However, JPEG does not compress certain types of images well, so it could not replace GIF for all applications.

Thomas Boutell organized what was to be called the PNG Development Group, started within days of Unisys's announcement that they would demand licenses for GIF usage. Development of the PNG standard proceeded at a rapid pace, with several drafts issued to the public. The final version was released on October 1, 1996, just over a year and half after the project began.

Byte Ordering

The PNG format stores multi-byte integers with the most significant byte first (big-endian). Bit strings are read from the least to the most significant bit. When a bit string crosses a byte boundary the bits in the second byte are the most significant.

Huffman codes within compressed data are stored with the code bits in reverse order. The most significant bits of the Huffman code are stored in the least significant bits of the data bytes.

File Format

A PNG file is organized into a sequence of blocks referred to as *chunks* in the PNG standard. Chunk types are defined by three sources. Some are defined by the PNG standard; these are the most important chunks a decoder has to deal with. The PNG Development Group also maintains a list of registered public chunk types. If someone creates a chunk type that may be of use to the general public, the creator can submit it to be considered for addition. Finally, there are private chunks defined by applications.

Chunks follow the format shown in Table 13.1. This format allows a decoder to skip over those chunks that it does not know how to process and those that the

	Field	Size	Description
Table 13.1 *PNG Chunk Format*	Length	4 bytes	Number of bytes in the Data field 0–2,147,483,647 (2^{31}–1) bytes.[1]
	Type	4 bytes	Chunk name.
	Data	Length bytes	Chunk data. The format depends upon the chunk type.
	CRC	4 bytes	CRC-32 value calculated from the data.

implementers feel are not important enough to implement. Being able to ignore unknown chunks is essential because decoders need to be able to process files containing private chunks created by other applications and new public chunks.

Chunk Naming

PNG chunks are given unique names that consist of four ASCII letters. The first, second, and last characters in a chunk type can be either upper or lower case. The case used for these characters follows the convention described below, which allows a decoder to determine information about the chunk from the name alone.

The third character in the chunk name must be in upper case. If an application encounters a chunk type containing any values other than ASCII letters, it should consider it invalid. Figure 13.1 shows some sample chunk names and their meanings.

Critical Chunks

If the first character of the chunk type is in upper case (bit 5 clear), the chunk is referred to as critical. A *critical chunk* is one that the decoder absolutely must process in order to decode the image. If a decoder encounters a critical chunk that it does not recognize, it should report an error. The PNG standard only defines four critical chunks: IHDR, PLTE, IDAT, and IEND.

Public and Private Chunks

The second character in the chunk type is upper case for chunks that are publicly defined. Public chunks types include all those defined by the PNG standard as well as additional chunk types that are registered with the PNG Development Group.

Applications can create private chunks of their own to store data that is specific to the application. These should have the second character in lower case to ensure that they do not conflict with publicly defined chunks.

---

[1]The size limitations in the PNG specification take into account programming languages that cannot handle unsigned integers.

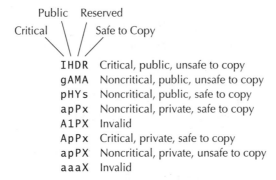

Figure 13.1
Sample PNG Chunk Names

IHDR	Critical, public, unsafe to copy
gAMA	Noncritical, public, unsafe to copy
pHYs	Noncritical, public, safe to copy
apPx	Noncritical, private, safe to copy
A1PX	Invalid
ApPx	Critical, private, safe to copy
apPX	Noncritical, private, unsafe to copy
aaaX	Invalid

> **While it is legal for an application to create private critical chunks, using such chunks will most likely make the images unreadable by other applications.**

Safe-to-Copy Chunks

The last character in the chunk type should be in lower case if the chunk is safe to copy and in upper case if it is not. An application should not copy chunks that it does not recognize if the fourth character in the chunk type is in upper case.

Suppose you are developing a PNG editor application that automatically puts a border and logo on an image and then saves the image to a new file. If the application encounters an unknown chunk it has two choices: it could pass that chunk on to the output file without making any modifications to it or discard it.

If the editing application encountered a private chunk created by an archiving program that stored indexing information within the image (e.g., subject, date, and photographer), it would not know how to interpret the information with it. However, copying the chunk to the output file would produce perfectly valid results. Such a private chunk would probably be made a safe-to-copy chunk.

On the other hand, suppose editor encountered a private chunk that contained information on the usage of colors with the image. After the border was added, the information in the chunk would no longer be valid. Such a private chunk should be unsafe to copy.

Cyclic Redundancy Check

Each PNG chunk contains a 32-bit CRC (Cyclic Redundancy Check) value that has been calculated from the chunk type code and chunk data. The CRC is a mathematical function that is commonly used in networking software to ensure that data in a network packet has been received correctly. Before sending a data packet the transmitter applies the CRC function to the data and then appends the CRC value to the packet. The receiver of the packet applies the CRC function to the data and then compares the calculated CRC value to the value in the packet. If the two values are not the same, the receiver can send a negative acknowledgment to the transmitter to request that the packet be resent.

The PNG file format applies the CRC function to each chunk so that decoders can verify that the data in the chunk has not been corrupted since the file was created. A decoder should calculate the CRC value for every chunk in a PNG file and ensure that the calculated value matches the CRC value stored in the chunk. A chunk where these two values do not match should be considered invalid.

The CRC function is based upon performing modulo 2 polynomial division on the input data, where each bit in the input stream is treated as a coefficient in a giant polynomial. The CRC function value is the remainder from the division operation. The choice of the polynomial determines the type of bit errors that can be detected. Both 16-bit and 32-bit CRC functions are in common use. A 32-bit CRC can detect more errors in larger packet sizes. PNG uses the 32-bit version, which is known as CRC-32. The polynomial used by PNG is

$$x^{32} + x^{26} + x^{23} + x^{22} + x^{16} + x^{12} + x^{11} + x^{10} + x^8 + x^7 + x^5 + x^4 + x^2 + x + 1$$

which is essentially the value

$$1\ 0000\ 0100\ 1100\ 0001\ 0001\ 1101\ 1011\ 0111_2$$

Software implementations of the CRC function invariably use a table lookup to calculate the CRC function. As each byte in the input stream is processed, a value known as the CRC register is updated using a value in the table. In the CRC function used by PNG, the CRC register is initialized with all bits set to 1. After the last byte has been processed the final CRC value is the 1s-complement of the value in the CRC register.

The CRC process used by PNG, when implemented using a lookup table, looks like this.

```
unsigned long CrcRegister ;

void CrcByte (unsigned char data)
{
  unsigned int index = (CrcRegister ^ data) & 0xFF ;
  CrcRegister = CrcTable [index] ^ ((CrcRegister >> 8) & 0x00FFFFFF) ;
  return ;
}

unsigned long Crc (unsigned char buffer [], unsigned int length)
{
  CrcRegister = 0xFFFFFFFFL ;
  for (unsigned int ii = 0 ; ii < length ; ++ ii)
  CrcByte (buffer [ii]) ;
  return ~CrcRegister ;
}
```

Before making any CRC calculations, the lookup table containing precalculated values for each possible byte integer value needs to be initialized using a function like this.

```
unsigned long CrcTable [256] ;
void MakeCrcTable ()
{
  for (unsigned int ii = 0 ; ii < 256 ; ++ ii)
  {
    CrcTable [ii] = ii ;
    for (unsigned int jj = 0 ; jj < 8 ; ++ jj)
    {
      if ((CrcTable [ii] & 0x1) == 0)
        CrcTable [ii] >>= 1 ;
      else
        CrcTable [ii] = 0xEDB88320L ^ (CrcTable [ii] >> 1) ;
    }
  }
  return ;
}
```

The mathematics of the CRC process is outside the scope of this book. However, to give you some idea of how it is done, compare the constant

$EDB88320_{16}$ = 1110 1101 1011 1000 1000 0011 0010 0000$_2$

used in generating the CRC lookup table to the value that we said was equivalent to the CRC. If you take this value, reverse the order of the bits, then prepend a 1-bit, you have the CRC-32 polynomial value

1 0000 0100 1100 0001 0001 1101 1011 0111$_2$.

Chunk Processing

Most PNG decoders will probably be implemented with a common function for reading the chunk data into memory. This common process would follow these steps:

1. Read the chunk data size.

2. Read and save the chunk type.

3. If the chunk data size is larger than the data buffer, allocate a larger buffer.

4. Read the chunk data.

5. Calculate the CRC value of the chunk data.

6. Read the chunk CRC from the file.

7. Compare the calculated CRC to the CRC read from the file. If they are not the same, the chunk is invalid.

After the last step the decoder can call a function to handle the specific chunk type.

File Organization

PNG Signature

IHDR Chunk

PLTE Chunk

IDAT Chunk 1

IDAT Chunk 2

IDAT Chunk 3

⋮

IDAT Chunk *n*

IEND Chunk

Figure 13.2
PNG File
Organization

Figure 13.2 shows the general organization of a PNG file. A PNG file must start with a PNG signature followed by an IHDR chunk and end with an IEND chunk. The ordering of the other chunks within a file is somewhat flexible. The ordering restrictions are covered in the discussions of chunk formats.

The PNG signature consists of 8 bytes that must have the values 137, 80, 78, 71, 13, 10, 26, and 10. These are the ASCII values 137, P, N, G, <RETURN>, <LINEFEED>, <CTRL/Z>, and <RETURN>. There is a bit of hidden logic in using these values in the signature. Other than the obvious device of including the string "PNG" to identify the format, most of the reasoning is rather subtle.

On Unix, a <LINEFEED> character is used to separate records in a text file. In MS-DOS, records are separated by a <RETURN><LINEFEED> pair. Many file transfer programs can operate in either binary or text mode. In binary mode these applications make a byte-to-byte copy, but in text mode they replace <LINE-FEED> characters with <RETURN><LINEFEED> pairs when going from Unix to DOS and replace <RETURN><LINEFEED> pairs with <LINEFEED> characters when going from DOS to Unix. If a PNG file is transferred employing text mode using one of these programs, either <RETURN><LINEFEED> or <LINEFEED> will be corrupted, so a decoder will have to go no further than the signature to know it has a bad file.

The first byte in the signature is not a displayable ASCII value, making it less likely that a decoder will confuse a text file with a PNG file. If you accidentally type a PNG file at the DOS command line, the <CTRL/Z> in the header stops it from printing beyond the signature.

Color Representation in PNG

The PNG format supports five different color types or methods for representing the color of pixels within an image. The method for representing color is specified in the file's IHDR chunk.

> **With the exception of BMP, the other file formats in this book use only one method to represent colors.**

RGB Triple

Like BMP, PNG can represent colors as an RGB triple. Each pixel is represented by three component values of either 8 or 16 bits. The components are stored in red, green, blue order (the opposite of BMP). RGB triples may only be used when the bit depth is 8 or 16 bits.

Palette

PNG images can also use a color palette in the same way BMP and GIF do. The size of the palette depends upon the sample precision. Images that use a palette must contain a PLTE chunk that defines the palette. Palettes may only be used when the bit depth is 1, 2, 4, or 8 bits.

Grayscale

In the grayscale color type there is one component per image, and it represents the relative intensity of the pixel. The grayscale color type can be used for all PNG bit depths. On most systems a decoder will need to create a palette to display grayscale images using a process like the one shown in Algorithm 13.1.

Algorithm 13.1
Grayscale Palette
Creation

```
MAXPIXELVALUE = 2^DISPLAYBITDEPTH - 1
For II = 0 To MAXPIXEVALUE Do
    Begin
    PALETTE [II].RED = II
    PALETTE [II].GREEN = II
    PALETTE [II].BLUE = II
    End
```

RGB with Alpha Channel

PNG images support the use of an Alpha channel to control the transparency of the image. The Alpha channel allows an image to be combined with its background. Each pixel value has an additional Alpha value whose size in bits is the same as the image bit depth. The RGB with Alpha color type can only be used with bit depths of 8 and 16.

An Alpha value of zero means that the pixel is fully transparent, in which case the background shows completely through. A value of $2^{Image\ Bit\ Depth} - 1$ is fully opaque, which means that the background is completely covered by the image. When the Alpha channel has an intermediate value, the pixel is merged with the background using the process in Algorithm 13.2.

```
MAXPIXELVALUE = (1 LeftShift BITDEPTH) - 1
OUTPUT.RED = (ALPHA * IMAGEVALUE.RED
             + (MAXPIXELVALUE - ALPHA) * BACKGROUND.RED) / MAXPIXELVALUE
OUTPUT.GREEN = (ALPHA * IMAGEVALUE.GREEN
             + (MAXPIXELVALUE - ALPHA) * BACKGROUND.GREEN) / MAXPIXELVALUE
OUTPUT.BLUE = (ALPHA * IMAGEVALUE.BLUE
             + (MAXPIXELVALUE - ALPHA) * BACKGROUND.BLUE) / MAXPIXELVALUE
```

Algorithm 13.2
Alpha Channel
Merging

Grayscale with Alpha Channel

An Alpha channel can also be used with grayscale images, but the image bit depth is restricted to 8 or 16. Each pixel using this color type is represented using two values containing the same number of bits, with the Alpha value following the pixel intensity value. The merging process for this color type is the same as for RGB with Alpha except that there is only one image color component.

Device-Independent Color

All of the colorspaces we have dealt with until now have been relative color spaces where color components have values from 0 to 2^{N-1}, where N is the number of bits used to represent a component. Zero represents the minimum component value for the device, and 2^{N-1} is the maximum value. Suppose that you worked for Coca-Cola and needed labels printed for bottles with the background color the same bright red used on all Coke bottles. If you told the printer you wanted the color to be (230,0,0) using the RGB colorspace with a sample precision of 8 bits, the color of the labels would depend upon the printing equipment. What you really need is a method to specify the absolute color.

The CIE 1931 standard (CIE stands for Committee Internationale de L'Éclairage, International Lighting Committee) has served exactly that purpose in photography, printing, and film since 1931. It uses three components that are usually designated XYZ. The Y component represents luminance, as it does in the YCbCr colorspace; the X and Z components represent chrominance. These are analogous to the Cb and Cr components, but the implementation is different.

If an application knows the XYZ color values for red, blue, green, and white for the device where the image was originally created, it is possible to convert the RGB values in the image to XYZ values giving absolute color. If these color values are known for the display image as well, it is possible to convert them to the corresponding RGB values for the display device so that the image will be displayed using the original colors. This assumes that the display device can actually display all of the XYZ colors in the image—something that is not always the case.

 Vendors of monitors for personal computers rarely include the monitors' XYZ values with the documentation. They generally have this information available if you ask them directly.

To make things even more confusing, the makers of monitors list the colors using a colorspace related to XYZ, known as xyY, which is a projection of the XYZ colorspace into two dimensions. The relationship between the xyY and XYZ colorspace is

Equation 13.1
xyY/XYZ Colorspace
Conversion

$$x = \frac{X}{X + Y + Z}$$

$$y = \frac{Y}{X + Y + Z}$$

$$Y = Y$$

$$X = \frac{x \quad Y}{y}$$

$$Z = \frac{Y \quad (1 - x - y)}{y}$$

Projecting the XYZ colorspace into two dimensions allows all possible colors to be represented on a piece of paper, although with the loss of luminance or brightness possibilities.

Figure 13.3 illustrates the xyY colorspace. The black triangle in the center represents the gamut, or range, of colors that can be displayed by a typical computer monitor. This triangular range is only a small subset of the visible colors. The gamut available to a particular device can vary substantially. For example, the gamut that can be displayed by the typical desktop color printer is a bit different than that for a computer monitor.

One of the reasons colors are not generally encoded within image files using XYZ colorspace is that it requires much more precision in the data. Using RGB, the data precision is only such that the possible colors for the device can be represented. Since XYZ covers all possible visible colors rather than the small subset a device can show, it requires more data bits to encode. The solution used by PNG is to encode values using RGB and create chunks that allow a decoder to determine the colors that were actually used at the source.

When I contacted the manufacturer of my monitors, the information they gave me was:

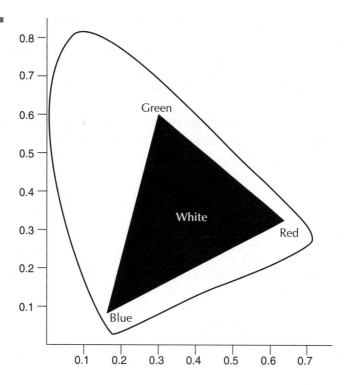

Figure 13.3
xyY Colorspace

Monitor 1

	x	y
Red	.612	.353
Green	.293	.595
Blue	.149	.068

White Point: 9300K

Monitor 2

	x	y
Red	.625	.340
Green	.280	.595
Blue	.155	.070

White Point: 9300K

Display devices are normally built so that the white point falls on or close to a set of data points known as the *black body curve*. 9300K is a standard white point value for a computer monitor that has an xy value of (0.285, 0.293). The *Y* value is implicitly 1.0. The white point in the XYZ colorspace is, then,

$$X = 0.973$$
$$Y = 1$$
$$Z = 1.440$$

for both monitors.

The conversion from RGB to XYZ is a matrix multiplication of the form

Equation 13.2
RGB to XYZ
Conversion

$$\begin{bmatrix} X \\ Y \\ Z \end{bmatrix} = \begin{bmatrix} C_R x_R & C_G x_G & C_B x_B \\ C_R y_R & C_G y_G & C_B y_B \\ C_R(1 - x_R - y_R) & C_G(1 - x_G - y_G) & C_B(1 - x_B - y_B) \end{bmatrix} \begin{bmatrix} R \\ G \\ B \end{bmatrix}$$

where C_R, C_G, and C_B are constants and the RGB values have been scaled to the range 0–1.0. The trick now is to find the values of these three constants.

If we substitute the xy values for the first monitor into Equation 13.2 we get

Equation 13.3

$$\begin{bmatrix} X \\ Y \\ Z \end{bmatrix} = \begin{bmatrix} C_R \times 0.612 & C_G \times 0.293 & C_B \times 0.149 \\ C_R \times 0.353 & C_G \times 0.595 & C_B \times 0.068 \\ C_R \times 0.035 & C_G \times 0.212 & C_B \times 0.783 \end{bmatrix} \begin{bmatrix} R \\ G \\ B \end{bmatrix}$$

We already calculated the white point XYZ coordinate and we know that the RGB value of the white point is (1.0, 1.0, 1.0). If we substitute that into the previous equation we get

Equation 13.4

$$\begin{bmatrix} 0.973 \\ 1.000 \\ 1.440 \end{bmatrix} = \begin{bmatrix} C_R \times 0.612 & C_G \times 0.293 & C_B \times 0.149 \\ C_R \times 0.353 & C_G \times 0.595 & C_B \times 0.068 \\ C_R \times 0.035 & C_G \times 0.212 & C_B \times 0.783 \end{bmatrix} \begin{bmatrix} 1 \\ 1 \\ 1 \end{bmatrix}$$

which can be factored into

Equation 13.5

$$\begin{bmatrix} 0.973 \\ 1.000 \\ 1.440 \end{bmatrix} = \begin{bmatrix} 0.612 & 0.293 & 0.149 \\ 0.353 & 0.595 & 0.068 \\ 0.035 & 0.212 & 0.783 \end{bmatrix} \begin{bmatrix} C_R \\ C_G \\ C_B \end{bmatrix}$$

This is a set of three linear equations with three unknown variables. We can now solve for C_R, C_G, and C_B, which gives (0.698, 1.094, 1.512). This makes the transform from RGB to XYZ for this monitor

Equation 13.6

$$\begin{bmatrix} X \\ Y \\ Z \end{bmatrix} = \begin{bmatrix} 0.427 & 0.321 & 0.225 \\ 0.246 & 0.651 & 0.103 \\ 0.024 & 0.232 & 1.184 \end{bmatrix} \begin{bmatrix} R \\ G \\ B \end{bmatrix}$$

To convert from XYZ back to RGB you have to invert the transform matrix. The easiest method is to use a Gaussian elimination. Row reduction and matrix inversions are beyond the scope of this book, but you will find an explanation of these techniques in any book on linear algebra, such as Anton (1981). This is the inverse function for the first monitor.

Equation 13.7

$$\begin{bmatrix} R \\ G \\ B \end{bmatrix} = \begin{bmatrix} 3.170 & -1.389 & -0.483 \\ -1.227 & 2.123 & 0.049 \\ 0.175 & -0.387 & 0.845 \end{bmatrix} \begin{bmatrix} X \\ Y \\ Z \end{bmatrix}$$

Gamma

The color models used with image files assume that there is a linear relationship between a component value and the color that appears on the screen. In reality, the display devices in use do not tend to respond in a linear manner to the input supplied to them. *Gamma* approximates the nonlinear behavior of these devices. It is simply a power function:

$$\Gamma(x) = x^{\varphi}$$
where
$$0 \le x \le 1$$
$$\varphi > 0$$

Adjusting the Gamma of an image can be used in conjunction with converting to the XYZ colorspace or on its own. Gamma adjustments have a greater effect on the appearance of an image on a computer monitor than does conversion to XYZ and back.

The effect of the Gamma function is to make component values generally darker or lighter. Gamma values greater than 1 make the image darker and those less than 1 make it lighter. Notice that the domain and range of the Gamma function are the same. If the input to the function is between 0 and 1 the output will always be in that range as well.

The Gamma value for a display system is the combined Gamma of the components.

Equation 13.8
Gamma
Combination

$$\Gamma_1(\Gamma_2(\ldots \Gamma_N(x))) = x^{\varphi_1 \varphi_2 \cdots \varphi_N} = x^{\varphi_1 \; \varphi_2 \; \cdots \; \varphi_N} = x^{\prod_{n}^{N} \varphi_n}$$

In other words, the Gamma value for a display system is the product of the Gamma values for all of its components.

The gAMA chunk allows an encoder to store the Gamma value for a system used to create the image. The implementer of a PNG decoder is faced with two issues:

- What Gamma values should be used to view the image?
- What is the Gamma of the system being used to display the image?

There is really no way for an application to determine what the viewing Gamma should be. In a well-lighted room it should probably be around 1.0. In a dark room it should be higher, around 1.5 or so. The problem here is that, unless the decoding software has access to a light sensor, there is no way for it to determine this. The best choice is either to allow the user to input a Gamma or to use a viewing Gamma of 1.0. Many image display programs allow the user to adjust the viewing Gamma after the image is displayed to get the best results.

Some high-end display systems allow the system's Gamma to be queried or even adjusted through software. If you are writing software for personal computers, you should assume that the Gamma for all of the components other than the monitor is 1. The PNG standard recommends a Gamma value of 2.5 for monitors if the exact value is unknown.[2] Most monitor vendors have this information available even though it is not in the printed documentation. The manufacturer says the Gamma value for the monitors in the previous section is 1.8.

Unless you have a high-end display system, a PNG viewing application cannot change the Gamma. If the PNG file contains a gAMA chunk giving the Gamma value for the image, that value is fixed as well. Since the total Gamma of the display system is

Equation 13.9

$$Desired\ Viewing\ Gamma = Application\ Gamma \times Display\ Gamma \times File\ Gamma$$

an application can adjust it by adjusting the pixel values. The Gamma correction the application should use is, then

Equation 13.10

$$Application\ Gamma = \frac{Desired\ Viewing\ Gamma}{Display\ Gamma \times File\ Gamma}$$

Applications should only apply Gamma correction to color components. Gamma correction is not applied to the Alpha channel.

Interlacing

Just as in GIF, PNG supports interlacing of images. The interlacing method used in the current PNG standard is called *Adam 7*.[3] Other interlacing methods may be added in the future, but this is the only one supported now. Adam 7 interlaces the image by pixels rather than by rows. It divides the image into 8×8 pixel blocks and updates it over seven passes. The Adam 7 interlace pattern is shown in Figure 13.4.

Adam 7 is considerably more difficult to implement than GIF's row interlacing. Fortunately the pattern contains regular intervals that can be exploited by a decoder. Figure 13.5 shows how a decoder would display an 8x8 block of pixels on the fly using the Adam 7 pattern. This illustration makes the regular pattern of the sequence more clear.

---

[2]The next version of the PNG standard is expected to recommend a value of 2.2 in order to be compatible with the sRGB standard.
[3]After the pattern's creator Adam M. Costello.

Figure 13.4
Adam 7 Interlace
Pattern

```
1  6  4  6  2  6  4  6
7  7  7  7  7  7  7  7
5  6  5  6  5  6  5  6
7  7  7  7  7  7  7  7
3  6  4  6  3  6  4  6
7  7  7  7  7  7  7  7
5  6  5  6  5  6  5  6
7  7  7  7  7  7  7  7
```

Figure 13.5
Adam 7 Interlace
Display

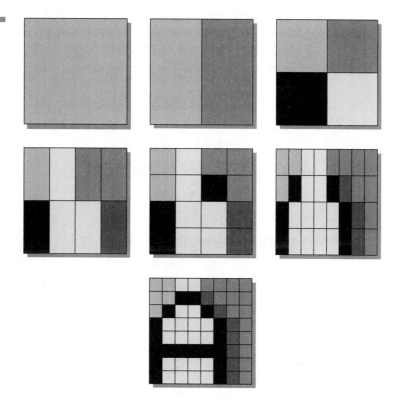

Critical Chunks

The PNG standard defines four critical chunks (IHDR, PLTE, IDAT, and IEND). Most PNG files need not contain any chunks other than these. The IHDR, IDAT, and IEND chunks must appear in every PNG file. For the critical chunks we have listed the general steps a decoder should take to process the chunk.

IHDR

Every PNG file contains one IHDR chunk, which must immediately follow the PNG signature. The IHDR block specifies the image dimensions, bit depth, and color type. The structure of the data block within an IHDR chunk is shown in Table 13.2. The length of the IHDR chunk data is 13 bytes. Decoders should consider any other length invalid.

A decoder needs to ensure that the bit depth and color type combination is valid. As discussed earlier, not every combination of bit depth and color type is legal. RGB and color types with Alpha channel are only valid with bit depths of 8 and 16; palette color types are invalid when the bit depth is 16.

The `Compression Method` and `Filter Method` fields are for future extensions of the PNG standard. Currently the only compression method supported is Deflate with a 32K-byte or smaller sliding window, and only one filtering method is defined. A decoder should ensure that these values are zero.

To process this chunk a decoder should

- Ensure that no other chunks have been processed.
- Validate the following:
  - Chunk data length should be 13.
  - Compression method and filter method should be 0.
  - Interlacing method should be 0 or 1.
  - Color type must be 0, 2, 3, 4, or 6.
  - Sample precision must be 1, 2, 4, 8, or 16.
  - Sample precision and color type must be consistent.
  - Storage for the image buffer and palette has been allocated.

Table 13.2 IHDR Data Format	Field Name	Field Size	Description
	Width	4 bytes	Image width in pixels.
	Height	4 byte	Image height in pixels.
	Bit Depth	1 byte	Sample precision (1, 2, 4, 8, or 16).
	Color Type	1 byte	Method for interpreting image data: 0—Grayscale image. 2—RGB triple. 3—Palette. 4—Grayscale with Alpha channel. 6—RGB with Alpha channel.
	Compression Method	1 byte	Must be zero.
	Filter Method	1 byte	Must be zero.
	Interlace Method	1 byte	0—The image is not interlaced. 1—Adam 7 interlacing.

PLTE

The PLTE chunk defines a color palette for the image. There may only be one PLTE chunk per image and it must occur before the first IDAT chunk. When the image's color type is palette the file must contain a PLTE chunk. The data within the PLTE chunk is an array of palette entry structures shown in Table 13.3. The number of palette entries is the number of data bytes in the PLTE chunk divided by 3, and is limited to a maximum of $2^{Bit\ Depth}$. The palette can contain fewer entries than the maximum allowed by the bit depth. The color values in the PLTE chunk are in the range 0–255 no matter what the image bit depth or color type is.

When the color type is RGB or RGB with Alpha channel, the PLTE chunk is optional. An encoder may include a palette for images with these color types in order to provide a recommended palette to use if the image needs to be quantized to 256 colors. A PLTE chunk is legal in this situation even when the bit depth is 16 bits. However, its component values are 8 bits no matter what the bit depth is. Grayscale images may not contain a PLTE chunk.

To process this chunk a decoder should

- Make sure that no other PLTE chunk has been processed.
- Ensure that the image color type is not grayscale or grayscale with Alpha.
- Validate chunk data:
    - The number of data bytes in a PLTE is a multiple of 3.
    - The number of palette entries is not greater than $2^{Bit\ Depth}$.
    - The number of palette entries is not greater than 256.
- Store the chunk's RGB values in the palette used to decode the chunk.

IDAT

IDAT chunks contain the compressed image data. All of the IDAT chunks within a PNG file must be consecutive with no intervening chunks. The IDAT blocks may occur anywhere after the IHDR block and before the IEND block. If the PNG file contains a PLTE block, the IDAT blocks must come after it. The size of the block data in an IDAT block can be in the range 0 to $2^{31} - 1$. The usual number of data bytes within an IDAT block is between 4K and 16K bytes. Of course,

Table 13.3
Palette Entry
Structure Format

Field Name	Size	Description
Red	1 byte	Red component intensity value (0–255)
Green	1 byte	Green component intensity value (0–255)
Blue	1 byte	Blue component intensity value (0–255)

the last IDAT block in a chain may have substantially fewer bytes. A PNG file that does not contain an IDAT block is invalid. The organization of the compressed data within IDAT blocks is covered in Chapter 13.

Unlike all other chunk types, most decoders will probably treat all the IDAT blocks as a group rather than process them independently. This makes the decompression process simpler and helps to ensure that all the IDAT blocks in the file are consecutive. When the first block in an IDAT block chain is encountered, the decoder should

- Ensure that no other IDAT block chains have been encountered.
- If the color type is Palette then make sure that a PLTE chunk has been processed.
- Decompress the image data.

IEND

The IEND chunk marks the end of PNG, so it obviously must be the last chunk in a PNG file.

To process this chunk a decoder should

- Ensure that at least one IDAT block has been processed.
- Make sure that the chunk data length is zero.
- Conclude the decoding process.

Noncritical Chunks

The PNG standard defines several noncritical or ancillary chunks. These are chunks that are not absolutely essential within a PNG file. An encoder does not have to create any of these chunks and a PNG decoder can simply ignore them. However, if you were writing a PNG decoder it would be desirable to implement as many of these standard chunks as possible. Likewise, an encoder should use them when applicable, rather than create application private chunks, in order to ensure the greatest portability. Many of the noncritical chunks are really only appropriate for specialized applications or when used for intermediate storage. For files that are going to be transmitted over the Internet or embedded in Web pages, a tEXt chunk or two and possibly a gAMA chunk are all that is appropriate in most cases.

bKGD

The bKGD chunk suggests a background color for the image. If the image is being displayed in a window that is larger than it is, a decoder can use this color to display the areas outside the image. If the image contains an Alpha channel the decoder can merge the background color with the image. The bKGD chunk must appear before the IDAT chunks in the image. If the image contains a PLTE chunk, then it must precede that bKGD chunk.

The format of the data within a bKGD chunk depends upon the image's color type.

Palette Color Type.   The chunk data consists of single byte that is an index into the color palette.

Grayscale or Grayscale with Alpha Channel.   The chunk data contains a single 2-byte integer that specifies the intensity of the background.

RGB or RGB with Alpha Channel.   The chunk data contains three 2-byte integers that specify the values for the red, green, and blue components of the background.

cHRM

An encoder can create a cHRM chunk to store the device-independent (1931 CIE) specification of the colors used to view the image on the source display. These values can be used to convert the RGB pixel values to absolute colors using the process described earlier in the chapter. The format of the cHRM chunk is shown in Table 13.4.

gAMA

If a PNG encoder knows the correct Gamma value used to view the original image, it can store this information in a gAMA chunk so the decoder can recreate the image as it was seen on the device that created it. The gAMA chunk data contains a 4-byte integer that holds the product of the Gamma value and 100,000. Thus, a Gamma value of 2.1 would be stored in the gAMA chunk as

Table 13.4
cHRM Chunk Data
Format

Field Name	Size	Description
White Point X	4 bytes	White point value × 100,000
White Point Y	4 bytes	White point value × 100,000
Red X	4 bytes	Red point value × 100,000
Red Y	4 bytes	Red point value × 100,000
Green X	4 bytes	Green point value × 100,000
Green Y	4 bytes	Green point value × 100,000
Blue X	4 bytes	Blue point value × 100,000
Blue Y	4 bytes	Blue point value × 100,000

210,000. A gAMA chunk must precede any PLTE and IDAT chunks in the file. The format of the gAMA chunk is shown in Table 13.5.

hIST

An encoder can place a hIST chunk in any PNG file that contains a PLTE chunk in order to supply decoders with the approximate usage frequencies for each color in the palette. The hIST chunk can assist a decoder in selecting the colors to use if it is unable to display all the colors in the palette. If an image contains a hIST chunk, it must follow the PLTE chunk and precede the IDAT chunks.

The hIST chunk data is an array of 2-byte, unsigned integers. The number of array elements in the hIST chunk must be the same as the number of color entries in the PLTE chunk. Each entry in the hIST array reflects the approximate relative usage of the corresponding color in the PLTE chunk.

If the encoder knows the absolute usage frequency of the colors within the palette, it can scale the values to fit into 16 bits. However, a zero frequency value should only be used when a color is not used at all. In the case of an RGB image, the frequency values will always be approximate and none should be zero.

pHYs

The pHYs chunk is used to store the absolute or relative pixel size of the device used to view the image when it was created. If a PNG file does not contain a pHYs chunk, the decoder should assume that the pixels are square and that the original physical size is unknown. A pHYs chunk must precede the IDAT chunks in the file. The format of the data for the pHYs chunk is shown in Table 13.6.

When the `Unit Specifier` field is 0, the X and Y pixel dimensions in the pHYs chunk give the relative sizes of the pixels on the source display. The decoder can use this information to scale the image on the output display. If the

Table 13.5 gAMA Chunk Data Format	Field Name	Size	Description
	Gamma Value	4 bytes	File Gamma × 100,000

Table 13.6 pHYs Chunk Data	Field Name	Size	Description
	Pixels Per Unit X	4 bytes	
	Pixels Per Unit Y	4 bytes	
	Unit Specifier	1 byte	0—The X and Y values give a ratio. 1—Unit is meters.

Unit Specifier field is 1, the X and Y dimensions give the number of pixels per meter on the source display. The decoder can use this information to output the image in the same size it was on the source display.

sBIT

An encoder can use an sBIT chunk to store the number of significant bits in the original sample data. If the original data uses a bit depth that is not supported by PNG—for example, 12—a decoder can use the information in an sBIT chunk to recreate the original sample values.

The format of the data within the sBIT depends upon the color type of the image.

> *Grayscale.*   The chunk data contains 1 byte giving the number of significant bits.

> *RGB and Palette.*   The chunk data contains 3 bytes giving the number of significant bits for the red, green and blue components.

> *Grayscale with Alpha Channel.*   The chunk data contains 2 bytes giving the number of significant bits for the grayscale data and Alpha channel.

> *RGB with Alpha Channel.*   The chunk data contains 4 bytes that specify the number of significant bits in the source for the red, green, and blue components and Alpha channel, respectively.

All data values within the sBIT chunk must be greater than zero and less than or equal to the bit depth.

A decoder can use a procedure like this to convert a sample value from a PNG file to the value at the original bit depth.

```
unsigned int sourcemax = 1 << sBITvalue ;
unsigned int filemax = 1 << BitDepth ;
sourcevalue = (filevalue * sourcemax + filemax - 1) / filemax ;
```

The process for an encoder is almost exactly the same.

```
unsigned int sourcemax = 1 << SourceBitDepth ;
unsigned int filemax = 1 << FileDepth ;
filevalue = (sourcevalue * filemax + sourcemax - 1) / sourcemax ;
```

tEXt

An encoder can use a tEXt chunk to store text information that does not affect the decoding of an image. The tEXt chunk can appear anywhere between the IHDR and IEND chunks (except among the IDAT chunks) and there can be any number of them in a file.

The chunk data contains a keyword and a keyword value. The chunk data format is shown in Table 13.7. The length of the Keyword field is determined by locating the NULL (0) terminator. This length may not be zero. The length of the Text field is the length of the chunk data minus the length of the Keyword and the Terminator. This length may be zero. Line breaks within the text should be represented with a single <LINEFEED> character.

The PNG standard defines the keywords shown in Table 13.8. An encoder can use these or create new keywords; however, a decoder should use the predefined keywords when they are applicable to maximize portability. Keywords are case sensitive.

tIME

The tIME chunk is used to store the last time the image was modified. The tEXt cnunk is used to store the creation time. The format of the tIME chunk data is shown in Table 13.9. Zulu (or Greenwich) time should be used rather than local time. Applications that do not modify the image data should not create a new tIME chunk. The tIME chunk may appear anywhere after the IHDR chunk and before the IEND chunk, except within the IDAT chunks.

Table 13.7
tEXt Chunk Format

Field Name	Size	Description
Keyword	Variable 1–79 bytes	ASCII string
Terminator	1 byte	A zero terminator for the keyword
Text	Variable	ASCII string

Table 13.8
tEXt Pre-defined
Keywords

Keyword	Description
Author	Name of the image's creator
Comment	Generic comment; conversion from GIF comment
Copyright	Copyright notice
Creation Time	Time the image was originally created
Description	Extended image description
Disclaimer	Legal disclaimer
Software	Application that created the image
Source	Device used to create the image
Title	Brief image description or title
Warning	Content warning

	Field Name	Size	Description
Table 13.9 *tIME Chunk Format*	Year	2 bytes	Gregorian year (2020, not 20)
	Month	1 byte	1–12
	Day	1 byte	1–31
	Hour	1-byte	1–23
	Minute	1 byte	0–59
	Second	1 byte	0–60

tRNS

The tRNS chunk is used to implement transparency without using an Alpha channel. Using this mechanism, the Alpha values are associated with colors rather than per pixel. A tRNS chunk must appear after the PLTE chunk, if present, and before the IDAT chunks. The format of the data within the tRNS chunk depends upon the color type used to store the image.

Palette.   The chunk data contains an array of bytes that specify the Alpha value to be associated with the color entries in the PLTE chunk. Each pixel with a color index of N has the Nth entry in the tRNS data as its Alpha value. The number of entries in the tRNS chunk must be less than or equal to the number of color entries in the PLTE chunk. Palette entries without an entry in the tRNS chunk have an Alpha value of 255.

Grayscale.   The chunk data contains a 2-byte integer that defines a transparent color. All pixels with this color value are fully transparent; pixels with any other value are fully opaque.

RGB.   The chunk data contains three 2-byte integers that specify an RGB color value. All pixels of this color are fully transparent; pixels of any other color are fully opaque.

The tRNS chunk may not be used when the color type has an Alpha channel.

zTXt

The zTXt chunk performs the same function as the tEXt chunk except that the text data is compressed using the Deflate compression method (the same method used to compress the image data). Just like the tEXt chunk, there can be any number of zTXt chunks and they can occur anywhere after the IHDR chunk and before the IEND chunk, except among the image's IDAT chunks. The format of the zTXt chunk is shown in Table 13.10.

	Field Name	Size	Description
Table 13.10 *zTXt Chunk Format*	Keyword	1–79 bytes	Uncompressed text string
	Separator	1-byte	Zero value keyword terminator
	Compression Method	1-Byte	Must be zero.
	Compressed Text	Variable	Deflate compressed text.

Conclusion

In this chapter we have introduced the PNG format and described its file and chunk structure. The PNG format contains support for device-independent color through Gamma correction and the XYZ color model. It is superior to GIF in all respects except one: animations. Unlike GIF, PNG files can only contain a single image. As this is being written a new multiple image standard called MNG is under development that will remove the final barrier to PNG completely replacing GIF.

The PNG file and block format is defined in the PNG standard, which is included on the accompanying CD-ROM. Foley et al. (1996) contains more information on Gamma correction, Alpha channel, and the XYZ colorspace. Blinn (1998) and Porter and Duff (1984) contain useful information on Alpha channel and compositing. Campbell (1987) and Ramabadran and Gaitonde (1988) give introductory descriptions of CRC calculations.

The source code example for this chapter is an application called PNGDUMP that displays the name, chunk data length, and CRC value for each chunk in a PNG file. The organization of this application is very similar to that of a functioning PNG decoder. For the critical chunks defined by the PNG standard, PNGDUMP performs appropriate validations. The major piece that a decoder would add is the decompression of the image data stored in the IDAT blocks (covered in the next chapter).

To run this application type

```
> PNGDUMP somefile.png
```

at the command line. Sample output from this program is shown in Figure 13.6.

Figure 13.6
Sample PNGDUMP
Output

```
{ IHDR
  Data Length: 13
  Data CRC: 9cc69707
  File CRC: 9cc69707
  Image Size: 383 x 262
  Bit Depth: 8
  Color Type: Palette Index
  Compression Method: deflate/inflate - 32k Sliding Window
  Filter Method: adaptive
  Interlace Method: none
}
{ PLTE
  Data Length: 768
  Data CRC: 9fe76824
  File CRC: 9fe76824
  Palette Color Count: 100
}
{ IDAT
  Data Length: 2000
  Data CRC: 710a2c5b
  File CRC: 710a2c5b
}
{ IDAT
  Data Length: 2000
  Data CRC: d857c86a
  File CRC: d857c86a
}
{ IDAT
  Data Length: 2000
  Data CRC: 119cab52
  File CRC: 119cab52
}
{ IDAT
  Data Length: 2000
  Data CRC: 1ab5b934
  File CRC: 1ab5b934
}
{ IDAT
  Data Length: 2000
  Data CRC: 610914db
  File CRC: 610914db
}
{ IDAT
  Data Length: 5b7
  Data CRC: cee96fbe
  File CRC: cee96fbe
}
{ IEND
  Data Length: 0
  Data CRC: ae426082
  File CRC: ae426082
}
```

Chapter 14

Decompressing PNG Image Data

The previous chapter explained how to decode a PNG file up to the point where the image data within the IDAT blocks is interpreted. This chapter covers the remaining topics needed to decode a PNG file. The main focus is the Deflate compression process that PNG uses to store pixel data in IDAT chunks.

Decompressing the Image Data

The first step in processing the image data is to decompress it. During the decompression process we treat the chunk data from the IDAT chunks in the image file as a continuous stream of bytes; then we pass them to a decompressor for the Deflate/Inflate processes. The segmentation of the compressed stream into IDAT chunks is irrelevant to the decompression processes. The sequence of compressed data bytes would be the same if one IDAT were used to hold the entire compressed block, if each compressed byte were placed in a separate IDAT chunk, or any combination between these two extremes.

ZLIB, Deflate, and PNG

Before Unisys started to demand licenses for its use in software, LZW had not been confined to GIF. It had also been used in many types of compression applications including the Unix *compress* program. When LZW could no longer be used in free software, there was an immediate need for a freely usable compression method to replace it. The solution came in the form of a general-purpose compression library known as ZLIB.

ZLIB employs an LZ77-based compression process known as Deflate, which had its origins in the ZIP and PKZIP programs. The compression source code within ZIP was too tightly bound to the application for general use, so Jean-Loupe Gailly and Mark Adler created ZLIB to implement Deflate compression in a manner that can be used by other applications. ZLIB has been used not only in PNG but in the GZIP archiving program as well. Currently, Deflate is the only compression method supported by ZLIB, but the ZLIB format has provisions for other methods to be added in the future.

For this discussion we are going to describe ZLIB and Deflate only as they apply to PNG. Not all settings that are valid in ZLIB/Deflate are legal when used in PNG files. The source code examples in this and the following chapters contain implementations of the PNG subset of Deflate.

LZ77 Compression

The LZ77 process uses a sliding window to maintain a dictionary of recently processed text. The compressed stream is a sequence of codes that are either literal values or commands for the decompressor to copy text from the window to the output stream.

An LZ77 decompressor reads each code in the compressed stream in sequence. Codes that represent literal values are copied directly to the output stream. Command codes are replaced in the output stream with text copied from the LZ window. In either case, the LZ window is advanced so that the last character copied to the output stream is included in the window. The big advantage of dictionary compression over Huffman coding is that compression can be done on the fly without having to process the entire stream, making it suitable for applications such as compression of data streams in a computer network.

Figure 14.1 contains a simplified example of LZ77 decompression using a 16-byte window. The data consists of 7-bit ASCII text, so by using 1 bit to differentiate a literal value from a command, each code in the compressed stream can be encoded using 8 bits. In this example copy commands are represented as <Offset:Length> where the offset is the number of bytes from the start of the LZ77 window and the length is the number of bytes to copy.

In this example the first six codes are literal values that are copied to the output stream. The seventh code copies two characters from the tenth position in the LZ Window ("A") to the output stream. As new codes are read, the window fills up and text starts to become lost to the compression processes. Notice that the final "MA" in the text could have been compressed into a code had that string not slid out of the window.

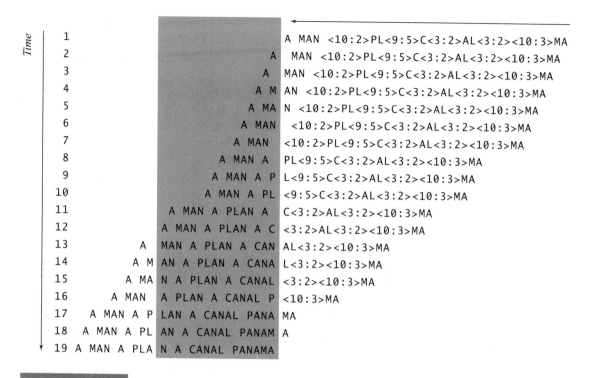

Figure 14.1
LZ77 Compression
Example

Deflate Compression

Data in the Deflate format is stored in blocks that are either uncompressed or compressed using a variation of the LZ77 process. For the moment we will concentrate on the format of compressed Deflate blocks. Deflate uses a 32K-byte (or smaller power of 2) sliding window into the most recently decoded text. During the decompression process this window holds the most recently decompressed data bytes.

The compressed stream contains codes that represent literal values or distance/length codes. When the decompressor encounters a literal value, it copies it to the output stream and then advances the sliding window by one position. When a distance/length code is read from the compressed stream, the decompressor uses the distance to locate the start of a previously decompressed string to copy to the output stream.

When copying a string from the sliding window you need to maintain two pointers or indices into the sliding window: one to the source text being copied and the other to the destination. Since the size of the window is a power of 2, it is easy to implement the window as a circular buffer rather than one that physically moves. Wrapping of indices in a 32K buffer is accomplished by performing a bitwise AND operation with an index and the value $7FF_{16}$ ($2^{15}-1$).

Algorithm 14.1 shows how a copy operation is implemented. It assumes that there is a function called OutputByte that processes each byte as it is decompressed. The arguments to the CopyData function are the number of bytes to copy and the distance from the current output position in the window.

Deflate uses codes in the range 0–285 in the compressed stream. The codes in the range 0–255 naturally represent literal bytes in the compressed stream. The code 256 is a special value that is used to mark the end of a compressed block, and codes 257–285 are used to start a command to copy from the sliding window.

The format for a copy command is shown in Figure 14.2. The codes 257–285 are part of the specifier for the length component of the copy command. Each length code has a base length value and a number of extra bits associated with it. After reading the code, the decoder reads the specified number of extra bits. The value of the extra bits is added to the base value to give the final copy length. The base values and number of extra bits for each length code are shown in Table 14.1.

Algorithm 14.1
LZ77 Data Copying

```
Global OUTPUTPOSITION
Constant WINDOWSIZE = 1 LeftShift 15
Constant WINDOWMASK = WINDOWSIZE - 1 // 7FF
PROCEDURE CopyData (LENGTH, DISTANCE)
  Begin

    // We add the window size to ensure the index is always positive.
    // The AND operation will get rid of any extras distance from
    // this addition.
    COPYPOSITION = (WINDOWSIZE + OUTPUTPOSITION - DISTANCE)
    COPYPOSITION = COPYPOSITION AND WINDOWMASK

    For II = 1 To LENGTH Do
      Begin
      WINDOW [OUTPUTPOSITION] = WINDOW [COPYPOSITION]
      OutputByte (WINDOW [OUTPUTPOSITION])
      // Advance to the next output position
      OUTPUTPOSITION = OUTPUTPOSITION + 1
      OUTPUTPOSITION = OUTPUTPOSITION And WINDOWMASK
      // Advance to the next byte to copy
      COPYPOSITION = COPYPOSITION + 1
      COPYPOSITION = COPYPOSITION And WINDOWMASK
      End
  End
```

Figure 14.2
Copy Command
Format

`<Length Code>[Length Extra Bits]<Distance Code>[Distance Extra Bits]`

The extra bits are followed by another distance code in the range $0-29$. This value specifies the base value for the distance from the current location in the buffer and the number of additional bits. The extra bits and base values for distance codes are shown in Table 14.2.

Table 14.1
Length Code Base
Values and Extra Bits

Length Code	Base Value	Extra Bits	Possible Length Values
257	3	0	3
258	4	0	4
259	5	0	5
260	6	0	6
261	7	0	7
262	8	0	8
263	9	0	9
264	10	0	10
265	11	1	11–12
266	13	1	13–14
267	15	1	15–16
268	17	1	17–18
269	19	2	19–22
270	23	2	23–26
271	27	2	27–30
272	31	2	31–34
273	35	3	35–42
274	43	3	43–50
275	51	3	51–58
276	59	3	59–66
277	67	4	67–82
278	83	4	83–98
279	99	4	99–114
280	115	4	115–130
281	131	5	131–162
282	163	5	163–195
283	195	5	195–226
284	227	5	227–257
285	258	0	258

Example

1. Read Length Code 275
   From Table 14.1 the Base Value is 51 and there are 3 extra bits.
2. Read 3 Bits giving 101_2 (5)
   Length Value is $5 + 51 = 56$
3. Read Distance Code 14
   From Table 14.2 the Base Value is 129 and there are 6 extra bits.
4. Read 6 Bits giving 001100_2 (12).
   The Distance value is $12 + 129 = 141$

This command copies the 56 characters located 129 positions before the current buffer position.

Table 14.2
Distance Code Base Values and Extra Bits

Distance Code	Base Value	Extra Bits	Possible Distance Values
0	1	0	1
1	2	0	2
2	3	0	3
3	4	0	4
4	5	1	5–6
5	7	1	7–8
6	9	2	9–12
7	13	2	13–16
8	17	3	17–24
9	25	3	25–32
10	33	4	33–48
11	49	4	49–64
12	65	5	65–96
13	97	5	97–128
14	129	6	129–192
15	193	6	193–256
16	257	7	257–384
17	385	7	385–512
18	513	8	513–768
19	769	8	769–1,025
20	1,025	9	1,025–1,536
21	1,537	9	1,537–2,048
22	2,049	10	2,049–3,072
23	3,073	10	3,073–4,096
24	4,097	11	4,097–6,144
25	6,145	11	6,145–6,145
26	8,193	12	8,193–12,288
27	12,289	12	12,289–16,384
28	16,385	13	16,385–24,575
29	24,577	13	24,577–32,768

One would normally expect value ranges that are limited by powers of 2. However, in Table 14.1 and Table 14.2 we have the values 0–285 and 0–29. So how are the lengths and distances efficiently coded?

The answer is Huffman coding. Two Huffman tables are used during most of the decompression process. One is used to decode length and literal values and the other is used to decode distance values.

Huffman Coding in Deflate

The Huffman coding process used in PNG with Deflate is almost identical to the one used in JPEG (Chapter 6). In fact, for the PNG decoder on the CD-ROM, we will only have to make small modifications to the JPEG Huffman decoder class. These are the differences you need to be aware of between Huffman coding in JPEG and in PNG:

- In JPEG, the Huffman codes containing all 1 bits are invalid. In PNG they are legal.

- In JPEG, the maximum Huffman code length is 16 bits. In PNG, lengths and distance codes are a maximum of 15 bits while the tables are encoded using a maximum of 4 bits.

- In PNG, if values of X and Y have Huffman codes of the same length and X is greater than Y, the Huffman code for X is greater than the Huffman code for Y. In JPEG, the ordering of Huffman codes matches the ordering of the values in the file.

- In PNG, the Huffman codes are stored with their bits reversed. The Huffman code 110_2 (6) is stored as 011_2 (3) in the compressed data.

- In PNG, Huffman table definitions contain the Huffman code length for every possible value. Unused values are given a code length of zero. In JPEG, code lengths are only given for values that are actually used.

As with JPEG, the input to the Huffman table generation process is an array of values and an array of Huffman code lengths. In PNG, the values are sorted by value rather than code length and the array contains zero length codes. We have to add a step to sort these arrays by code length, and during the Huffman code generation we have to take into account the values with zero length codes.

Algorithm 14.2 illustrates the process for decoding a compressed block. The procedures `DecodeUsingLengthTable` and `DecodeUsingDistanceTable` are assumed to Huffman decode the next value in the input stream using the literal/length and distance Huffman tables, respectively. `ReadLiteralBits (n)` is a function that returns the next *n* bits from the input stream and `CopyData` is the function defined in Algorithm 14.1.

<table>
<tr><td>Algorithm 14.2
Deflate Process</td></tr>
</table>

```
Procedure DecodeBlock
    Begin
    While True Do
        Begin
        CODE = DecodeUsingLengthTable ()
        If CODE = 256 Then
            Return
        Else If CODE < 256 Then
            OutputByte (CODE)
        Else
            Begin
            EXTRA = LENGTHEXTRABITS [CODE]
            BASE = LENGTHBASES [CODE]
            LENGTH = BASE + ReadLiteralBits (EXTRA)
            CODE = DecodeUsingDistanceTable ()
            EXTRA = DISTANCEEXTRABITS [CODE]
            BASE = DISTANCEBASES [CODE]
            DISTANCE = BASE + ReadLiteralBits (EXTRA)
            CopyData (LENGTH, DISTANCE)
            End
        End
    End
```

Compressed Data Format

Until now we have dealt with the PNG compression from the top down. Now we are going to back up and examine the ZLIB/Deflate compressed data format.

The structure of the compressed data is shown in Table 14.3. Notice that most of the fields are not complete bytes and that when used with PNG most have mandatory values. The Compression Level field is an advisory field. It gives a clue as to whether there may be any benefit in recompressing the data. The value in the Check Bits field is used to ensure that the header value is a multiple of 31. A 2-byte header that is not evenly divisible by 31 is invalid.

The Adler-32 checksum serves the same function the CRC-32 does for PNG blocks. The major difference is in how it is used. The CRC-32 value for a PNG block is calculated using the bytes stored in the file. The Adler-32 value for a compressed stream is calculated on the uncompressed bytes. As each byte is decompressed, the decoder should update the Alder-32 value. After all the data has been decompressed, a decoder should compare the Adler-32 calculated from the decompressed data with the value stored in the field. If the two values are not the same, the decoder should assume that the data has been corrupted.

The following source code illustrates how to implement the Adler-32 checksum. The UpdateAdler function updates the value in the AdlerRegister variable for each byte as it is decompressed. The Adler register is initialized to 1

Table 14.3 Compressed Data Format	Field Name	Size	Description
	Header	2 bytes	
	Compression Method	4 bits	Must be 8.
	Window Size	4 bits	Must be 7 or less.
	Check Bits	5 bits	Makes the first 2 bytes a multiple of 31.
	Preset Dictionary	1 bit	Must be zero.
	Compression Level	2 bits	0—Fastest compression used. 1—Fast compression used. 2—Default compression used. 3—Maximum compression used.
	Compressed Blocks	Variable	
	Adler Checksum	4 bytes	Adler-32 Checksum calculated from the uncompressed data.

before calculating the checksum. The Adler value stored in the file is the value of the Adler register after the last byte has been processed. No modification needs to be made, as with CRC-32.

```
unsigned long AdlerRegister = 1 ;
const unsigned long PRIME = 65521L ;
void UpdateAdler(unsigned char value)
{
  unsigned long low = AdlerRegister & 0x0000FFFFL ;
  unsigned long high = (AdlerRegister >> 16) & 0x0000FFFFL ;
  low = (low + value) % PRIME ;
  high = (low + high) % PRIME ;
  AdlerRegister = (high << 16) | low ;
}
```

Compressed Data Blocks

The compressed data can be divided into any number of compressed blocks. It is possible for the encoder to compress the entire image into a single block, but in some cases using multiple blocks can improve compression. Each block starts with a 3-bit header with the format shown in Table 14.4. The header specifies the method used to compress the block and if more blocks follow this one. If the Final bit is set, the Adler-32 value follows this block.

Deflate compressed blocks have no relationship to IDAT blocks. A compressed block does not even have to begin on a byte boundary.

	Field Name	Size	Description
Table 14.4 *Compressed Block* *Header Format*	Final	1 bit	1—This is the last compressed block. 0—There are additional compressed blocks after this one.
	Type	2 bits	0—The data is uncompressed. 1—Compressed with fixed Huffman codes. 2—Compressed with dynamic Huffman codes. 3—Invalid.

Uncompressed Block Format

If the Type field in the block header specifies that the data is uncompressed, the remaining data in the block is byte aligned. Any unused bits following the header are discarded. The format of an uncompressed data block is shown in Table 14.5. A decompressor simply copies the uncompressed bytes to the output stream.

Dynamic Huffman Codes

Dynamic Huffman codes is the most useful compression method. The bit fields shown in Table 14.6 immediately follow the compressed block header. These values give the number of values that are actually used in the compressed data. While two Huffman tables are used to decompress the data, there are three lengths defined here. The reason for the extra field is that the code lengths for the length/literal and distance Huffman tables themselves are Huffman encoded.

The structure in Table 14.6 is followed by a sequence of up to 19 3-bit fields. The actual number of bit fields is the value of the Lengths field plus 4. These bit fields contain the Huffman code lengths for the values 0–18. The lengths are stored in the order

16 17 18 0 8 7 9 6 10 5 11 4 12 3 13 2 14 1 15

	Field Name	Length	Description
Table 14.5 *Uncompressed* *Block Format*	Length	2 bytes	The number of data bytes in the block.
	NLength	2 bytes	The 1's-complement of Length. Used for validation.
	Block Data	Length bytes	The uncompressed data bytes.

	Field Name	Length	Description
Table 14.6 *Dynamic Huffman* *Code Fields*	Literals	5 bits	Number of length/literal codes—257 (257–286).
	Distances	5 bits	Number of distance codes—1 (1–32).
	Lengths	4 bits	Number of code length codes—4 (4–19).

Entries at the end of the list are less likely to have a corresponding length value stored in the file. Values without an entry are assigned a code length of zero. Using these length codes, a decompressor creates the Huffman table used to decode the code lengths for the other literal/length and distance Huffman tables.

The Huffman-encoded values 0–18 are used to encode the literal/length and distance Huffman tables. Table 14.7 shows the meanings of these codes. The codes 16, 17, and 18 have a number of extra bits associated with them. When a decoder encounters one of these codes, it is followed by the specified number of literal bits.

Example

Decoder reads the Huffman encoded value 17 from the input stream. Following Algorithm 14.7, the decoder reads the 3 extra bits 101_2 (5). This value is added to the base value giving 8 (= 3 + 5). This command sets the next 8 code lengths to zero.

The code lengths for the literal/length Huffman table come next in the input stream. The number of code lengths is the value of the Literals field in Table 14.6 plus 257. A decompressor reads Huffman-encoded command values (0–18) and processes them according to Table 14.7 until the specified number of code lengths has been read.

The distance Huffman table code lengths immediately follow. The number of distance codes is the value of the Distance field in Table 14.7 plus 1. Distance table length codes are encoded in the same manner as they are in the literal/length table.

Algorithm 14.3 illustrates how to read the code lengths for a Huffman table from the input stream. The parameters to the ReadLengths function are the number of code lengths to read (from Table 14.6) and an output array of code lengths where LENGTHS [n] is the Huffman code length for the value n.

After the code lengths have been read, they are used to generate the literal/length and distance Huffman tables. The compressed data format is identical to that used with fixed Huffman codes.

Table 14.7
Length Encodings

Code	Description	Base Value	Extra Bits
0–15	Literal value.	N/A	0
16	Repeat the previous code 3–6 times.	3	2
17	Repeat length 0 3–10 times.	3	3
18	Repeat length 0 11–138 times.	11	7

Algorithm 14.3
Reading
Compressed
Huffman Tables

```
Procedure ReadLengths (LENGTHCOUNT, LENGTHS [])
    Begin
    INDEX = 0
    While INDEX < LENGTHCOUNT DO
        Begin
        CODE = HuffmanDecodeInputStream ()
        If CODE < 16 Then
            Begin
            LENGTHS [INDEX] = CODE
            INDEX = INDEX + 1
            End
        Else If CODE = 16 Then
            Begin
            COUNT = 3 + ReadRawBitsFromInputStream (3)
            For I = 1 To COUNT Do
                Begin
                LENGTHS [INDEX] = LENGTHS [INDEX - 1]
                INDEX = INDEX + 1
                End
            End
        Else If CODE = 17 Then
            Begin
            COUNT = 3 + ReadRawBitsFromInputStream (3)
            For I = 1 To COUNT Do
                Begin
                LENGTHS [INDEX] = 0
                INDEX = INDEX + 1
                End
            End
        Else If CODE = 18 Then
            Begin
            COUNT = 11 + ReadRawBitsFromInputStream (7)
            For I = 1 To COUNT Do
                Begin
                LENGTHS [INDEX] = 0
                INDEX = INDEX + 1
                End
            End
        End
    End
End
```

Fixed Huffman Codes

When fixed Huffman codes are used, the compressed data in the block immediately follows the block header. The compressed data may or may not be byte aligned. This block uses a predefined set of Huffman codes rather than codes generated from usage frequencies.

A block that uses fixed Huffman codes is decompressed in the same manner as is one with dynamic Huffman codes. The only difference in processing

Table 14.8
Literal/Length
Huffman Code
Lengths for Fixed
Huffman Codes

Value	Code Length
0–143	8
144–255	9
256–279	7
280–287	8

is that the Huffman table lengths are not stored in the input stream. The Huffman table for length/literal codes is generated using the code lengths shown in Table 14.8. The Huffman table for distance code uses a length of 5 for all possible values (0–29).

Writing the Decompressed Data to the Image

The process described in the previous sections in this chapter shows how to convert a stream of compressed bytes contained in a sequence of IDAT blocks into a stream of uncompressed data bytes. We need to perform interlacing, filtering, and color conversion on this stream before writing it to the image.

Interlacing

When an image is interlaced, it is divided into a series of seven passes. We can exploit the regularities in the Adam 7 interlace pattern to create a structure like the one shown in Table 14.9. This structure gives the location of the first pixel within an 8 × 8 block that is updated by each pass and the row and column intervals between the next pixels. All of the row and column intervals are maintained across adjacent 8 × 8 blocks. This example shows how the information in Table 14.9 would be used to determine the sequence of pixels to process in a pass of an interlaced image.

Algorithm 14.4
Interlace Processing
Using a Table

```
Procedure ProcessPass
  Begin
  ROW = FirstRow
  While ROW < IMAGEHEIGHT Do
    Begin
    COL = FirstColumn
    While COL < IMAGEWIDTH Do
      Begin
      ProcessDataForPixel (ROW, COL)
      COL = COL + ColumnInterval
      End
    ROW = ROW + RowInterval
    End
  End
```

Table 14.9
Adam 7 Pixel
Update Intervals

Pass	First Row	First Column	Row Interval	Column Interval
1	1	1	8	8
2	1	5	8	8
3	5	1	8	4
4	1	3	4	4
5	3	1	4	2
6	1	2	2	2
7	2	1	2	1

Using Table 14.9, the number of pixels per row in a given pass in an interlaced image is

$$Pixels\ per\ Row\ =\ \frac{Image\ Width\ +\ Column\ Interval\ -\ 1}{Column\ Interval}$$

If the image is not interlaced, the number of pixels per row is simply the image width and there is only one pass. The number of bits required to represent a pixel for each color type is shown in Table 14.10. The number of bits to represent each row is, then,

$$Bits\ per\ Row\ =\ Bits\ per\ Pixel\ \times\ Pixels\ per\ Row$$

and the number of bytes per row is

$$Pixels\ per\ Row\ =\ \frac{Bits\ per\ Row\ +\ 7}{8}$$

Filtering

A filter is a function that transforms the data in a pixel row into a format that is more compressible. The pixel data for each row is preceded by a single byte that specifies the filtering method applied to each row. Table 14.11 lists the possible values for the filter byte and the corresponding filter type. Values outside the range 0–4 are invalid. If the filter type is zero, the row was not filtered, so the row data contains the actual pixel values.

Table 14.10
Bits per Pixel for
PNG Color Types

Color Type	Bits per Pixel
RGB	3 × Bit depth
RGB with Alpha	4 × Bit depth
Grayscale	Bit depth
Grayscale with Alpha	2 × Bit depth
Palette	Bit depth

Code	Filter Type
0	Unfiltered
1	Sub filter
2	Up filter
3	Average filter
4	Paeth filter

Table 14.11
Row Filter Codes

 Since we are dealing with decoding PNG images in this chapter, this section will deal only with reversing the filtering process. The filtering process is covered in the next chapter.

Some of the filters are calculated from the unfiltered data generated for the previous row. A PNG decoder needs to maintain two buffers large enough to hold the pixel data for an entire row. One buffer contains the data for the current row and the other contains the data for the previous row.

The filtering process involves calculations based upon values of adjacent pixels. Filtering is performed on a per-byte basis rather than per pixel and filtering is performed relative to corresponding bytes within pixels. For example, if you are processing an image using the RGB color type with a bit depth of 16, the high-order byte for the red component of one pixel is always used with the high-order byte for the red component of another pixel. If the bit depth is less than 8, filtering is performed on adjacent bytes. Table 14.12 gives the intervals between corresponding bytes for the possible bit depth and color type combinations.

The following sections describe how the filtering process is reversed for the various filter types. In these descriptions `buffer [previous]` contains the unfiltered bytes from the previous row and `buffer [current]` contains the filtered bytes for the current row. The variable `interval` is obtained from Table 14.12.

Table 14.12
Interval between
Corresponding
Bytes When Filtering

Color Type	Bit Depth	Interval
Grayscale	1, 2, 3, 4, 8	1
Grayscale	16	2
Grayscale with Alpha	8	2
Grayscale with Alpha	16	4
Palette	1, 2, 3, 4, 8	1
RGB	8	3
RGB	16	6
RGB with Alpha	8	4
RGB with Alpha	16	8

If X is the first byte in a row, the value of buffer [N][X-1] is zero. Likewise, if the current row is the first row for the pass, all of the values of buffer [previous] are implicitly zero.

All filters are performed using integer arithmetic and the data bytes are treated as signed (Algorithms 14.5–14.8). If the result from reversing a filter is greater than 255, only the least significant byte in the result is used.

Algorithm 14.5
Reverse Sub Filter

```
Function ReverseSub (X)
   Begin
   Return buffer [current][X] + buffer [current][X-Interval]
   End
```

Algorithm 14.6
Reverse Up Filter

```
Function ReverseUp (X)
   Begin
   Return buffer [current][X] + buffer [previous][X]
   End
```

Algorithm 14.7
Reverse Average
Filter

```
Function ReverseAverage (X)
   Begin
   Return buffer [current][X] +
                  (buffer [current][X-Interval]
                  + buffer [previous][X]) / 2
   End
```

Algorithm 14.8
Reverse Paeth Filter

```
Function PaethPreductor (Left, Above, UpperLeft)
   Begin
   pa = abs (above - upperleft)
   pb = abs (left - upperleft)
   pc = abs (left - upperleft + above - upperleft)

   If pa <= pb AND pa <= pc Then
     Return Left
   Else if pb <= pc
    Return Above
   Else
    Return UpperLeft
   End

Fuction ReversePaeth (X)
   Begin
   Return buffer [current][X] + PaethPredictor (
                  buffer [current][X-Interval],
                  buffer [previous][X],
                  buffer [previous][X-Interval])
   End
```

Color Correction

In many cases, after the reverse filtering process is complete the data is ready to display. If an application has the required information, the decoder can color correct the pixel data. If the PNG file contains a cHRM chunk, the decoder can convert the pixel data to CIE 1931 format to get the exact colors shown on the source display, then correct the data for the destination display. If the file contains a gAMA chunk, the data can be Gamma corrected for the output display.

16- to 8-bit Conversion

Most current computer systems only support bit depths of up to 8. Unless you are writing a decoder for a specialized system that supports greater bit depths, you are going to have to convert 16-bit data values to 8 bits. The technically correct method to convert pixel values from one bit depth to another is

Equation 14.1
Bit Depth
Conversion

$$New\ Value\ =\ Old\ Value\ \ \frac{2^{NewBitDepth}-1}{2^{OldBitDepth}-1}$$

The easiest method to convert from 16 to 8 bits is to discard the low-order byte of each 16-bit color value after applying color correction (if applicable). The results are virtually indistinguishable from that of Equation 14.1.

Either of these two methods could create large, solid blocks of colors that could look odd, especially in photographs. In some situations you may wish to apply dithering during the color conversion.

Transparency

If the color type is RGB with Alpha or grayscale with Alpha, or if the PNG file contains a tRNS chunk, transparency can be applied if desired. If the image is being drawn on a background and the decoder has access to the background's color data, the image in the PNG file can be combined with the background pixels using the process described in the previous chapter. Another possibility is to combine the image with a solid background that is specified by the application or from a bKGD chunk.

Conclusion

In this chapter we have covered the remaining aspects of PNG that are required to implement a PNG decoder. Besides explaining the Deflate compression process, we have covered the format of the pixel data, including the filtering process.

The compressed data format for PNG is defined in Deutsch and Gailley (1996a) and Deutsch (1996b). Both of these documents are on the accompanying CD-ROM. Blinn (1998) contains a description of a dithering process suitable for 16-bit to 8-bit conversion.

The source code example for this chapter on the accompanying CD-ROM is a complete PNG decoder class, `PngDecoder`. This class uses the same process all of the other decoders covered in this book use to read a PNG file and convert it to a `BitmapImage` object.

There is also a sample PNG decoding application that converts a PNG file to the Windows BMP format.

The command format for this application is

```
DECODER input.png output.bmp
```

Chapter 15

Creating PNG Files

This is the last chapter on the PNG format. It covers the process for creating files in the PNG format, which is essentially the reverse of the one used in the previous chapter to read PNG files.

Overview

The basic process for creating a PNG file is fairly simple.

1. Write the PNG signature.
2. Write the PNG IHDR chunk.
3. Create a PLTE chunk if the image requires a palette.
4. Compress the image data into a series of IDAT blocks.
5. Write an IEND chunk.

An encoder can be designed so that it adds optional PNG chunks if needed. The optional chunks can be either predefined public chunks or application specific. However, in most situations the steps listed above are all that is needed.

With the exception of creating the IDAT blocks, all of the steps listed above are trivial. This chapter will deal almost exclusively with storing data in the IDAT chain. For information on the other chunks refer to Chapter 13.

Deflate Compression Process

The previous chapter covered the format of the Deflate compressed data within a chain of IDAT blocks. While clearly a compressor uses the same structures for the data a decompressor does, compression is not simply a reversal of decompression.

The Deflate specification gives an outline of a compression process. It recommends that this process be followed because of the patent minefield that surrounds any LZ compression process.

To implement Deflate compression we need to maintain a 32K or smaller power-of-2 window into the most recently processed uncompressed data bytes, just like the one used with decompression. The compression process requires an additional lookahead window into the data yet to be compressed. Starting from the beginning of the lookahead buffer we try to find the longest substring that has a match in the LZ77 sliding window. Since the longest match allowed by Deflate is 258 bytes, the lookahead window needs to be at least this long to get the longest possible matches. Rounding the lookahead window up to the next power of 2 (512) makes wrapping in the window simpler.

Algorithm 15.1 illustrates the general compression process for PNG image data. This is roughly the inverse of the DecodeBlock function shown in the previous chapter. The length and distance values are converted to codes and literal bits using the code also shown in the previous chapter.

There are two significant omissions in Algorithm 15.1. In a PNG file the Huffman tables precede the image data, so the encoder needs to generate them first. The other missing piece is the method the encoder uses to locate matching strings in the LZ77 windows.

Finding Matching Strings in the LZ77 Window

Finding the best match for the start of the lookahead buffer is the most time-consuming part of compressing PNG files. A simple linear search would require 32K searches per string being compressed, which could easily amount to billions of search operations to compress an image file. Instead of brute force, the approach recommended by the Deflate specification is to use a hash table where hash values are calculated using 3-byte sequences.

A *hash table* is a structure used to store objects that are accessed using a key, when the number of possible key values greatly exceeds the number of table entries at any given time. Hash tables are most commonly used with string keys. Many compiler implementations use hash tables to store variables defined by a module. A typical source module for a compiler may have a few hundred variable names out of the billions upon billions of possibilities. During PNG compression we have 32,768 entries with a maximum of 16 million possible values.

Algorithm 15.1
Deflate
Compression
Process

```
While MOREIMAGEDATA Do
  Begin
  FindLongestMatchInLZ77Window (LENGTH, DISTANCE)
  If LENGTH < 3 Then
    Begin
    ConvertLengthToCode (LENGTH, CODE, EXTRABITS, BITCOUNT)
    HuffmanEncodeLength (CODE)
    OutputLiteralBits (EXTRABITS, BITCOUNT)
    ConvertDistanceToCode (DISTANCE, CODE, EXTRABITS, BITCOUNT)
    HuffmanEncodeDistance (CODE)
    OutputLiteralBits (EXTRABITS, BITCOUNT)
    CopyFromLookaheadBuffer (LENGTH)
    End
  Else
    Begin
    HuffmanEncodeLength (FirstLookahead ())
    CopyFromLookaheadBuffer (1)
    End
  End
```

Entries in a hash table are referenced using a hash value. Figure 15.1 illustrates the structure of a hash table. The *hash value* is generated from a key by using a hash function. A *hash function* takes a key as input and returns an integer value within some fixed range. The hash value is used as an index into an array that contains a list of objects with the same hash value. A good hash function should distribute the possible key values evenly across the range of index values.

Since we are dealing with pixel values that have an equal probability of occurring, we can use a simple hash function which returns values in the range $0 \ldots 2^{3N} - 1$.

```
const int mask = (1<<N) - 1 ;
unsigned int Hash (unsigned char v1,
                   unsigned char v2,
                   unsigned char v3)
{
  return (v1 & mask) | ((v2 & mask) << N)
                     | ((v3 & mask) << (2 * N)) ;
}
```

The big problem with a hash table, especially in PNG compression, is how to handle entries with the same hash value. This is known as a *hash collision*. Unless we create a hash table with 16 million entries, something that may be feasible in a few years, we are going to have different 3-byte sequences with the same hash value. In addition, we are counting on having identical 3-byte

Figure 15.1
Hash Table
Structure

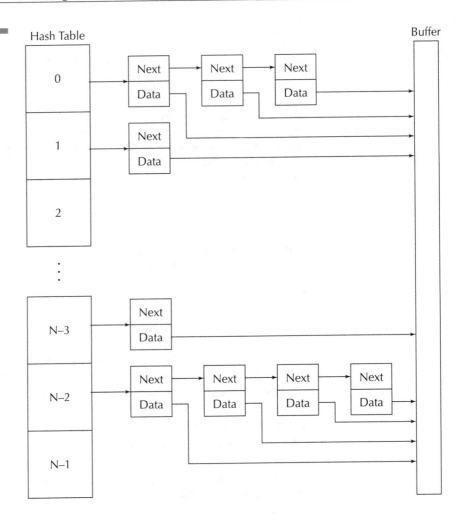

sequences appear within the LZ77 window to be able to replace strings with length/distance codes. Identical sequences will have identical hash values. Imagine an image with a solid background. It is entirely possible that the entire LZ77 window will contain entries with the same hash value.

To resolve collisions we chain entries with identical hash values. For storing 3-byte sequences we can define the hash table as something like this.

```
Structure HashEntry
   Begin
   INDEX : Unsigned Integer
   NEXT : Pointer To HashEntry
   End

Global HashTable [0..(1 LeftShift (3 * N) - 1] Of Pointer To HashEntry
```

The hash function returns an index to the first entry in the hash table. The other entries with the same hash value are located by following the pointer to the next entry. Algorithm 15.2 illustrates the basic procedure for finding the best match within the LZ77 window.

A compressor can use additional criteria for determining the best match. For example, it may take the distance into consideration as well as the code length. As the distance value becomes larger so does the number of additional bits required to encode it. If the distance value for a 3-byte match is large enough to require 13 additional bits, it is most likely that the compressor can encode the string with fewer bits using three literal values rather than a length and distance code.

Think about what happens when the procedure just described is used with an image containing relatively few colors. The hash chains could become quite large, which would make searching them end to end very slow. A good solution to this problem is to put a limit on the number of entries in a hash chain that the compressor will search for the best match. This limit can be configured to allow the amount of compression to be traded off against compression time. Limiting the number of entries searched in each hash chain does not have a significant negative impact on compression. However, it can result in a major reduction in compression time. The search limit can be made a configurable parameter so that the user can trade off time for compression.

Algorithm 15.2
Matching Entries in
the Hash Table

```
Procedure BestMatch (BESTLENGTH, BESTOFFSET)
  Begin
  BESTLENGTH = 0
  BESTOFFSET = 0

  HASHVALUE = Hash (LOOKAHEAD [0], LOOKAHEAD [1], LOOKAHEAD [2])
  HASHENTRY = HashTable [HashValue]
  If HASHENTRY = NULL Then
    Return // No possible Match

  While HASHENTRY <> NULL Do
    Begin
    II = 0
    While LZWINDOW [HASHENTRY.INDEX + II] = LOOKAHEAD [I] Do
      II = II + 1
    If II > BESTLENGTH Then
      Begin
      BESTLENGTH = II
      BESTOFFSET = HASHENTRY.INDEX
      End
    HASHENTRY = HASHENTRY.NEXT
    End
  End
```

Each time we move a character from the lookahead buffer to the LZ77 window, we need to create a hash table entry that references the character's position when added to the buffer. The hash value for the new hash entry needs to be calculated using values in the lookahead buffer because the hash function requires the value of the next two characters, which will not yet have been added to the LZ77 window.

> A PNG encoder should maintain a fixed pool of hash table entries rather than constantly allocating and freeing them. Since there are 2^{15} characters in the LZ77 window, that is the size of the hash entry pool as well.

If the compressor adds a hash entry to a hash chain that is not empty, it should be at the start of the chain rather than the end. This causes the most recently processed string to be matched first when searching the LZ77 for strings. Strings with smaller distance values can be encoded using fewer bits.

Huffman Table Generation

A PNG encoder can either use the fixed Huffman codes shown in Table 14.9 or generate Huffman codes based on usage frequencies. It is simpler to implement fixed Huffman codes but there is obviously a penalty when it comes to compression. Unless you are working with an application where compression speed is critical, there is really no reason to use fixed Huffman codes.

Chapter 6 covered Huffman coding as it applies to JPEG. The same process with a few modifications will work with a Huffman encoder. The differences between Huffman table generation in JPEG and PNG were listed in the previous chapter.

When we used Huffman coding in JPEG, we generated the Huffman table by making two nearly identical passes over the image data. The first pass gathered usage frequencies. After generating the Huffman tables from the usage frequencies, the second pass repeated the steps of the first pass except that the data was Huffman encoded.

Such a scheme can be used to encode PNG image data but there are a couple of significant drawbacks. The main problem with having two nearly identical passes is the time required to compress an image. The process of searching the LZ77 window for matching strings is significantly more processing intensive than is JPEG entropy encoding. Performing PNG compression process twice lengthens the compression time noticeably.

A good solution to this problem is to store the literal/length and distance codes in a buffer. A simple method for implementing such a buffer would be to use an array of 2-byte integers. A length/distance code would be stored in the buffer using 2 bytes while a literal value would use only 1 byte. The first pass through the data gathers usage statistics and writes to this buffer. After generating the Huffman tables, the second pass simply encodes the values stored in the buffer. Algorithm 15.3 illustrates how the first pass would be implemented.

How large does a buffer need to be to encode an entire image? The answer is that we do not need to hold the entire image in the buffer. The Deflate process allows the compressed data to be stored in multiple compressed blocks. The compressor can allocate a buffer at the start of image compression. When the buffer is full, the compressor ends the first pass. After the data is encoded in the second pass, the encoder starts a new Deflate block and resumes the first pass where it left off. In other words, instead of having two passes that process the entire image, we have multiple alternating passes.

Naturally the size of the buffer affects the size of the resulting image file. The smaller the buffer, the greater the number of compressed blocks, which results in more overhead from additional Huffman tables in the compressed stream. However, making the buffer too large can actually make the compressed image larger. When too much image data is written to a single compressed block, so many Huffman codes get defined that the overhead from the Huffman code lengths becomes greater than the overhead from additional Huffman tables. The optimal buffer size varies from image to image. A compressor could conceivably determine when it should create a new block from the Huffman code usage. This, in conjunction with a large buffer, would produce the best compression.

Once the Huffman codes have been generated for the length/literal and distance tables, the tables have to be written to the compressed output stream. The

Algorithm 15.3
Gathering Huffman
Usage Statistics

```
Procedure GatherData
  Begin
  While MOREIMAGEDATA And COUNT + 1 < BUFFERSIZE Do
  If LENGTH > 3 Then
    Begin
    IncrementLengthFrequency (ConvertLengthToCode (LENGTH))
    IncrementDistanceFrequency (ConvertDistanceToCode (DISTANCE))
    BUFFER [COUNT] = LENGTH + 256
    COUNT = COUNT + 1
    BUFFER [COUNT] = DISTANCE
    COUNT = COUNT + 1
    End
  Else
    Begin
    BUFFER [COUNT] = CopyFromLookaheadBuffer (1)
    COUNT = COUNT + 1
    End
  End
```

Huffman tables stored are Huffman encoded using the codes shown in the previous chapter. The easiest method for generating the Huffman codes for encoding the code lengths is a function that takes pointers to functions as parameters like the ones we used for JPEG. This function is called twice each time lengths are written to the output file—the first time it is called with a function for gathering Huffman statistics; the second time it is called with a function that outputs the Huffman-encoded lengths.

Algorithm 15.4 illustrates the process for compressing Deflate blocks using a buffer.

One oddity of PNG compression is that Huffman codes within the compressed data are stored with the bits in reverse order. The Huffman decoding

Algorithm 15.4
Deflate
Compression

```
Procedure OutputDataBlock
  Begin
  II = 0
  While II < COUNT Do
    Begin
    If BUFFER [II] > 255 Then
      Begin
      ConvertLength (BUFFER [II], CODE, EXTRABITS, BITCOUNT)
      HuffmanEncodeUsingLengthTable (CODE)
      OutputLiteralBits (EXTRABITS, BITCOUNT)
      II = II + 1
      ConvertDistance (BUFFER [COUNT], CODE, EXTRABITS, BITCOUNT)
      HuffmanEncodeUsingDistanceTable (CODE)
      OutputLiteralBits (EXTRABITS, BITCOUNT)
      II = I + 1
      End
    Else
      Begin
      HuffmanEncodeUsingLengthTable (BUFFER [COUNT])
      II = II + 1
      End
    End
  HuffmanEncodeUsingLengthTable (ENDCODE)
  End

Procedure CompressImage
  Begin
  While MOREIMAGEDATA Do
    Begin
    GatherData
    GenerateHuffmanTables
    WriteDeflateBlockHeader
    OutputDataBlock
    End
  End
```

process reads the most significant bit of the code first and then adds the least significant bits. However, within PNG compressed data, bits are read from the least significant bit to the most significant. If the Huffman codes were stored in the normal order, the decompressor would read their least significant bits first, which would defeat the entire Huffman coding process. This example illustrates the reversal of bits in a Huffman code.

```
unsigned short ReverseHuffmanCode (unsigned short input)
{
  unsigned short value = 0 ;
  for (unsigned int ii = 0 ; ii < 16 ; ++ ii)
  {
    if ((input & (1 << (15 - ii))) != 0)
      value |= (1 << ii) ;
  }
  return value ;
}
```

Filtering

Each data row in a PNG file is preceded by a byte that specifies the filter method applied to the row data before compression. The possible values for this byte and the corresponding filter method were given in the previous chapter. The filter functions are similar to their inverses shown previously.

Sub Filter

```
filteredvalue = image [row][X] - image [row][X-Interval]
```

Up Filter

```
filteredvalue = image [row][X] - image [row-1][X]
```

Average Filter

```
filteredvalue = image [row][X] - (image [row][X-Interval]
                                  + image [row-1][X]) / 2
```

Paeth Filter

```
filteredvalue = buffer [row][X] - PaethPredictor (
                        image [row][X-Interval],
                        image [row-1][X],
                        image [row-1][X-Interval])
```

where PaethPredictor and Interval are as defined in the previous chapter.

Why Use Filtering?

The purpose of applying row filters is to make the image data more compressible. Suppose you have an image containing a gradient background where the color of each pixel varies by a fixed amount from the pixel next to it. This is familiar to Windows users from its use in software installation screens. For a blue to black gradient, the color data of a typical row would look something like

0 0 1 0 0 2 0 0 3 0 0 4 0 0 5 0 0 6 0 0 7 0 0 8 ...

While the data has a very orderly pattern, there are no repeating strings of 3 bytes or greater, thus reducing its compressibility through the Deflate process. If this same data row were to be run through the sub filter defined above, the data would become

0 0 1 0 0 1 0 0 1 0 0 1 0 0 1 0 0 1 0 0 1 0 0 1 ...

which compresses much better in a PNG file. It turns out that filtering is generally the best method for improving the compression of an image file. Using filters can generally reduce the image size by about 30–40%.

On the other hand, filtering can increase the size of a PNG file. For images that use a color palette, no filtering should be used. Filtering takes advantage of similar adjacent color values, but palette indices have no relation to the actual color value. Since filtering operates on bytes rather than bits, using filters with images with bit depths of fewer than 8 does not produce the same sort of results as it does with larger bit depths. Consequently, filtering would be effective with these images only in the rarest of cases.

What Filter to Use?

Filters are applied on a row-by-row basis and can be changed from row to row. This raises the question of which filter is best for a given row, the answer to which is that we really do not know. This remains an area for experimentation and discovery.

The PNG specification suggests performing all filters on each row. Each filtered value is treated as a signed byte ($-128..127$) and all are then summed together. The filter that produces the smallest sum is selected. Another possibility is to find the filter that produces the longest repetitions of the same values.

The simplest method for an encoder to automatically select a filter is to not use filtering for images that use a palette or for images with a bit depth of fewer than 8 bits. For other image types, the sub filter should be used for the first row and the Paeth filter for the remaining rows. In most situations, this method does not produce results that are significantly worse than either of the methods described earlier.

Conclusion

In this chapter we have covered the process for creating PNG files, which is essentially the reverse of the one used to read them. As in JPEG, the implementer of a compressor has to make arbitrary choices about the how to do the compression process, such as how big to make the IDAT chunks, when to create a new Deflate block, how far to search in the hash chains, and which filters to use. Methods for selecting the best filter are still an area of exploration. The PNG format should become more common in the near future.

The source code for this chapter on the accompanying CD-ROM is a PNG encoding class, PngEncoder, which uses a PNG Huffman encoding class that is nearly identical to the equivalent JPEG class shown in Chapter 6. The only significant differences are in the BuildTable function. The PNG version does not have a special value to ensure that no Huffman code consists of all 1-bits and it ensures that the ordering of Huffman codes matches the ordering of the values.

The encoder class's SetUseFilters function specifies whether or not filters are used in the compression process. The SetCompressionLevel function controls the maximum depth to which the hash chains are searched and the SetBlocksize function controls the size of the compression buffer.

There is also a sample encoder that converts Windows BMP files to PNG format. The command sequence for this application is

```
ENCODER [-f -F -M] input.bmp output.png

-f Use Filters
-F Use Fastest Compression
-M Use Maximum Compression
```

This brings to an end our discussion of the PNG format and with it an end to the book. We hope that you have learned how to read and write images using the most common formats.

Glossary

AC Coefficient In JPEG, all of the DCT coefficients except for the single lowest-order coefficient. These coefficients represent the addition of cosine functions of increasing frequency.

Additive Color Model A color model where component values add color to black. Higher component values produce colors closer to white.

Alpha Channel A pixel value (in addition to the color components) that represents the transparency of the pixel.

Baseline JPEG A subset mode of sequential JPEG where the number of tables is restricted and the sample precision must be 8 bits.

Big-Endian The representation of integers with the individual bytes ordered from most to least significant. *See* Little-Endian.

Bitmap Format An image format where the data consists of a set of values that represents the color at discrete points or pixels.

Coefficient *See* DCT Coefficient.

Chrominance A component in a color model that represents the color of a pixel as opposed to its intensity. In the YCbCr color model Cb and Cr are chrominance components.

Chunk The basic division of a PNG file.

Color Model A method for specifying how colors are represented. Most color models represent colors using three dimensions or components. RGB, YCbCr, and CMYK are examples of color models.

Color Quantization The process of reducing the number of colors in an image. Usually quantization is used to allow an image to be displayed on a device with a limited number of colors or to store the image in a file format that does not support as many colors as the original image.

Colorspace   The set of all colors that can be represented using a particular color model.

Component   One of a set of values used to represent a pixel in a particular color model. Most color models represent a color value using three component values.

CRC   Cyclical Redundancy Check. A polynomial-based method for detecting corrupted data.

Data Unit   In JPEG, an 8×8 block of sample values for a single component.

DC Coefficient   The lowest-order DCT coefficient. It represents a constant value.

DCT   Discrete Cosine Transform. A mathematical process that converts a set of values into an equivalent representation as the sum of cosine functions.

Deflate   The compression process used in PNG. It is a variant of the LZ77 process that incorporates Huffman coding.

Down-Sampling   The process of reducing the resolution of a component in an image.

Frame   In JPEG, a group of one or more scans. For the JPEG modes in common use a frame is indistinguishable from an image.

Gamut   The range of colors that can be displayed on a particular output device.

Gamma   A model commonly used to correct colors in an image based upon the properties of the system and the viewing environment.

Hierarchical JPEG   A little used JPEG mode where the image is broken into a number of frames that refine the image.

Huffman Coding   A compression technique that uses variable-length codes to represent data.

Inflate   The decompression process used in PNG. It is the reverse of the Deflate process.

Interleaved Scan   In JPEG, a scan that consists of more than one component.

Interlaced Image   An image that is not displayed sequentially, but rather by using a pattern of lines or pixels.

JFIF   JPEG File Interchange Format. The format used for JPEG files.

JPEG-LS   A new JPEG lossless compression technique.

Little-Endian   A format for representing integers where the individual bytes are ordered from least to most significant.

Logical Screen   In GIF, a logical display area for the images stored in the file. The individual images specify their size and location within the logical screen.

Lossy Compression   A compression method that creates a close approximation of the original data. Lossy compression methods discard information that is considered less important in order to increase compression.

Lossless Compression   A compression method that allows an exact copy of the original image to be retrieved.

Lossless JPEG   A rarely used JPEG mode that implements a lossless compression technique. Lossless JPEG is now considered obsolete.

Luminance   A color component that represents brightness.

LZ   A family of compression algorithms named after their creators, Abraham Lempel and Jacob Ziv.

LZW   (Lempel-Ziv-Welch) The LZ variant used in GIF.

MCU   (Minimum Coded Unit) In JPEG, the number of data units that are encoded as a group.

Median Cut Algorithm   Heckbert's algorithm for color quantization.

Network Order   Identical to "big-endian." It refers to the fact that in Internet Protocol integers are transmitted with the most significant byte first.

Noninterleaved Scan   In JPEG, a scan that contains only one component.

Pixel   A discrete location on a display device or an individual point within a bitmap image format.

Point Transform   The process used to reduce the precision of data in progressive JPEG when successive approximation is used. For DC coefficients, the point transform is a bit shift. For AC coefficients, the point transform is integer division.

Progressive JPEG   A JPEG mode where the image is divided into multiple scans. The initial scans are a coarse representation of the image. Subsequent scans refine the image.

Quantization   In JPEG, the process for reducing the number of DCT coefficients used to represent a data unit. *See also* Color Quantization.

Raster Format   Identical to "bitmap format."

RGB Colorspace   A colorspace where the components represent the relative amounts of red, green, and blue light to be added to black.

RLE   (Run Length Encoding) A compression method where consecutive runs of the same value are encoded using run-length/value pairs.

Sampling Frequency   In JPEG, the relative frequency at which a component is sampled with respect to the other components in the image.

Sample Precision   The number of bits used to represent a component value.

Scan   In JPEG, a set of compressed data that represents a single pass through the image for one or more components.

Sequential JPEG   A JPEG mode where the image is stored from top to bottom, left to right.

Spectral Selection In Progressive JPEG, the process of dividing components into a range of spectral bands or DCT coefficients, used by all progressive JPEG images. Spectral selection can optionally be used in conjunction with successive approximation.

SPIFF (Still Picture Interchange File Format). The official JPEG file format. It is intended to replace JFIF.

Subtractive Color Model A color model where components subtract color from white. Higher component values create colors closer to black.

Successive Approximation In Progressive JPEG, the process of dividing components into multiple scans by reducing the precision of the data in the initial scan and using subsequent scans to refine the data. Successive approximation is not required in progressive JPEG.

Truecolor Any system where 2^{24} or more colors can be represented simultaneously. The name reflects the fact that this is approximately the limit of colors humans can distinguish.

Up-Sampling The process of increasing the resolution of a color component.

Vector Format A graphics format where images consists of a sequence of drawing commands.

XYZ Colorspace The three-component color model defined by the Commission Internationale de l'Éclairage (CIE) in 1931. It defines absolute, rather than relative, colors.

YCbCr Colorspace The color model used in JPEG. YCbCr uses three components that represent luminance (Y) and chrominance (Cb and CR).

Bibliography

Anton, Howard, *Elementary Linear Algebra,* John Wiley & Sons, New York, NY, 1981.

Blinn, Jim, *Jim Blinn's Corner: Dirty Pixels,* Morgan Kaufmann, San Francisco, CA, 1998.

Boutell, Thomas et al., "PNG Specification," Version 1.0, PNG Development Group, October 1996.

Brown, C. Wayne and Shepherd, Barry J., *Graphics File Formats,* Manning, Greenwich, CT, 1995.

Burden, Richard L., Faires, J. Douglas, Reynolds, Albert C., *Numerical Analysis,* Prindle, Weber & Schmidt, Boston, MA, 1981.

Campbell, Joe, *C Programmer's Guide to Serial Communications,* Howard W. Sams & Company, Carmel, IN, 1987.

Deutsch, L. Peter and Gailly, Jean-Loup, "ZLIB Compressed Data Format Specification," Version 3.3, RFC 1950, 1996.

Deutsch, L. Peter, "DEFLATE Compressed Data Format Specification," Version 1.3, RFC 1951, 1996.

Foley, James D., van Dam, Andries, Feiner, Steven K., and Hughes John F., *Computer Graphics Principles and Practice,* Addison-Wesley, Reading, MA, 1996.

CompuServe, Inc, "Graphics Interchange Format (GIF) Specification," CompuServe, Columbus, OH, 1987.

CompuServe, Inc, "Graphics Interchange Format (GIF) Specification," Version 89a, CompuServe, Columbus, OH, 1989.

Graham, Ian S., *The HTML Source Book,* John Wiley & Sons, New York, NY, 1997.

Hamilton, Eric, "JPEG File Interchange Format," Version 1.02, C-Cube Microsystems, September 1, 1992.

Heckbert, Paul, "Color Image Quantization for Frame Buffer Display," *ACM Computer Graphics Journal,* Volume 16, Number 3, July 1982.

Huffman, D. A., "A Method for the Construction of Minimum Redundancy Codes," *Proceedings of the IRE,* Volume 40, Number 9, pages 1098–1101.

JPEG (1994), *Digital Compression and Coding of Continuous-tone Still Images, Part I: Requirements and Guidelines.* ISE/IEC IS 10918-1, American National Standards Institute, New York, NY, 1994.

Lindley, Craig A., *Photographic Imaging Techniques in C++,* John Wiley & Sons, New York, NY, 1995.

Microsoft Corporation, *Win32 Programmer's Reference Volume 5: Messages, Structures, and Macros,* Microsoft Press, Redmond, WA, 1993.

Murray, James D. and vanRyper, William, *Encyclopedia of Graphics File Formats,* O'Reilly & Associates, Sebastopol, CA, 1994.

Nelson, Mark, *The Data Compression Book,* M&T Books, San Mateo, CA, 1992.

Nye, Adrian, *Xlib Programming Manual,* O'Reilly & Associates, Sebastopol, CA, 1988.

Pennebaker, William B. and Mitchell, Joan L., *JPEG Still Image Data Compression Standard,* Van Nostrand Reinhold, New York, NY, 1993.

Porter, Thomas and Duff, Tom, "Compositing Digital Images," *Computer Graphics,* Volume 18, Number 3, July 1984.

Ramabadran, Tenkasi V. and Gaitonde, Sunil S., "A Tutorial on CRC Computations," *IEEE Micro,* August 1988, pages 62–75.

Rao, K. R. and Yip, P., *Discrete Cosine Transform,* Academic Press, New York, NY, 1990.

Rimmer, Steve, *Windows Bitmapped Graphics,* Windcrest Books, Blue Ridge Summit, PA, 1993.

Scheifler, Robert W. and Gettys, James, *X Window System,* Digital Press, Bedford, MA, 1990.

Stroustrup, Bjarne, *The C++ Programming Language, Third Edition,* Addison-Wesley, Reading, MA, 1997.

Swan, Tom, *Inside Windows File Formats,* SAMS, Indianapolis, IN, 1993.

Welsh, Terry, "A Technique for High-Performance Data Compression," *IEEE Computer,* Volume 17, Number 6, June 1984, pages 8–19.

Ziv, J. and Lempel, A., "A Universal Algorithm for Sequential Data Compression," *IEEE Transactions on Information Theory,* Volume 23, Number 3, May 1977, pages 337–343.

Ziv, J. and Lempel, A., "Compression of Individual Sequences via Variable-Rate Coding," *IEEE Transactions on Information Theory,* Volume 24, Number 5, September 1978, pages 530–536.

Internet Sites

Since Web sites have a tendency to move or disappear, rather than creating an exhaustive list, we are only listing those sites that we consider the most useful.

JPEG

www.jpeg.org—Home of the JPEG committee

www.ijg.org—Independent JPEG Group

PNG

www.cdrom.com/pub/png/—The PNG Home Page

www.cdrom.com/pub/infozip/zlib/—ZLIB Home Page

www.cdrom.com/pub/mng—Multiple Image Network Graphics

GIF

www.geocities.co.jp/SiliconValley/3453/gif_info/index_en.html—GIF Info Page

members.aol.com/royalef—GIF Animation on the WWW

General

www.wotsit.org—Wotsit's Format Page

www.dcs.ed.ac.uk/~mxr/gfx/—The Graphics File Formats Page

Index

The SIGGRAPH Series of ACM Press Books

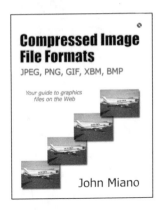

Compressed Image File Formats
JPEG, PNG, GIF, XBM, BMP
By John Miano

This comprehensive reference on the major graphics file formats and the compression technologies they employ is an indispensable resource for graphics programmers, especially those developing graphical applications for the Web. It examines the most common graphics file formats in detail and demonstrates how to encode and decode image files for each. If you want to learn how to read and write graphics file formats for the Web, there is no better reference than this book.

0-201-60443-4 • 320 pages • ©1999 • Paperback with CD-ROM

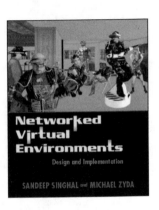

Networked Virtual Environments
Design and Implementation
By Sandeep Singhal and Michael Zyda

Networked virtual environments (Net-VEs) offer a three-dimensional, virtual "space" in which users around the world can interact in real time. Net-VE applications have already been adopted by the military and aerospace and entertainment industries. They are also used to enhance engineering design, scientific research, and electronic commerce. Written by two of the field's leaders, this book provides a comprehensive examination of Net-VEs, explains the underlying technologies, and furnishes a roadmap for designing and building interactive 3D virtual environments.

0-201-32557-8 • 352 pages • ©1999 • Hardcover

The Computer Image
By Alan Watt and Fabio Policarpo

The three main fields of computer imagery—computer graphics, image processing, and computer vision—are merging in many applications. Computer vision techniques are used in computer graphics to collect and model complex scenes; computer graphics techniques are used to constrain the recognition of 3D objects by computers; image processing techniques are routinely used by graphic designers to manipulate photographs. This book is the first to bring all three areas together in a coherent overview.

0-201-42298-0 • 752 pages • ©1998 • Hardcover with CD-ROM

Digital Illusion

Entertaining the Future with High Technology
By Clark Dodsworth, Jr., Contributing Editor

This book is the first to detail the design and implementation of computer-based entertainment. In it Clark Dodsworth has pulled together key players in the field to share their keen insights and invaluable experiences. First, the contributors describe recent developments in graphics, simulation, and animation that have led to advances in interactive entertainment. The book then describes, with examples, the infrastructure required to develop the new technologies of illusion, and it also explores some of the practical issues involved in designing virtual environments. In addition, the history and economics of the field are examined, with a critical eye to future developments.

0-201-84780-9 • 576 pages • ©1998 • Paperback

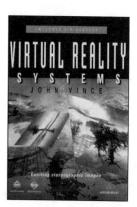

Virtual Reality Systems

By John Vince

Virtual Reality Systems is an accessible introduction to the underlying technologies used to create today's virtual environments: real-time computer graphics, color displays, and simulation software. It provides balanced coverage of both hardware and software issues and provides optional explanations of the underlying mathematical algorithms and techniques.

0-201-87687-6 • 384 pages • ©1995 • Hardcover

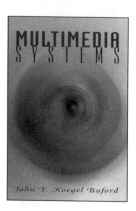

Multimedia Systems

By John F. Koegel Buford

This carefully edited book provides a technical introduction to key issues in multimedia, including detailed discussion of new technologies, principles, current research, and future directions. It furnishes a unified treatment of recent developments in the field, bringing together, in one volume, multimedia elements common to a range of computing areas such as operating systems, database management systems, network communications, and user-interface technology.

0-201-53258-1 • 464 pages • ©1994 • Hardcover

ACM Press Books: Other Titles Available

Advanced Animation and Rendering Techniques

Theory and Practice
By Alan Watt and Mark Watt

Dealing with state-of-the-art techniques in rendering and animation, this book provides a unique synthesis of advanced techniques not previously available in one coherent source. It offers a balance between theoretical concepts and implementation detail that will be invaluable to professional programmers and students alike.

0-201-54412-1 • 472 pages • ©1992 • Hardcover

Mobility

Processes, Computers, and Agents
Edited by Dejan Milojicic, Frederick Douglis, and Richard Wheeler

This book brings together in one single resource leading edge research and practice in three areas of mobility: process migration, mobile computing, and mobile agents. Presented chronologically, the chapters in this book—each written by a leading expert in that particular area—track the development of critical technologies that have influenced mobility. Introductions by the editors and original afterwords by many of the authors provide information on implementation and practical application, technological context, and updates on the most recent advances.

0-201-37928-7 • 704 pages • ©1999 • Paperback

Software for Use

*A Practical Guide to the Models and Methods
of Usage-Centered Design*
By Larry L. Constantine and Lucy A.D. Lockwood

In this book, two well-known authors present the models and methods of a revolutionary approach to software that will help programmers deliver more *usable* software. Much more than just another set of rules for good user-interface design, the book guides readers through a systematic software development process—*usage-centered design*, which weaves together two major threads in software development methods: use cases (also used with UML) and essential modeling. With numerous examples and case studies of both conventional and specialized software applications, the authors illustrate what has been shown to work in practice and what has proved to be of the greatest practical value.

0-201-92478-1 • 608 pages • ©1999 • Hardcover

ACM Press Books: Other Titles Available

Requirements Engineering and Rapid Development
An Object-Oriented Approach
By Ian Graham

The message of this book is simple—software development should be done quickly and effectively. Systems that take years to develop can often end up out of synch with their users' evolving requirements and business objectives by the time they are delivered. This book shows how to solve the problem by using a systematic approach to requirements gathering and business modeling. Packed full of practical advice and tried-and-tested techniques for object modeling, it illustrates how these techniques may be applied not only to models of computer systems, but to models of the world in which they have to operate.

0-201-36047-0 • 288 pages • ©1999 • Hardcover

Information Warfare and Security
By Dorothy E. Denning

This book tells what individuals, corporations, and governments need to know about information-related attacks and defenses. Every day, we hear reports of hackers who have penetrated computer networks, vandalized Web pages, and accessed sensitive information. We hear how they have tampered with medical records, disrupted 911 emergency systems, and siphoned money from bank accounts. Could information terrorists, using nothing more than a personal computer, cause planes to crash, widespread power blackouts, or financial chaos? Such real and imaginary scenarios, and defenses against them, are the stuff of information warfare—operations that target or exploit information media to win some objective over an adversary.

0-201-43303-6 • 544 pages • ©1999 • Paperback

Also of Interest:

The Computer in the Visual Arts
By Anne Morgan Spalter

Uniquely focused on the computer as a medium for artistic expression and graphic communication, this book is an introduction to computer graphics. It is the first comprehensive work to combine technical and theoretical aspects of the emerging field of computer art and design. Integrating theory, examples, and the concepts underlying all the major types of graphics software, the author explains the principles and practices that artists, designers, illustrators, and photographers simply must understand to take full advantage of this dynamic, visual medium.

0-201-38600-3 • 500 pages • ©1999 • Hardcover

Warranty

Addison Wesley Longman warrants the enclosed disc to be free of defects in materials and faulty workmanship under normal use for a period of ninety days after purchase. If a defect is discovered in the disc during this warranty period, a replacement disc can be obtained at no charge by sending the defective disc, postage prepaid, with proof of purchase to:

Addison Wesley Longman, Inc.
Computer and Engineering Publishing Group
One Jacob Way
Reading, MA 01867

After the 90-day period, a replacement will be sent upon receipt of the defective disc and a check or money order for $10.00, payable to Addison Wesley Longman, Inc.

Addison Wesley Longman makes no warranty or representation, either express or implied, with respect to this software, its quality, performance, merchantability, or fitness for a particular purpose. In no event will Addison Wesley Longman, its distributors, or dealers be liable for direct, indirect, special, incidental, or consequential damages arising out of the use or inability to use the software. The exclusion of implied warranties is not permitted in some states. Therefore, the above exclusion may not apply to you. This warranty provides you with specific legal rights. There may be other rights that you may have that vary from state to state.

System Requirements:
Windows '95 or Windows NT
Borland C++ Builder, v.3 or Microsoft Visual C++, v.5